How Do Churches Grow?

How Do Churches Grow?

Roy Pointer

Marshalls

Marshalls Paperbacks
Marshall Morgan & Scott
3 Beggarwood Lane, Basingstoke, Hants., UK.

Copyright © 1984 by Roy Pointer
First published by Marshall Morgan & Scott 1984

British Library Cataloguing in Publication Data
Pointer, Roy
  How do churches grow?
  1. Church renewal
  I. Title
  262'.0017   BV600.2
ISBN 0 551 01070 3

Phototypeset by Input Typesetting Ltd, London
Printed in Great Britain by Camelot Press, Southampton

This book is dedicated to
the memory of the late
Rev. John E. Summers, BD,
of Balham Baptist Church, London, 1972–79.
A friend and fellow-pioneer in British Church Growth.

Contents

viii

List of Diagrams

Acknowledgements

This book would never have been written without the help of many people. I am grateful to Dr C Peter Wagner of Fuller Theological Seminary, who first challenged me to write it. I would like to thank him and the other faculty members of the School of World Mission, who are training me to be a missionary to my own nation.

A special word of appreciation is due to my friend and colleague, the Rev Eddie Gibbs, who 'nagged' me until the manuscript was completed! Other friends and colleagues, in Bible Society, notably the Rev Tom Houston (now President elect of World Vision), Peter Brierley (now Director of MARC, Europe) and Jan Harrison (Programmes Director) have been generous with encouragement, statistical information and the development of the questionnaires.

I am grateful to the many ministers and churches who have given me the privilege of learning from their experience and using their testimony. John Hunt, Editor of Marshall Morgan and Scott, has been particularly gracious and patient in his encouragement. I am also very grateful to Rev Tom Houston for kindly writing the Foreword.

Finally, this book would never have been written without the constant love, support and understanding of my wife Dorothy, who really is a gift from God. And also my children, Angela, Timothy, Stephen, Sharon and Andrew, who see little enough of Dad normally and saw even less while this project was under way.

Foreword

This book had to be written. Roy Pointer has made such a careful and wide ranging study of both the literature and the growing edge of British church life, that it would have been a great loss if it had not been written down for the benefit of a wider audience than he can personally address.

Church Growth has arrived in Britain from the Third World via the United States. It was as recently as 1976 that its way of thinking came into our strategic Christian vocabulary in the report 'Let My People Grow', produced by the Evangelical Alliance. Since then, it has needed to be thought through in the U.K. context and be illustrated by British examples. *How do Churches Grow?* is the latest snapshot of the progress of recovery from decline that is under way in U.K. with a perceptive analysis of its essential components.

It is a practical introduction to the subject that anyone will find eminently usable, who is serious about applying the principles. Every chapter is valuable but perhaps the most original and crucial is chapter five 'Organised for Growth'. If the prescriptions for effective leadership set out here were followed in our churches they would soon have a new lease of life.

Though written from the standpoint of one kind of churchmanship, the book shows an unusual awareness of the whole spectrum of church life and will be valuable to readers of all denominations and of none.

I am happy to commend this book not only to a British readership but to all in every country who want to live and work on the frontiers of Kingdom and Church and see Jesus Christ more and more widely known and loved.

Tom Houston

What This Book Is All About

This book has been written to introduce the theory and practice of Church Growth to British churches. There are various missionary schools of thought but this particular school offers the British Church what it most needs in this period of its long and sometimes glorious history – guidance on how to make disciples of British people and nurture them in healthy growing churches.

The Church Growth Movement causes mixed reactions in Christians and these have been borne in mind in the writing of this book.

APATHY

Many Christians are unconcerned or uninterested in the decline of the British Church. The fact that 36 million British people are 'unchurched' and probably many more do not know Jesus Christ as their personal Lord and Saviour leaves many Christians unmoved. Therefore, this Movement, that urges them to reach out and bring people to Christ and into their fellowship, has little appeal. Some are apathetic because they are 'doing all right' or are resigned to the present state of affairs and are 'doing their bit'.

Some are more concerned about their church's welfare than the welfare of those who are outside it, and unlike Jesus, are apathetic to the plight of the lost. This book has been written to overcome such apathy.

ATTACK

Church Growth emphases in the context of decline or maintenance or even limited growth, appear so challenging and disturbing that hostility is a common reaction. The Church Growth Movement has and will continue to develop in fervent debate with its critics. Sadly, many criticisms stem from ignorance or are based upon caricature. Hopefully, this book will increase understanding and present a comprehensive picture of what Church Growth has to offer.

If this book does disturb you I trust your response will be amicable and the continuing debate enlightening. As the Scripture says, 'No doubt there must be divisions among you so that the ones who are in the right may be clearly seen' (1 Cor. 11.19).

AMAZEMENT

Some Christians are surprised that Church Growth has a firm theological foundation, historical perspective and contemporary relevance, and that the stress upon evangelisation and church growth is both biblical and spiritual. Church Growth acknowledges the authority of the Bible and the activity of the Holy Spirit in the life of the Church, which is the traditional position of all orthodox Christians.

In writing this book I have therefore attempted to write without bias or prejudice and in an ecumenical and eirenical spirit, believing that the task of re-evangelising the British Isles requires the mobilisation of the whole Church proclaiming the whole gospel.

APPLICATION

Church Growth is concerned with the practical dimensions of mission and therefore offers the Christian leader insights and principles that will improve performance in ministry. Issues arresting renewal and growth are honestly faced, and solutions to problems found, so that Church Growth principles call for application. They work!

I have tried to limit the contents of this book to issues that need to be faced by *local churches* wanting to experience growth in quality and quantity. The principles described should lead to correct assessment, wise decisions and effective action in any local church, regardless of denomination. I have therefore tried to avoid denominational bias or terminology and provide insights that any Christian leader could use. This book has been written to help Christian leaders overhaul their church or churches and develop effective programmes leading to church growth. Hopefully, what has been written will be applied!

The first chapter describes the remarkable growth of the world Church in contrast to the appalling decline of the British Church and sketches the origins of the Church Growth Movement. Chapter 2 explores four important emphases of the Movement and the third chapter describes ten 'signs of growth' found in growing churches.

Chapter 4 stresses the importance of fact-finding to prepare for effective mission and a local church survey is provided in Appendix 5, 'Understanding Your Church'.

Chapters 5 and 6 offer guidelines for organisation and planning for a local church to experience and sustain renewal and growth.

Throughout the book 'Church' refers to the universal Church or denomination and 'church' is always the local community of believers. The book has been written with a general readership in mind and theological terminology and the use of the biblical languages has been kept to a minimum. Church Growth has developed a technical language of its own and that should suffice!

I have not used page footnotes but included references from other books in the text. Each reference is followed by the author's surname, the date of publication and the page number. The title and a brief description of the book appears in Appendix 2.

1 Why Church Growth?

'A bench mark in our understanding of the true religious state of the planet' is how *Time Magazine* described the publication of the *World Christian Encyclopaedia* in 1982. Editor, Dr David B Barrett, an Anglican missionary and Director of the Centre for the study of World Evangelisation in Nairobi, Kenya, took fourteen years to compile the data and draw together the many contributions that fill this fascinating fact-filled volume of 1,010 pages.

Dr Barrett successfully obtained the co-operation of religious and secular authorities throughout the world, and personally visited 212 countries and territories, in his attempt to 'count every soul on earth'. He even obtained top-level clearance from the Russian government to work with Communist Party statisticians researching the spread of atheism – they discovered 137 million Soviet citizens were irreligious but 97 million boldly remained Christian!

This world-wide research revealed that during this century Christianity has become the first truly universal religion in history with Christian communities in all nations and among almost all peoples. The goal of world evangelisation set at the beginning of the century may not have been achieved totally but has been much more successfully accomplished than most Christians and non-Christians believed.

However, Dr Barrett cautions against 'two pitfalls' when examining the statistics. Firstly, he urges readers to avoid triumphalism, 'spectacular growth or numerical success do not in themselves spell spiritual depth or significant progress.' And, 'Neither should we fall into the trap of equating the fortunes of organised Christianity and institutionalised religion with the fortunes of the Kingdom of God.'

Secondly, statistics should not be regarded as impersonal. Numbers represent people who can be counted. Dr Barrett illustrates the point when he writes, 'If you and your family are charismatic Christians (or Evangelicals, or a similar tradition), you all feature in a total of 780 absolute numbers here. If you are a Christian worker, you feature as an individual in an addition thirty-five sets of absolute numbers. If you are a worker in a foreign land, you feature in a further twenty. And so on. Since you and I permeate these statistical tables to that extent, they cannot be so impersonal after all.'

THE GROWTH OF THE WORLD CHURCH

The *World Christian Encyclopaedia* estimates that the world's Christian population has grown from 558 million in 1900 to 1,433 million in 1980. This phenomenal growth of the world Church within the period of a long lifetime and within living memory has taken place despite the appalling decline of the European churches and the rapid and considerable growth of non-religious and atheistic groups.

In 1900 Christians represented thirty-four per cent of the world's population of 1,620 million and in 1980 were thirty-three per cent of 4,374 million. In 1900 two-thirds of Christians were predominately European and white, whereas in 1980 the Church had a non-white majority for the first time in 1,200 years. Dr Barrett estimates that by 2000 AD three-fifths of all Christians will live in Africa, Asia and Latin America.

At a time when Westerners cease to be practising Christians at a rate of 7,600 per day, Africa is gaining 16,400 Christians daily, with 4,000 converted every day from other religions. In 1910 at the Edinburgh Missionary Conference it was feared that Africa, south of the Sahara, would turn to Islam. In fact the sub-continent has been turning to Christ and by 2000 AD about twenty per cent of all Christians will be African.

In Latin America in 1900 there were 62 million Christians comprising eleven per cent of the population and by 1980 they had become twenty-four per cent and numbered 349 million! (See Figure 1, The Growth of Latin American Christianity.)

In East and South Asia there are 807,000 nett new converts (converts minus defections or apostasies) annually in addition to the increase by births among the Christian communities. The South Korean Church is one that has seen particularly vigorous growth with 42,700 Christians in 1900 and an estimated 11.5 million (thirty per cent of the population) by the mid 1980s.

When all these facts were added together the world Church was growing in 1980 by 59,200 people daily and there was a nett increase of 460 new churches every week.

Third World Missions to other countries are also growing in number and personnel and missionary strategists believe South Korea will become one of the major centres for World evangelisation in the remaining years of this century with missionaries already being sent to Europe.

In 1981 the Rev Michael Banks, Rector of Loughborough, was travelling incognito on the London Underground. He had heard that the Korean Church was sending out missionaries but was surprised when an Asian gentleman sitting next to him enquired, 'Are you a Christian?' When asked why he wanted to know, the Asian intro-

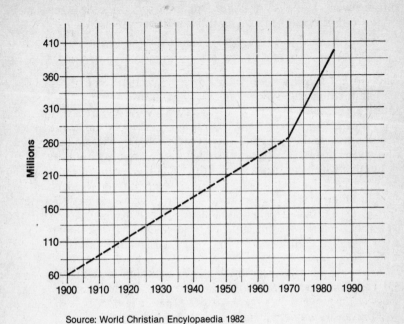

Source: World Christian Encylopaedia 1982

Figure 1. The Growth of Latin American Christianity

duced himself as a South Korean pastor training to be a missionary in England!

It may be distressing to realise that the United Kingdom is seen by many Christians from overseas as a mission field with 30–40 million people unreached by the gospel, but as long as the vast majority of British Christians remain indifferent to the plight of their countrymen, we must rejoice and be thankful that others are prepared to undertake the urgent task of re-evangelising these islands.

THE DECLINE OF THE BRITISH CHURCH

Decline in Church Membership

The 1970s was another decade of decline when the British Church lost 1 million members, 2,500 ministers and closed 1,000 churches. In reporting these sad statistics the *UK Christian Handbook* (1983 Edition) reveals that Church membership has slumped to thirteen per cent in England, twenty-three per cent in Wales, thirty-seven per cent in Scotland, and only in Northern Ireland remains high at eighty per cent (see figure 2, Proportions of Adult Population who are Church Members).

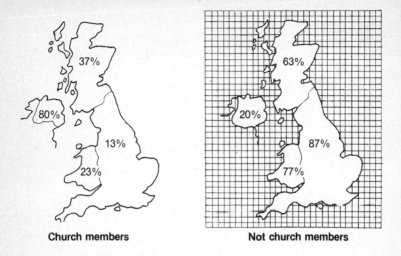

Church members   **Not church members**

Figure 2. Proportion of Adult Population who are Church Members.
(Source: *UK Christian Handbook*: 1983)

Decline in Church Attendance

Church attendance is even lower than Church membership with an estimated 36 million British people who do not go to church. Peter Brierley, editor of the *UK Christian Handbook* and Director of MARC Europe, suggests that there are 31.4 million unchurched people in England, 2.5 million in Scotland, 1.7 million in Wales and 0.2 million in Northern Ireland.

The average percentage of the population attending church in England revealed by the Nationwide Initiative in Evangelism survey and reported in 'Prospect for the Eighties' is eleven per cent. This is inflated by the number of those who attend church twice on Sundays and a more accurate figure is probably nearer nine per cent (see the percentages by English county in Figure 3, The Unchurched of England).

Decline in Church Size

The decline in church membership and attendance, which has been unremitting for most of this century, has produced a situation where there are 51,000 churches in the United Kingdom (39,000 in England, 6,000 in Scotland, 4,000 in Wales and 2,000 in Northern Ireland), attended by fewer and fewer people. Consequently many have small and aged congregations, which are vulnerable to further decline and eventual closure. Protestant local church size in the United Kingdom has also become generally small, as the N.I.E. survey shows (see Figure 4, Protestant Church Size in England).

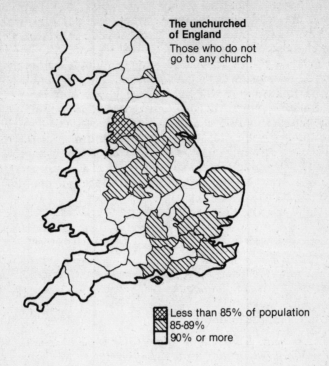

Figure 3. The Unchurched of England

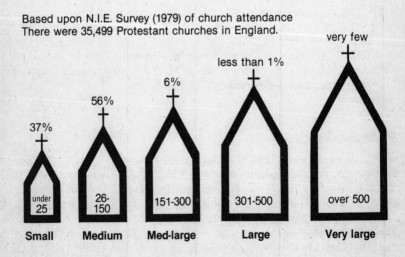

Figure 4. Protestant Church Size in England

Roman Catholic churches (only 4,200 throughout the United Kingdom) are predominantly large (twenty-one per cent) or very large (thirty-seven per cent) which is mainly due to the practice of building churches in areas with large Catholic communities, the stress upon worship and Mass attendance, and the multiple staff of priests.

However, the Roman Catholics are also declining in church attendance as the trends in the NIE Survey reveal. (See Figure 5, Percentages of English Church Attendance by Denomination). This is based upon the findings in 1975 and has a projection for 2000 AD. While this is of limited value statistically, it does illustrate where growth and decline are currently taking place. Free Church growth, however does not represent the traditional mainline Free Church denominations, but rather the House Churches and other Independent and Pentecostal groups.

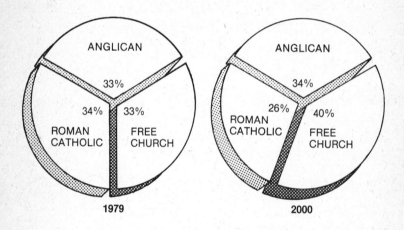

Figure 5. Percentage of English Church Attendance by Denomination

Denominational Decline

While the mainline denominations are declining steadily with only Baptist Church attendance improving, the denominational decline is not consistent, and some are growing quite rapidly. Most noticeable growth is among the Pentecostal, African/West Indian and Independent Churches (See Figure 3. Growth or Decline of British Denominations), but these are very small denominational groupings and the combined nett increase in membership between 1975 and 1980 is less than 70,000 members, with the Pentecostal increase just over 5,000.

African/West Indian Church growth is particularly encouraging

with considerable potential for more. This is a recent phenomenon
requiring further study, for there are valuable lessons to be learnt
from many of these flourishing churches. Growth among the Independent churches is mainly House Church growth which tends to be
produced by transfer from other denominations. While there is great
evangelistic potential among these new churches the vast majority
have yet to realise it.

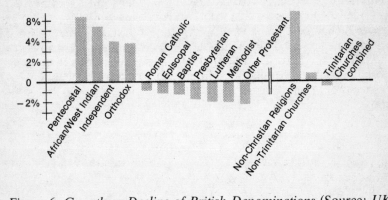

Figure 6. Growth or Decline of British Denominations (Source: *UK Christian Handbook* 1983)

Mainline denominational decline is not, however, uniform, for
within each denomination some local churches are growing while
others decline. A recent study of the growing churches in the NIE
Survey has revealed that some churches are growing in every county
of England and within every denomination. *Church growth is
undoubtedly possible but currently eludes the British Church on a
national scale.*

There is on the other hand another side to the story which cannot
escape those with faith and confidence in the gospel. If all these
51,000 local churches of every denomination could become outposts
of the Kingdom of God and for effective evangelism the prospect
for church growth throughout the United Kingdom would be
considerable.

*In fact if every local church added TWO more members annually
than it lost by death, transfer or lapse, the British Church would be
on the path to growth again.* This book has been written to help your
local church in that grand task.

Calls to Evangelise

It would be wrong to suggest that this decline of the British Church
has been accepted with complacency and indifference by Church
leaders. Many attempts and projects to evangelise the United
Kingdom have been, and continue to be, placed before the churches.

In this century the Church of England has made two major attempts to promote evangelism.

During the First World War, in 1917, the Archbishops set up a 'Committee of Enquiry on the Evangelistic Work of the Church'. The second attempt, during World War Two, produced the booklet *Towards the Conversion of England* published in 1945. This booklet described the evangelistic task in terms of the conversion of the vast majority of English people and even a large proportion of Church people. It would appear that the position remains unchanged a generation later.

Other denominations and Christian agencies have endeavoured to call the country to Christ. Evangelistic crusades have been sponsored; evangelistic programmes based on local churches have been devised; national and even international conferences on evangelism have been convened, and now we find ourselves in a 'Decade of Evangelism'.

These efforts and activities through the years have been limited in their success and today every committed Christian must surely be praying for a spiritual breakthrough that will arrest the decline and bring thousands of British people to Christ before it is too late. Many Church leaders have great expectations for the next few years. Forces are at work in the nation and the churches that would appear to indicate that God is preparing a harvest. The wind of the Spirit is blowing and signs of hope are being reported within several denominations and from many quarters.

One of the encouraging signs is the willingness of many British Christians to look to the growing churches of the world to see what may be learned from their experience. Modern travel and communications now make it possible for Christians to come from overseas to engage in missions, preaching, teaching and evaluation. This input from the world Church is very important, for, as Bishop John V. Taylor said as long ago as 1963 to the Commission on World Mission and Evangelism at Mexico City:

> I could point to one situation after another in my own country where it is becoming patently clear that British Christians on their own can never meet the need. However faithful and enthusiastic our mission to our own people may be, we are too small, too burdened with our own history, to be able to break through with newness and surprise. And the very essence of the Gospel is surprise. We must call in the partners the Lord has given us.'
>
> (TAYLOR 1964:60)

In 1981 the Church of England opened its doors to a group of Third World Christian leaders – 'Partners in Mission' – and invited them to assess their life and mission. Their findings are written up in the report *To a Rebellious House*.

Evangelists are coming to these shores from North and South

America, India and Africa. As this book is being written we are
actively involved in preparing for the extended visits of Dr Billy
Graham and Dr Luis Palau in Mission England and Mission to
London in 1983 and 1984. One other import from overseas is the
Church Growth Movement.

Despite the constant and continuing church decline the subject at
the top of many agendas is 'Church Growth'. Whether motivated by
faith, curiosity or desperation, it is a fact that many British Church
leaders are looking to this Movement for help. It is therefore
important that we understand its origins.

THE ORIGINS OF CHURCH GROWTH

Five years ago the term 'Church Growth' was little known and of
no significance to most Church leaders in the United Kingdom.
Only missionary scholars realised it was a technical term describing
principles and procedures of Christian mission developed from the
foundational research of an American missionary scholar, Dr Donald
A. McGavran.

Donald MacGavran is a third-generation missionary veteran of
over thirty years service with the United Christian Missionary
Society. Born in India of missionary parents, he was educated in the
United States and served in the country of his birth from 1923 to
1954, specialising in the fields of education and the administration
of medical work.

Research in India

His pioneering research and writing was done in association with the
Methodist Bishop J. Waskom Pickett. McGavran acknowledges his
indebtedness to Dr Pickett in this initial research into the remarkable
movements to Christ among the lower caste and outcaste peoples of
India. By asking fundamental questions and carefully analysing the
missionary enterprise, they became convinced that the work of
missions could be better administered and employed.

Little interest was aroused in missionary circles when this research
was published in the 1930s, but McGavran continued his research to
discover how people are converted to Christ and churches grow. The
results of his studies were eventually published in 1955 as *The Bridges
of God: A Study in the Strategy of Missions*.

The publishers were World Dominion Press of London who had
earlier published the works of Anglican missionary scholar Roland
Allen. In his preface to the book, the late Sir Kenneth Grubb of the
Church Missionary Society commends *Bridges of God* as a 'tract for
the times' with its strategies for church growth. He also likened
McGavran's ideas to those of Roland Allen.

Mission historian, Professor Kenneth Scott Latourette, author of
the seven-volume *History of the Expansion of Christianity* wrote the

foreword and described it as, 'One of the most important books on missionary methods that has appeared in many years.' *The publication of* Bridges of God *is regarded as the launching of the Church Growth Movement.*

In 1959 McGavran published *How Churches Grow* which challenged missionary leaders to reconsider their priorities and strategies in mission. It called for a major revision of methods to take advantage of the tremendous opportunities for evangelism and church planting in many parts of the world.

As a mission executive with his denomination McGavran was able to extend his research to such countries as Mexico, Puerto Rico, the Philippines, Congo, Jamaica and Thailand and develop his insights into formal principles of Church Growth.

The Institute of Church Growth

In 1961 McGavran opened an Institute of Church Growth for the training of an international body of students on the campus of North West Christian College at Eugene, Oregon. The influence and activity of the Institute grew until the facilities proved inadequate. A solution to the problem came when McGavran was invited to become the founding Dean of the School of World Mission at the Fuller Theological Seminary, Pasadena, California. So in 1965 the Institute moved to Pasadena, its present home.

The School of World Mission has experienced remarkable growth and increasing influence in missionary affairs. An international faculty offers post-graduate degree courses to missionary candidates, missionaries on furlough and church leaders from all over the world. The increasing demand has resulted in the introduction of extension ministries through international lecturing programmes by the faculty and an 'In-Service-Programme' of studies for students who remain overseas.

While critical of some of the emphases of the Church Growth Movement, Dr Lesslie Newbigin writes:

'The calling of men and women to be converted, to follow Jesus, and to be part of his community is and must always be at the centre of mission.

'One of today's most influential schools of missiology takes this as its central emphasis. The Institute of Church Growth, located at the Fuller Theological Seminary and under the leadership of Dr Donald McGavran, has forced missionary agencies in many parts of the world to ask why churches do not grow and to plan deliberately for church growth and expect it as the normal experience of missions'.

(NEWBIGIN 1978:136)

Church Growth theory has developed through the research of the faculty, their students and supporters of the Movement. Hundreds of research papers are now available with major studies of church growth published for such areas as Mexico, Brazil, Argentina, Jamaica, Fiji, New Guinea, Taiwan, Nigeria, Ethiopia, Spain, Italy, Scandinavia and England. These findings from growing churches around the world are related to the growth of churches throughout Church history and compared with the growth of churches in the Bible. The resulting principles of Church Growth are then available for application in the churches of all lands, (see Figure 7, The Development of Church Growth Principles).

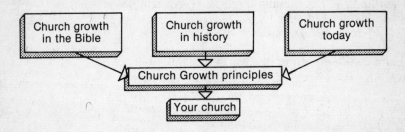

Figure 7. The Development of Church Growth Principles

Will these Church Growth principles developed from the theology, history and contemporary experience of missions bring growth to your church? Not necessarily, but they will help you *overhaul your church and prepare for the activity of the Spirit of God*, who alone is able to make your church effective in the mission of God and bring true church growth.

Church Growth in America

Dr McGavran's original and abiding concern is the propagation of the gospel and the establishment of churches among the millions who have never heard of Jesus Christ. While recognising that Church Growth principles apply throughout the world his concern is to make disciples of the exploding populations of the Third World.

As early as the late 1950s American students had urged the application of these principles in the USA. During the 1960s others called for the expertise and emphases of the developing Movement to be available to the American Church. In 1970 McGavran published *Understanding Church Growth* and Dr C Peter Wagner, professor of Church Growth at the School of World Mission, says of the book:

'It played a part in preparing America for Church Growth. It treated Church Growth on a global basis, vigorously exposed the fallacy of defensive thinking, and stated the universal principles which characterize it. He illustrated growth principles almost entirely from the expansion of churches overseas. It must be considered the Magna Carta of the Church Growth Movement.'

(WAGNER 1976:14)

The first conscious attempt to introduce Church Growth to the USA was a seminar for American Church leaders in 1972. This was in response to a demand for the School of World Mission to recognise the USA as part of the world! Since then many courses and conferences have been offered at Pasadena and throughout North America. An increasing number of American denominational colleges and agencies offer training and local church consultancy and the Movement continues to grow in influence and experience.

After two years' research of growing American churches, in 1976 Dr Wagner published *Your Church Can Grow*. This popular book introduced 'Seven vital signs of a healthy church' and offered the Movement's insights in less technical terms to a wider Christian audience.

Church Growth literature has multiplied during the past decade. It may be classified in four groups: 1. technical books based upon research and mainly devoted to Third World churches; 2. general books on American Church Growth; 3. national or denominational adaptations of Church Growth principles; and 4. books related to specific areas of Church Growth theory. New titles are promoted in the monthly Church Growth Bulletin and made available at discount from the associated Book Club.

Church Growth in the United Kingdom

In 1978 Dr Wagner joined a group of British Church leaders for a Church Growth consultation at the London Bible College. The consultation attempted to draw together various agencies and individuals who were interested in, or promoting Church Growth principles in the United Kingdom.

In his description of the purpose of the gathering, Dr Peter Cotterell, Director of Missionary Studies at LBC and one of the original convenors of the consultation, drew attention to the failure of the great majority of British churches to bring men and women to Christ. He commended Church Growth principles that had helped churches in many parts of the world to improve their health and effectiveness and hoped that the consultation would stimulate the sensitive introduction of Church Growth principles in British churches to promote their renewal and growth.

Two Bible Society staff, the Rev Tom Houston and the Rev Eddie Gibbs, were keynote speakers at the consultation as the Society had taken a bold step in offering basic Church Growth courses earlier in the year. There had been increasing concern in the Society about the declining British Church in the context of the ever increasing needs of the growing world Church and it was believed that lessons learned from the mission field needed to be applied at home.

Since 1978 the Bible Society has held 200 courses throughout the United Kingdom, attended by 13,500 ministers and lay leaders of all denominations. The demand for this and similar ministries continues and an increasing number of books, publications and agencies are available to serve the British churches.

Denominational adaptations of Church Growth theory are being applied within home and foreign mission departments and the day may not be far off when the vision of Canon Alexander Wedderspoon of Winchester Cathedral for the development of the Church Growth Movement in England is realised:

'It is likely that there will be three main stages:
(a) The initial training of selected clergy and lay leaders by existing trained consultants.
(b) The further training of some of the best of these men and women as *church growth consultants*.
(c) The setting up of a central agency responsible for the co-ordination of research, publications, training and forward planning.'

(WEDDERSPOON 1981:133)

British Church Growth Association

On 14 September 1981 the British Church Growth Association was formed with the intention of gathering together researchers, consultants, teachers and practitioners to promote the growth of British churches. It was supported by representatives of many denominations and societies in the United Kingdom and it is hoped that the Association will provide an increasing wealth of information and insight about British church growth. Details of the Association and other agencies will be found in Appendix 1. A list of books mentioned throughout this book is in Appendix 2.

SUMMARY

In this chapter we have contrasted the phenomenal growth of the world Church with the appalling decline of the British Church.

The value of lessons about growth from overseas and therefore the potential contribution of the Church Growth Movement have been stressed. The origins of the Movement and its introduction to the United Kingdom by Bible Society and other agencies, and the formation of the British Church Growth Association has been described.

2 What's So Special About Church Growth?

Church Growth is a technical term. It was chosen by Dr McGavran because he believed 'evangelism' and 'missions' had lost their true meaning. They had been defined so many times that they no longer represented the burning zeal of the Church to obey the great commission to preach the gospel to the whole world and 'make disciples' of all peoples everywhere.

Church Growth is not to be confused with the tremendous growth of the Church during the past two centuries that has produced a truly 'universal' religion with a Christian presence in every nation for the first time in history. It is not the study of great 'people movements' as whole tribes have turned to Christ; nor is it simply the study of growing churches.

While Church Growth has benefitted from the study of these phenomena, the term is limited to the *missionary school of thought* that has developed from the work of Dr McGavran. In order to protect and clarify the term, a formal definition has been introduced by the Academy of American Church Growth, and adopted with minor modifications by international Church Growth agencies around the world.

The definition adopted by the British Church Growth Association is as follows:

Church Growth investigates the nature, function, structure, health and multiplication of Christian churches as they relate to the effective implementation of Christ's commission to 'Go, then, to all peoples everywhere and make them my disciples' (Matt. 28.19–20).

Church Growth seeks to combine the revealed truths of the Bible with related insights from contemporary social and behavioural sciences.

This definition contains several important and distinctive emphases and in this chapter I want to consider four:

THE TASK OF EVANGELISM

In 1980 three international conferences were organised to discuss the mission of the Church. In May, the World Council of Churches' *Commission on World Mission and Evangelism* convened a conference at Melbourne, Australia with the theme 'Your Kingdom Come'. The main concern was the liberation of the poor of the earth from economic, political and social oppression.

In June a *Consultation on World Evangelisation* was held at Pattaya, Thailand, under the sponsorship of the Lausanne Committee. Meeting under the banner 'How Shall They Hear' the delegates endeavoured to identify and plan the evangelisation of the unreached and 'hidden peoples' of the earth – Muslims, Buddhists, Hindus, Jews, nominal Christians, animists and others.

In September, mission agencies from around the world came together at Edinburgh, site of the great World Missionary Conference of 1910, to clarify priorities and draw up plans for crossing 16,750 culturally definable frontiers with the gospel. One of the organisers, Dr Ralph D. Winter, considered this conference to be an ideal complement to Melbourne and Pattaya. Called the *World Consultation on Frontier Mission*, its purpose was 'to clarify the key administrative decisions that will move from facts, strategies and dreams to plans, bold moves and realities'.

Even a cursory reading of the papers presented at these conferences reveals the confusion and, sadly, the divisions in the Church over the nature and priorities of Christian mission today. In the midst of this confusion the Church Growth Movement, claiming biblical authority, continues to stress the task of evangelism; '. . . *the effective implementation of Christ's Commission to "Go, then, to all peoples everywhere and make them my disciples" (Matt. 28:19).'*

Church Growth believes that the Scriptures and supremely the Cross of Christ bear witness to the fact that man's greatest need is personal reconciliation to God. Therefore the task of evangelism is the fundamental expression of the Church's mission.

Evangelism and Social Concern

Of course evangelism cannot be separate from compassionate *social service* that deals with the immediate physical and social needs of those peoples being evangelised. When the great eighteenth century evangelist George Whitefield went to America, in addition to his sermons and prayer books he carried medicines for the sick and provisions for the destitute. In conjunction with his fervent preaching of the gospel he established an orphanage, provided food for the hungry, employed ex-convicts and engaged in many other 'acts of mercy'.

There is also no doubt that evangelisation leads to radical changes in the social order of evangelised peoples. As new converts submit to the reign of Christ they confront the practices of their society with the ideals of the Kingdom of God. As the people of God they speak to their peoples on his behalf and exercise a prophetic ministry which summons the existing social order to conform to divine standards of justice and righteousness.

Social action attempts to change the structure of society that cause injustice and deprivation. For example, many of the social reforms within British society in the eighteenth and nineteenth centuries were the result of the *evangelistic* zeal of Methodism and the Salvation Army.

When William Booth and the Salvation Army pioneers publicised the scandal of child prostitution in Victorian Britain they were engaged in *evangelising* hundreds of juvenile prostitutes. Some were converted to Christ and told their story. They exposed the horror of children sold like slaves to procurers to serve in the brothels of Britian and the Continent. Many, as young virgins, had been drugged and violated by wealthy men who paid huge sums to the brothel-keepers. Clients included Members of Parliament, the nobility and even foreign royalty. This vile practice was protected by inadequate legislation, indifference to the plight of the poor, the corruption of the police and judiciary and the immorality of many rich and powerful people. The Salvationists and others had to endure violence, false accusation, ridicule and even imprisonment before the nation's conscience was stirred. Eventually Parliament acted with the Criminal Amendment Act of 1885 that raised the age of consent to sixteen years old and gave authority to the agencies of reform.

As the Church considers world mission at the close of the twentieth century it cannot fail to be deeply moved by the contemporary sufferings of mankind. It is estimated that 800 million people are destitute and 10,000 die of starvation every day. Millions more are socially oppressed by the political regimes of the extreme right or left. The world's dwindling resources are unequally shared and the economic and technological imbalance between 'North and South' aggravate the situation. Our mass media vividly and constantly portray the horrors of famine, disease and oppression. How are we to respond to these obvious needs around us?

The temptation is to concentrate all our energies and resources upon the alleviation of these physical and social needs. We are stirred by the compassion of Christ to loving service, and if we are not on our guard it is possible to neglect and even forget the commission of Christ to 'make disciples'.

The Priority of Evangelism

The Church will not forget her Commission if she stresses the priority of evangelism, 'symbiotically' related to our social service with social action following in the wake of true evangelisation. Dr McGavran comments on these issues when he says:

'The Church today faces deep cleavage among her members at just this point. Some are so deeply impressed by the physical needs of man – and who can deny their urgency? – that meeting these needs becomes for them the highest present purpose of God and the Church. Deeply as I sympathise with the problem and long as I have ministered to desperate physical need – for years I superintended a leprosy home – I cannot ally myself with these brethren. On the contrary, my conviction is that the salvation granted to those who believe in Jesus Christ is still the supreme need of man, and all other human good flows from that prior reconciliation to God.'

(McGAVRAN 1970:51)

The priority of evangelism in the mission of the Church was recognised at the *Congress on World Evangelisation* at Lausanne, Switzerland in July 1974. This gathering of almost 3,000 evangelical leaders from 150 nations was described by *Time Magazine* as, 'a formidable forum, possibly the widest-ranging meeting of Christians ever held'. The Congress summarised its conclusions and expressed its commitment to world evangelisation in the *Lausanne Covenant*, and gave two reasons for this priority:

(a) The Immensity of the Task
The Church has been commissioned to preach the gospel to the whole world until the end of time. Every generation of all races must be evangelised and today sixty-seven per cent of the world's population continue to owe no allegiance to Jesus Christ. The World Christian Encyclopaedia estimates that in 1980 there were 1,561 million evangelised non-Christians who were aware of Christianity, Christ and the gospel but had not accepted them. A further 1,381 million remain completely unevangelised. Therefore world evangelisation requires the resources of the whole Church to take the whole gospel to the whole world.

(b) The Nature of the Church
The Church is at the centre of God's plan and purpose for the Universe (Eph. 1.9, 10, 20–35) and is, 'the appointed means of spreading the Gospel'. Other humanitarian agencies seek to alleviate human suffering, only the Church will also preach the gospel and exercise the ministry of reconciliation (1 Cor. 5.18–20).

Additional reasons for this priority of evangelism are:

(c) The Example of Jesus
With prayer (John 17.38), and by commission (John 20.21), our Lord sends his people to follow his example and continue his ministry. Christ's mission is the model for the Church's mission. If we study the life of Jesus we realise that he prayerfully made plans and established priorities for his ministry. The recruitment and deploy-

ment of his disciples are obvious occasions (Luke 4.12,13; 9.1–6; 10.1–16).

During his ministry he was also conscious of the limited time available for his mission (Mark 8.31) and therefore restricted his travels (Luke 13.22) and contacts (Matt. 15.24). It is not surprising that these constraints forced him to make difficult decisions many times. On one occasion, when he could have remained to heal the reached, he chose to leave and evangelise the unreached (Luke 4.31). He gave priority to evangelism.

The Church follows the example of her Lord when she does the same.

(d) The Example of the Apostles

The apostles enjoyed the confidence of our Lord during his ministry (Luke 12.41) and following his resurrection (Acts 1.3). In obedience to the Great Commission (Matt. 28.16–20; Mark 16.14–18; Luke 24.36–51; John 20.19–23; Acts 1.1–11) and in submission to the Holy Spirit they evangelised and planted churches throughout the Roman Empire and beyond its frontiers.

It is hard to believe that they misunderstood the Saviour or were misdirected by the Spirit in the priorities of their mission. The Church is apostolic when it acts upon the priority of evangelism.

(e) The Prospect of Christ's Return

Christ's promise (Matt. 28.20) and the angelic testimony (Acts 1.11) have placed the Church's mission in an eschatological context. Every time we pray, 'They Kingdom come' we anticipate the coming of the King and realise that time and opportunity are limited. Professor Johannes Verkuyl of Amsterdam recognises the importance of the 'Eschatological Motive' and the 'Motive of Haste' in the history of Christian missions and says:

'. . . any church which does not eagerly long for the kingdom and for the "fulness of the heathen" to come into it is no longer a church, it has become an exclusive club. Churches on every continent must begin to feel the throbbing desire to gather all peoples under one Head, Jesus Christ, the only rightful owner of human lives.

'Anyone acquainted with the biographies of the pioneers in world mission knows of their strong drive to get the message out quickly, but no generation of Christians should ever be without it, and therefore Karl Barth could cite sluggishness as one of the major sins of the church today.

'We must as Christians be alert to what the New Testament calls the "times and seasons" and take appreciative advantage of them while it is still daylight for the night is coming when no man can work.'

(VERKUYL 1978:167)

The urgency of the hour calls for the priority of evangelism.

(f) The Cause of Social Liberation

The suggestion that the priority of evangelism is necessary to the cause of social liberation is based upon the conviction that transformed individuals transform society. There have been numerous occasions in the history of the Church when rapid and radical changes in the social order of a tribe or nation have followed the conversion of its leaders and members. As McGavran points out:

'. . . the only way toward his reconstructed society is reconstructed men. The only certain foundation to a Christ-ruled social order is Christ's rulership in the hearts of the men and women who compose it. A corollary of this truth is that full implementation of total Christianity is impossible till there has been tremendous increase in the numbers of real Christians.'

(McGAVRAN 1959:27)

The social liberation of peoples by the Church logically requires the priority of evangelism. In certain circumstances however where lives are at risk through famine, disease or war, social ministries must take precedence.

(g) The Plight of Man

Probably the most compelling reason for the priority of evangelism is the plight of man. The Scriptures reveal man as alienated from God and subject to his judgement. Man is lost and needs to be saved. In the words of the Lausanne Covenant:

'Such a salvation (a rescue that is from the guilt of sin and from the judgement of God upon it) is urgently needed because *all men are perishing because of sin*. "Perishing" is a terrible word, but Jesus himself used it (e.g. Matthew 18.14; Luke 13.3,5; cf. John 3.15,16) and so did the apostles (e.g. 1 Corinthians 1.18); therefore we must not shy away from it. *All men* are in this plight until and unless they are saved by Christ. Yet there is something else we know about all men, namely that God loves *all men*. And because of His great love Scripture says that he is forbearing and patient towards sinners, *not wishing that any should perish*, but that all should *repent* (2 Peter 3.9). Although this is the wish of God (for he says, "I have no pleasure in the death of any one" Ezekiel 18.32), we have to add that some will refuse to repent and believe, will instead *reject Christ*, and so will repudiate the joy of salvation and condemn themselves to eternal separation from God (cf. Thessalonians 1.7–9). The prospect is almost too dreadful to contemplate; we should be able to speak of hell only with tears.'

(LAUSANNE 1975:17)

There is little understanding and even less sympathy with this doctrine in contemporary British churches. But I would be less than true to the Scriptures and indeed my own heart, if I failed to give it prominence. One also hesitates to quote a reference to the plight of man and tears. Very few tears are shed for the 36 million or so lost men and women of these British Isles, even by those who believe the doctrine. Surely their plight and the plight of all men demands the priority of evangelism?

A Decade of Evangelism?

In 1980 British churches were offered two major national conferences to motivate and encourage evangelism through local churches. In April, the Evangelical Alliance sponsored the *National Congress on Evangelism* at Prestatyn to launch a 'Decade of Evangelism'. In September the *Nationwide Initiative in Evangelism Assembly* was held at Nottingham, in an attempt to involve the mainstream denominations in evangelism.

The support and attendances at these conferences represented a pitifully small percentage of the 52,000 churches in the United Kingdom. It was a further indication of the low priority given to evangelism, even by 'evangelical' churches. The subsequent run-down of the N.I.E. and the lack of support for Mission England and Mission to London by so many churches are further indications of the lack of interest in evangelism. We may therefore find that this emphasis upon the task and priority of evangelism by the Church Growth Movement will be its greatest contribution to the renewal and growth of British churches.

THE GROWTH OF THE CHURCH

The second distinctive emphasis of the Church Growth Movement is the scientific analysis of the '. . . *nature, function, structure, health and multiplication of Christian churches*' in order to promote their growth among the peoples of the earth. The Great Commission is seen as the justification for this emphasis and the mandate for church growth. The Church Growth Movement stresses the fact that every church should grow.

The authors of the Gospels are unanimous in declaring that the work of Jesus Christ as the Messiah and Servant of God entailed the calling of men to believe in him and become his followers. Those who responded became his disciples. This calling to faith and learning cannot be limited to the period before the Crucifixion. Firstly, because Jesus taught that the relationship would survive death (Matt. 19.23–30; Luke 12.8,9; John 11.25–27) and secondly because the Evangelists are equally unanimous that the risen Lord commanded the surviving community of disciples to continue his ministry by preaching the gospel and making disciples of all peoples everywhere

(Matt. 28.16–20; Mark 16.14–18; Luke 24.36–51; John 20.19–23; Acts 1.1–11).

Obviously the term disciple primarily describes the individual's relationship to the teacher. John the Baptist, the Pharisees, Moses and many others had disciples who were contemporaries with the disciples of Jesus. A disciple was a pupil bound to a teacher to acquire practical and theoretical knowledge. The word could also describe a person related as an apprentice to a tradesman, doctor, philosopher, rabbi or prophet and, occasionally, someone who was actually following the master on his journeys.

The disciples certainly recognised Jesus as their teacher, but their discipleship included much more, for he was their Master and Lord (John 13.13). A disciple of Jesus had faith in his person and unreserved commitment to his mission; anything less was inadequate (John 6.66–69). Those who followed him were called to take up a cross, lay down their lives for his sake, and leave family and forsake fortune (Mark 8.34–38; Luke 14.33). It is clear that these demands cut across all social obligations outside the company of the disciples. In fact they served to produce, as they were intended to, a social group with obligations to each other (Mark 10.43–44; John 13.34–35). They were called to be a community of disciples gathered around Jesus.

These disciples of Jesus, at least 500 at the time of his death (1 Cor. 15:6) with about 120 at Jerusalem (Acts 2:15), were committed to him and each other. But they were not allowed to become introverted or exclusive. Discipleship included a call to service (Mark 1:17; 6:7–13; Luke 5:10; 10:1–13) and suffering (Matt. 10:16–25) on behalf of others. They were a community of men and women who were committed to the mission of Christ in the world from which they had been called (John 17:14–18). They were, in fact, the 'embryonic' Church.

When the risen Lord charged his disciples to 'make disciples', he undoubtedly intended the formation of similar communities and this is precisely what is recorded in the Acts of the Apostles. Gathered communities of disciples were formed when individuals responded to the proclamation of the gospel, whether in Jerusalem (2:41,42,47), Samaria (8:5–8, 14–16) or the 'ends of the earth' (14:19–22).

A variety of names were used to describe the disciples and their communities. They were *believers* (5:14) who shared a common faith; *brethren* (6:3) who were born into God's family and related to each other; *Christians* (11:26) with a common allegiance to Christ; *witnesses* (3:15) with a story to tell; *people of the Way* (9:12) who followed the same rule of life; *the flock* (20:28) under one Shepherd and *the Church* (14:23) who, as the 'called-out-ones', assembled together. These terms illustrate that becoming and being a disciple is entirely personal, but the Christian life is maintained and matured by the fellowship of other believers.

In obedience to the Great Commission the disciples evangelised individuals and formed the converts together in local churches. *Therefore the Commission to 'make disciples' is a call for church planting, and the basic mandate for church growth.*

When we turn to the remainder of the New Testament the apostolic authors, especially the apostle Paul, describe the nature and function of the Church with her universal and local dimensions, cosmic destiny and present duties. The term *disciple* is no longer used as the community is addressed, but the Commission abides in all its simplicity, 'make disciples' by evangelism and church planting. *The Great Commission is a command to grow churches.*

The Four Dimensions of Growth

The growth of the church by the addition of new converts is the fundamental dimension of growth but there are obviously many other areas of growth that relate to the '. . . *nature, function, structure, health and multiplication of Christian churches'.* Church Growth thinking embraces more than an interest in numbers and includes a concern for quality as well as quantity. Latin American missionary scholar Dr Orlando Costas suggests 'holistic expansion' as a suitable term to describe the multidimensional growth of the body of Christ, and defines *four dimensions* (see figure 8):

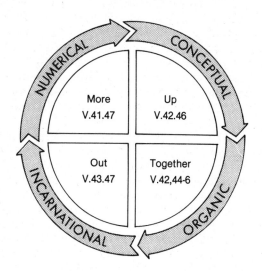

Figure 8: The Four Dimensions of Growth – Acts 2.41–7

'In order for church growth to be holistic expansion it must encompass four major areas: the numerical, organic, conceptual and incarnational.'

(COSTAS 1974:89)

(a) *Growing More in Numbers – Numerical Growth*
This describes the recruitment of individuals to active membership
of the church (Acts 2.47; 4.4; 6.7; 9,31, 35; 16.5 etc.). They are
incorporated into the fellowship of believers and share its corporate
life of worship and witness. Members are recruited in four ways:

Biological Growth occurs when the children of Christian parents
come to a personal faith in Jesus Christ as Saviour and Lord and
join the Church, usually by a rite that recognises their status as
responsible members. This may be by confirmation, believer's
baptism, putting on the Salvation Army uniform, etc.

Despite the emphasis upon 'children's work' many children fail to
follow their parents in their commitment to Christ and the Church.
Of course, there is no guarantee that children will automatically
embrace their parent's faith, (John 3.5–8; Luke 12.51–53; 1 Tim.
3.4,12) but constant failure in this area indicates weaknesses in the
methods and materials used for sunday school and youth
programmes, and also in Christian family life.

Transfer Growth is the recruitment of members who are already
committed Christians, by transfer from other congregations. This
may be due to Christians moving from one area to another but
occasionally is the result of Christians changing churches for social
or doctrinal reasons. During a coffee-break at one of our Courses a
lady anxiously asked me to justify her move across the street from
a Methodist to a United Reform Church, because they had a youth
programme for her daughter. After several years she had become
an elder in the U.R.C., but assured me she was a Methodist at heart!

Many charisimatic and house churches have experienced tremendous numerical growth through the transfer of Christians attracted
by their worship and activities. One prominent house church leader
has estimated as many as ninety per cent! Tragically these churches
often fail to realise that new people are not new converts and consequently neglect their evangelistic responsibilities.

A recent study of a London church, recognised as a centre for
Charismatic renewal throughout the seventies, has shown that the
church added an average of *one member per year by conversion*
throughout the decade. It hosted conventions and celebrations led
by leading Charismatic preachers and groups, attracting coach loads
of people. Obviously many Christians benefitted from the ministry
offered by this church but its members failed miserably in the task
of evangelising their own community and they are now experiencing
serious decline.

Restoration Growth describes the restoration of lapsed Christians to
an active membership of regular worship and service.

It is invidious to single out a denomination but the following
example serves to illustrate a typical challenge for the mainline deno-

minations. Between 1933 and 1969 the Methodist Church lost a total of 1.2 million members of which thirty-nine per cent had died and forty-three per cent had voluntarily terminated their membership. Therefore, in one generation 500,000 Methodists left their churches. Some may have joined other denominations but a large number allowed their membership to lapse and ceased to worship. There are many reasons why these Christians became disillusioned with their churches, but the plain fact remains that hundreds of thousands of former Methodists need to return to the Shepherd and be restored to their fold.

Conversion Growth takes place when those outside the Church are brought to repentance and faith in Christ and join a local church as responsible members. There is a desperate need for all British churches to recruit by Conversion Growth and *unfortunately most are structured for Biological or Transfer Growth.*

Conversion to Christ will be evident in changed attitudes of mind and patterns of behaviour (Acts 9.20–22; 1 Cor. 6.9–11); 2 Cor. 5.17). These are the result of spiritual rebirth and the activity of the Holy Spirit within the believer (John 1.11, 12; 3.3–8; Rom. 8.9–17; Gal. 3.1–5, 1 Pet. 1.1, 3,23). The new birth is the means of entry to the family and Kingdom of God and the 'invisible' Church, and this new life is sustained by the local church where, ideally, the family meets and the King reigns.

(b) *Growing Up in Maturity – Conceptual Growth*
This second dimension of growth describes the personal and corporate development of Christian understanding (Acts 2.42; Col. 1.9,10,28; 2 Tim. 3.14–16; Heb. 5.11–6.8; 1 Pet. 2.2). Dr Costas defines it as 'the degree of consciousness that a community of faith has with regard to its nature and mission to the world.' This knowledge comes from the Word of God.

The Great Commission includes the teaching of disciples as a fundamental activity (Matt. 28.20) and therefore, by implication, the responsibility of learning the faith as a basic responsibility. The primitive fellowships of believers were constituted on the basis of the Lord's teaching through the apostles (Acts 2.42). After further illumination and revelation (John 16.12–13; Acts 15.28; 1 Cor. 14.37; Rev. 1.1,2), this teaching took written form under the direction of the Holy Spirit and became the New Testament. These writings, together with those of the Old Testament, were recognised as the authoritative Scriptures of the Church and the ultimate source of its doctrine and practice (2 Tim. 3.14–16; 2 Pet. 3.15–16).

Ignorance of the Scriptures and insensitivity to the Holy Spirit led to such ills as immaturity (1 Pet. 2.2), disunity (1 Cor. 3.1–4), impotence and apostasy (Heb. 5.11–6:8) and destructive heresy (2 Pet. 1.20–22). Consequently the Christian and the Church were in constant need of reformation by the Word of God and renewal by the Spirit of God (cf. Matt. 22.29) – and still are.

The local church is a community formed and nurtured by the preaching and teaching of the Word of God (Acts 15.36). The progress of the gospel and the growth of the Church are even described as the increase of the Word (Acts 6.7; 12.24; 19.20). Therefore the progress of a Christian or church in every age and all cultures may be measured against this 'yardstick' of Scripture.

Taking into account variations of illumination, interpretation and culture we may gauge the maturity and ministry of every Christian and church throughout history. We may assess Irenaeus and a second century church in France; or Augustine and a fourth century church in North Africa; or Cranmer and a sixteenth century church in England; or Hudson Taylor and a nineteenth century church in China or any church at the close of this twentieth century.

Whether we evangelise and plant churches among the Karen of Burma, or the Quechua of Peru or the flat-dwellers of London, the Bible is the manual for mission and the guide for growth. It is therefore imperative that Christians grow in their understanding of biblical truth (Col. 1.9,10,21).

(c) *Growing Together in Community – Organic Growth*

Dr Paul Tournier, the well-known Christian psychologist, has said, 'Two things you cannot do alone . . . marry and be a Christian!' He affirms that while becoming and being a Christian are entirely dependent upon an intimate and personal relationship to Christ (Rom. 8.9), the Christian faith can only be lived in relationship (Acts 2.42–47) and in service to others (1 Pet. 4.10).

The New Testament describes these personal and corporate dimensions of Christianity in such passages as:

1 Cor. 12.27	'All of you are Christ's body, and each one is a part of it.'
Eph. 4.25	'Everyone must tell the truth to his fellow-believers, because we are all members together in the body of Christ.'
Heb. 10.25	'Let us not give up the habit of meeting together, as some are doing. Instead, let us encourage one another all the more, since you see that the Day of the Lord is coming nearer.'

Commitment to Christ includes commitment to a community and Organic Growth describes the formation and functioning of this communal life of the local church. Dr Costas defines it as:

'. . . the internal development of a local community of faith, i.e. the system of relationships among its members – its form of government, financial structure, leadership, types of activities in which its time and resources are invested etc.'

(COSTAS 1974:90)

Organic growth is concerned with such issues as depth of fellowship: quality of worship; training of new members; discovery of gifts and the exercise of ministry; appointment and role of leaders; practice of corporate prayer; celebration of the ordinances or sacraments – all that relates to the corporate organisation and activity of the local church.

(d) *Growing Out in Service and Witness – Incarnational Growth*
Dr Costas defines this as:

'. . . the degree of involvement of a community of faith in the life and problems of her social environment, i.e. her participation in the afflictions of her world; her prophetic, intercessory and liberating action on behalf of the weak and destitute; the intensity of her preaching to the poor, the brokenhearted, the captives, the blind, and the oppressed (Lk 4.18–21).'

(COSTAS 1974:90)

Incarnational Growth describes the development of the ministry of a local church as an extension and continuation of Christ's ministry.

In his final book, *I believe in the Great Commission*, Dr Max Warren evaluates the history of Christian missions by comparing it with the 'four-fold pattern' of our Lord's ministry. He shows that down the centuries the Church has endeavoured, however inadequately, to follow her Master in his ministry of preaching, teaching, healing and witness, (Matt. 4.23).

Today, as always every local church is called to demonstrate by word and deed the presence of Christ in society. This calls for an involvement in society that western Christianity finds hard to accept and more difficult to implement. We must avoid the twin dangers of absorption by or withdrawal from the world and learn afresh how to permeate society in the way Christ intended, as 'salt and light' (Matt. 5.13–16).

We have to learn anew how to preach the unchanging gospel to a rapidly changing society. Charles Spurgeon ministered very effectively in the 1880s but I am sure that even he would have done things very differently in the 1980s.

We have the responsibility of teaching the truths of God and his Kingdom today. Jesus and the apostles used many of the known methods and most of the available media to communicate the Good News of the Kingdom. Today the contemporary Church must be willing to claim for Christ the technology of modern communications to get the message across.

A local church should engage in a healing ministry even if many within the Church reject the miracle that underlines the message and the wonders that signify the Lord is with his people (Mark 16.20). While we rejoice in the progress of modern medicine surely we also believe in the extraordinary intervention of God in the healing process.

We must also learn to tap by prayer the unlimited spiritual resources available for the progress of God's mission.

Christians are called to stand against the forces of evil and the rebellion of men. As 'Christ-bearers', they must be known by their faith, hope and love. They are to contend for truth, righteousness and peace, in the market-place, factory-floor and home at the close of this twentieth century.

In all these ways churches must develop and grow, and as they do they experience Incarnational Growth.

Quality or Quantity?

The relationship and interdependence of these four dimensions of growth shows how impossible it is to separate quality from quantity in the church. A growing church should strive to grow in all four dimensions and recognise that numerical growth is as valid as any other dimension of growth. *In fact, failure to grow in quantity usually indicates weakness in quality*. An analysis of the causes of decline in numbers of church members always raises questions about the quality of a church's life.

This was well illustrated by British Baptists. At the 1977 Assembly of the Baptist Union, the Council received a request, 'to set up an interdepartmental commission to examine the causes of the numerical and spiritual decline of our denomination'. There was some debate about spiritual decline but the ski-slope graphs of membership confirmed the decline in numbers.

In response, the Council appointed a group to undertake an enquiry and publish a report. This was presented at the 1979 Assembly under the title, *Signs of Hope* and the denomination was asked for comments and suggestions that would lead to a 'strategy for action' to set before the 1980 Assembly. This strategy for 'Baptist Christians through the 80s' is described as a 'Call to Commitment' and covers six main areas of commitment:

to worship and pray	(Growing Together)
to evangelism	(Growing Out)
to learn	(Growing Up)
to care	(Growing Together and Out)
to serve	(Growing Out)
to leadership	(Growing Together)

As Baptists respond to this 'Call' for growth in quality of Christian life there should be a corresponding growth in quantity of members. I expect the Baptist denomination to grow more in numbers throughout the eighties as its members respond to these commitments, and confirm there is no dichotomy between quality and quantity in the principles of Church Growth.

THE COMPLEXITY OF CHURCH GROWTH

A minister was asked why he believed his church was growing so rapidly. He confidently replied, 'Because I preach the Word of God.' The minister of a neighbouring church was asked why his church had lost so many members and the congregation was now reduced to a handful. His equally confident reply was, 'Because I preach the Word of God.' Both ministers failed to recognise the complexity of factors at work in their churches. There are many reasons why churches grow or decline, but these men, like so many other Christians, had simple solutions and easy answers to the complex issues of the Church's mission.

Church Growth research and principles recognise that many factors contribute to the growth or decline of churches. This is a *third emphasis* contained within the definition. The stated intent of the Movement, '. . . *to combine the revealed truths of the Bible with related insights from the contemporary social and behavioural sciences'*, acknowledges the combination of factors that affect the local church. These have been identified within six main areas (see Figure 9).

Local Church Factors

These are factors *within the local church* that affect its growth or decline. Generally they relate to the activities of the minister and members but may also include such matters as the size, design and use of the church buildings.

Ministers who preach like the great C. H. Spurgeon are probably factors for growth. If, however, their sermons last an hour they are probably not! Churches that are poor in prayer and slack in service cannot expect to grow and churches that abandon the faith and lose their devotion to Christ will certainly die. Dan Taylor, the eighteenth century Baptist revivalist, identified this problem in the dying unitarian churches of his day. 'They degraded Christ and He degraded them,' was his verdict.

There are innumerable local church factors and many will be considered in the next chapter. There are also examples in the Bible. In Acts 6.1–6 the apostles were faced with the problems of priorities, leadership and pastoral care in the church of Jerusalem. When these were resolved, growth followed (Acts 6.7).

When Paul chastised the immoral church leader at Corinth (1 Cor. 5.1–13) he was concerned for the holiness, health and growth of the church among the residents of that immoral city. The awful condition of the church was an obstacle to effective mission in that community.

The Letters to the Seven Churches (Rev. 2.1–3.22) contain many references to local church factors which affected their vitality and

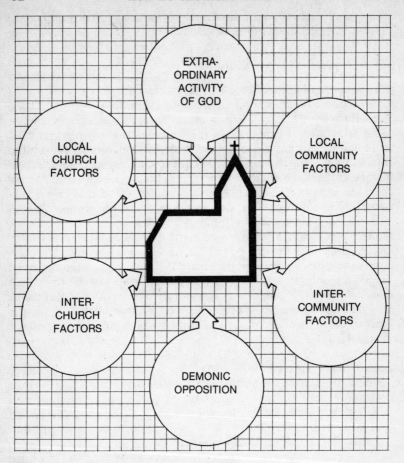

Figure 9. Church Growth is Complex

mission. In fact they are threatened with extinction if they do not deal
with such internal problems as lovelessness, heresy, compromise,
immorality, lethargy and nominality.

Local Community Factors

The local church is greatly influenced by the area in which it is
situated. Local community factors describe the influences for growth
or decline that arise *from the local community*. These are more
common than most churches realise and what may be obvious to the
outside observer often remains undetected by the local church.

For example, the mobility of the population in the local community
has a considerable effect on the church. The development of new
towns, the building of large housing estates and the redevelopment

of inner city areas cause the rapid movement of large numbers of people. Many city churches have seen their immediate area demolished and have been left standing like proud and lone survivors of the London Blitz. Churches have to survive the exodus of their members and must face the challenge of reaching new residents who are often of a different social, racial or religious group.

Churches have declined because the local population were dependent upon a particular industry or activity that has become redundant. Many Welsh Chapels have declined or even closed because a mine has been exhausted and shut down. The miners move to other pits and take their incomes and families with them. The Baptist Chapel at Coelbren in West Glamorgan has lost about sixty per cent of its members in recent years because of the closure of the local mines. Churches and Chapels in similar circumstances may remain faithful in all things, but will inevitably decline. Any calls to more fervent prayer and zealous service must be balanced by a recognition of this Local Community Factor.

Failure to recognise the influence of the local community upon church growth may create a false picture of the health and vitality of a church. The statistics of a Methodist Church in Bedfordshire revealed very rapid growth throughout the seventies. Attendance had grown from forty to 150, so we asked for the completion of a brief questionnaire that would reveal the causes of this remarkable growth. The reply proved disappointing as the usual signs of growth were absent. The clue to the growth lay in the concluding statement, 'There is much new building going on in our area'. The growing community had produced a growing church.

There are numerous biblical examples of the influence of the community upon a church. It is impossible to understand many sections of the letters of the apostle Paul without a knowledge of the places he wrote to. His own ministry in Ephesus would have been very different had the Temple of Diana not been there (Acts 19.1–41).

In the Letters to the Seven Churches (Rev. 2.1–3.22), there are many allusions to the communities. Smyrna had its 'synagogue of Satan' and Pergamum had 'Satan's throne'. These two churches could not escape the harmful influence of the large and hostile Jewish community at Smyrna or the multitudes of credulous and superstitious pilgrims to the Temples of Asklepios, Zeus and Caesar at Pergamum.

If the church of the first century was charged by Christ to be sensitive to *local community factors*, so must the church of the twentieth century.

Inter-Church Factors

The local church is greatly influenced by links, whether formal or informal, *with the wider Christian community*. Other churches, denominational leaders, parachurch agencies, ecumenical events, Christian literature, etc. all have considerable effect on the local church.

Very few churches have not been influenced for good or ill, by the charismatic movement, or the World Council of Churches, or Bible Society, or Bishops, or Jesuits, or Karl Barth, or Charles Wesley! Obviously our willingness to be influenced will depend upon our denomination, churchmanship, or theology, but none of us are completely insulated from the great universal Church to which we all belong.

The vast majority of British churches have formal links with each other within denominations or fellowships. Some, like the Anglicans or Roman Catholics, have several levels of leadership above the local church and clearly defined territorial boundaries and associations. Local parish churches are grouped into a Diocese with a Bishop exercising authority and oversight. Church government above the local church is by Synod or Council and decisions taken at this level may greatly affect the parish church. A Bishop's refusal to replace a curate or provide certain funds could prove to be the final and fatal blow in the life of a church.

Methodist Conference or Circuit decisions may cause a Methodist Chapel to grow or decline. The Salvation Army's short-term deployment of its officers may have disastrous effects upon their Citadels. And even local Baptist churches are influenced by emphases and decisions at Association or Union levels.

When the London Baptist Association was formed in 1865 it had three main objectives: 'fellowship – co-operation and unity: evangelism – to advance the Kingdom of Christ; and church extension – a continuing programme of church building.' Every Baptist church in London had these priorities on its agenda. It is not surprising, therefore, that in the first hundred years this Association grew from a fellowship of fifty-nine to 279 churches.

Biblical examples of Inter-Church Factors are found throughout the letters of the apostles. In fact the letters are an example in themselves.

The apostle Paul commends the Thessalonians for their tremendous influence and example (1 Thess. 1.2–8). They had become a model for other Christians and churches to copy.

In Acts 15.1–35 we have the account of the Jerusalem Council and the debate on the crucial question of Gentile evangelisation. The outcome was of considerable importance for church planting throughout the Gentile regions of the Roman Empire and beyond. The issue was quite clear. Did Gentiles have to become Jews to become Christians? The Council agreed they did not, but had only to conform to a few 'necessary rules' (Acts 15.28). No wonder the missionary minded church of Antioch rejoiced (Acts 15.31). They knew the right *Inter-Church* decision had been taken and local church growth could advance and even accelerate throughout the Gentile regions of the Empire.

Inter-community Factors

These are the social, ideological and technological factors *within the social systems of nations or regions* that help or hinder the growth of local churches. These factors provide the cultural background or milieu of the local community. The community of a fishing village on the North East coast of Scotland, for example, has a distinctive character. If we were to study the causes of growth or decline of the local Presbyterian church we might begin by talking to the minister and members (*local church*) and then call at the local government offices for the plans and population statistics of the village (*local community*). We would also need to assess the influence of the Presbyterian denomination and especially the area Presbytery (*inter-church*). But our research would be incomplete if we ignored the fact that this was a British church in Scotland. However isolated the village may be, it cannot escape the attention of the British Government or the influence of the British media. Nor would this village and its church, however remote, be unaffected by the regional development of this part of Scotland because of the discovery and refining of North Sea oil. These would be *inter-community factors* and they may have considerable effect upon the growth or decline of the local church.

In Galatians 4.4 we are told that Christ came at the 'right time'. Church historians have identified a number of factors that providentially prepared the world for the coming of the Son of God. A very significant 'inter-community factor' was the *Pax Romana*, the peace and rule of the Roman Empire. This provided safe travel and easy communication. It was possible to travel from London to Alexandria on excellent roads and by safe sea voyages. There was a common currency and one language, Greek, was spoken by large numbers of people everywhere. In many ways it was probably easier to travel through Europe and the Mediterranean World in the days of the Apostles than it is today.

The Early Church took full advantage of these 'inter-community factors' and spread abroad to preach the gospel throughout the Empire and beyond its frontiers. Within decades of Pentecost thousands of churches had been established and millions were following Christ. Not only the great missionary, Paul, but other itinerant apostles, prophets, teachers and evangelists toured the churches to strengthen their faith and correct any false doctrine or practice. In the providence of God, prevailing conditions contributed to the planting and growth of churches.

In his book *Towards the Dawn*, Dr Clifford Hill has analysed the condition of Great Britain at the beginning of the 1980s. His conclusion is that we are in grave danger and at the mercy of uncontrollable political, economic, social and cultural forces. We have but one hope: that the nation will repent and turn to God. He calls for the Church in Britain to grasp the opportunity of the hour, recover its authentic voice of prophecy and call the nation back to God through Christ. Lamenting the weakness of the Church, he says:

> 'The central tragedy of our age is that those forces of social change that we have been noting are reaching their point of ultimate crisis at precisely the point in history when the Church in Britain is weaker than at any time for hundreds of years . . . never before has the challenge to Christianity been greater, and yet equally never before has the opportunity for the Gospel been greater.'
> (HILL 1980:173)

Whether we agree with Dr Hill's analysis or not, the condition of Britain in the eighties is the *inter-community factor* that will affect every British church throughout the decade.

Demonic Opposition

Satan and demonic forces oppose the growth of the Church and the Kingdom. They constantly attack the ministry of the Word (Mark 5.15) and the servants of Christ (Luke 22.31). They work through people who are within and outside the Church (John 8.44; 13.27; Acts 5.3; 13.8) and they are able to manipulate human affairs to their advantage (1 Thess. 2.18).

Satan's opposition to the mission of God is a recurring theme of Scripture and even a cursory reading of the Bible reveals the perpetual warfare against Satan for the welfare of man and the world.

Jesus entered into this conflict in a decisive way through his ministry. The personal encounter with the Devil at the beginning established the supremacy of Jesus (Matt. 4.1–11) but the conflict continued throughout His ministry (Luke 4.13). The mission of the Seventy achieved a significant victory (Luke 10.18) and Jesus, who came, 'to destroy what the Devil had done' (1 John 3.8), won the final and complete victory by his death and resurrection (Col. 2.15; Heb. 2.14). The Devil's defeat will be fully realised when Christ comes again to judge and reign (Phil. 2.6–11; 1 Cor. 15.26). Satan's destiny is known, his end prepared and he is now restrained (Matt. 25.41; Rev. 20.7–10), but until Judgement Day the Church on earth has the same task as her Master and must engage the enemy. Therefore the context of mission is conflict and those who want their churches to grow must be willing to join the battle.

Satan, as the prince of this fallen world (John 14.30) has mankind under his rule (1 John 5.19). The missionary task, therefore, includes the release of humanity from this bondage (Luke 4.18; Acts 26.18), in order that mankind may become children of God (Col. 2.20). The Devil and demonic forces resist this ministry of liberation and fight to keep control. They attack Christians and churches ceaselessly and ferociously (1 Pet. 5.8) using deceit, stealth and cunning (2 Cor. 11.14; Eph. 6.11; 1 Tim. 3.7).

The apostles warned the churches to be cautious and vigilant (2 Cor. 2.11; Jas. 4.7; 1 John 4.1) and Church leaders throughout history, such as Cyprian, Luther and Wesley, have shared this apostolic concern.

Contemporary theology, however, stresses the socio-political dimensions of demonic activity, 'the principalities and powers' (Eph. 6.12), and is reluctant to recognise its direct influence upon personal and church affairs. Many Church leaders are also unwilling to accept the activity of supernatural evil in the 'christianised' societies of the West. They relegate the Devil and demons to the naive and prescientific world views of earlier ages or the highly exaggerated accounts of modern missionaries. Demons may exist in New Guinea but not in Newcastle!

The occult explosion of the sixties and seventies should have changed all that. The activity of the evil supernatural is widely publicised and the vast majority of British people in the eighties have heard about or experienced psychic phenomena. Only two per cent of respondents to a *Times* questionnaire on the paranormal did not believe in the possibility of psychic experience. The results of the survey were published in *The Times* of December 20th, 1980, and the response to the following question is most revealing:

'*Q3.* Which of the following sources of information acquainted you with ESP or other psychic phenomena?

Newspaper and magazine articles, media, popular books.	52 per cent
Personal experiences of your own	66 per cent
Experiences to persons you know	54 per cent
Literature from scientific studies of the paranormal	36 per cent
Lectures on the subject	9 per cent

In addition to this general awareness of the psychic and supernatural, there are many who are actively involved in occult practices. There is widespread use of Ouija Boards and Tarot cards for contacting 'the spirits' and predicting the future. Millions of books on astrology are sold annually and even Marks and Spencer's find them marketable.

Britain today is an occult-conscious society, but surprisingly there are many within the churches who deny or avoid the supernatural and are ill-equipped to deal with the problem. The Rev John Richards, former Secretary to the Study Group for Exorcism for the Church of England, draws attention to the dilemma when he says:

'The so-called "modern" theologian who glibly dismisses any diabolic or demonic reality is certainly out of step with modern society, when in America, sixty-five per cent now believe in a

personal devil, and the Church of England – of all churches –
officially states the need for an exorcist in every diocese!'

(RICHARDS 32:1974)

C. S. Lewis warned against 'two equal and opposite errors' when
dealing with demons. We must not disbelieve in their existence or
be excessively interested in them. While stating our belief in the
reality of demonic opposition to church growth, we do not want
to exaggerate their power or significance, for whenever they are
encountered victory is assured in the name of Christ (Acts 13.10;
16.16–17; 19.11–20).

We have included this factor for two important reasons. Firstly,
the failure to discern the demonic cause of some local church
problems means that the problem remains unsolved. Demonic
infiltration and assault upon the churches of the New Testament
resulted in moral and doctrinal error. When the cause of the problem
was discerned the apostles acted swiftly with Christ's authority to
correct the situation (Acts 5.1–10; 1 Cor. 5.1–5).

A contemporary church that is being attacked by demonic powers
must realise its need of spiritual weapons for the conflict (2 Cor.
10.4). Its members must pray for the power and gifts of the Holy
Spirit that are essential for this warfare (Mark 9.29; 1 Cor. 12.10).

Secondly, the occult practice of so many people has important
implications for evangelism. Those who have been involved in occult
activity, and fail to confess and renounce it, are hindered from
turning to Christ or progressing in their Christian walk. The evangelist, witness or minister who is insensitive to the *power encounter*
(Acts 26.18) between the forces of darkness and the Spirit of God
will be unable to help such people.

Some groups are more involved in occult practices than others
and the factor of demonic opposition will be correspondingly more
important when evangelising and planting churches among them.
Paul's experiences at the ancient occult centre of Ephesus (Acts
19.18–20) will be matched on many occasions in the re-evangelisation
of occult-ridden England.

Extraordinary Activity of God

God never does anything 'ordinary' so 'extraordinary' is used to
describe the activity of the Spirit of God in ways that produce
remarkable and rapid church growth.

Throughout the history of the Church the Holy Spirit has acted
sovereignly and often spectacularly to advance the mission of God.
These movements or 'visitations' of the Spirit supplement the
continuous missionary endeavours of God's people and bring large
numbers of people to Christ. This is achieved in two distinct ways;
by Revivals and by People Movements.

Revivals

When the Holy Spirit acts upon an individual or group *who are already Christians*, and revives their spiritual life this may be properly called 'Revival'. If those who are revived channel their renewed experience into witness, then large numbers of unbelievers within the network of relationships of these Christians are won for Christ.

Dr J. Edwin Orr, a recognised authority on revivals, prefers the term 'Evangelical Awakenings' because of the phenomena that accompany them. He says:

'An Evangelical Awakening is a movement of the Holy Spirit in the Church of Christ bringing about a revival of New Testament Christianity. Such an awakening may change in a significant way an individual only; or it may affect a larger group of people; or it may move a congregation, or the whole body of believers throughout a country or continent; or indeed a larger body of believers throughout the World. Such an awakening may run its course briefly, or it may last a whole lifetime. Such awakenings come about in various ways but there is a pattern which is common to all.

'The main effect of an Evangelical Awakening is always the repetition of the phenomena of the Acts of the Apostles, which narrative gives a simple account of an Evangelical Awakening, one that revived believers, then converted sinners to God.'

(ORR, 1965:265)

The impact of revival upon the numerical growth of churches is well illustrated by the linear graph of the Baptist Association of West Glamorgan. This is the county where the Welsh Revival of 1904 began and the rapid growth in church membership is clearly seen (see figure 10). This graph is typical of all churches except the Roman Catholic churches of South Wales and confirms the reports of those who witnessed these events.

The subsequent decline of the Baptists is reflected in all the Welsh churches and is the cause of much heart searching among Free Church leaders. Many believe the Revival was superficial and the decline confirms their suspicions. However, the graph shows that the pre-revival Church has also declined.

The causes of this decline are complex, as we should now realise. The local churches and chapels may have been weak, especially in Christian education and the nurture of new converts (*Local Church Factors*). The denominations may have lacked the strategic foresight to take full advantage of the Revival and its effects upon Wales (*Inter-Church Factors*). Satan may have fiercely attacked the revivalists and the post-Revival churches (*Demonic Opposition*). But the most likely causes of decline are the combined effects of the First World War, the Depression, the modernisation of the mining industry, the defence of the Welsh language and culture and the mobility

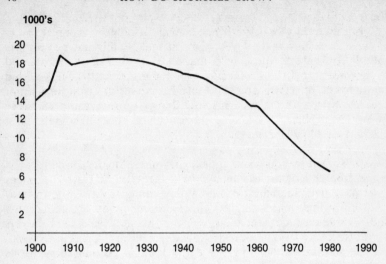

Figure 10. The West Glamorgan Baptist Association 1900–1981

of the Welsh people (*Local and Inter-Community Factors*). When we recognise this complexity of church decline we are in a better position to evaluate the Revival, and assess its impact upon church growth in Wales.

When all the facts have been examined we must give thanks to God for the thousands of Welsh people who were converted to Christ and swept into the churches. News of what God had done spread abroad and sparked off revivals in many parts of the world. The revivals in Assam and Korea are at least two that are attributed to the influence of this extraordinary activity of God in Wales at the turn of the century.

Revival, as God's gift, is not subject to or dependent upon the will of man. It cannot be produced by human enterprise or endeavour. When revival comes it takes the ongoing service of God's people and multiplies its effect. One of the missionaries reporting the Korean Revival of 1907 said of the Holy Spirit's extraordinary activity, 'He has accomplished more in half a day than all of us missionaries could have accomplished in half a year' – over 365 times more effective! When we consider the inability of the British Church to advance the mission of God in Britain today we confess we need nothing less than revival.

This was the conviction expressed by Dr W. E. Sangster in his final address to his beloved denomination at the Methodist Conference of 1958. He knew that all revivals have been preceded and accompanied by prayer and he called Methodism to passionate, pleading and persistent prayer for revival. Dr Sangster was concerned for the plight of the nation and the role of his own denomination. All who share his concern and long for revival to return to Britain will heed his wise counsel and turn to God in fervent prayer.

People Movements

Revival is one extraordinary activity of the Holy Spirit that produces rapid church growth. Another activity of God that we may describe as extraordinary is the way groups of people turn to Christ in large numbers.

The Good News Bible translates Christ's commission in Matthew 28.19, 'Go, then, to all *peoples* everywhere and make them my disciples.' The word *peoples* translates a Greek word that has given us 'ethnic', which we use in reference to race. The word may be translated 'tribes, clans or families'. It is unfortunately translated 'nations' in many versions (e.g. KJV, RSV, NEB, NIV) and suggests to the modern reader that the Church is sent to make disciples of nation states such as Kenya, France and Thailand. While this is not untrue, it loses sight of the great variety of groups that may exist within one nation. As the different groups may require different approaches with the gospel it is important to recognise the distinction between 'peoples' and 'nations' in the actual command of Christ.

There have been many instances in the history of Christian missions when groups or peoples decide for Christ in a 'multi-individual' way. Each member of the tribe or clan or family decides for Christ and everyone in the group becomes a Christian. When the Holy Spirit acts upon *a group of non-Christians* and they are collectively converted to Christ we may describe this as a People Movement. It would appear that the Holy Spirit has used the network of relationships within the group to produce a period of ripeness. When this phenomenon takes place among large groups many churches are formed in a very short period of time.

When Peter evangelised Lydda and Sharon it is reported that 'All the people . . . turned to the Lord' (Acts 9.35) and a sizeable group from Joppa did the same (Acts 9.42). All who heard the gospel in the household of Cornelius became Christians (Acts 10.44–48) and that similar events accompanied the ministry of Paul and Silas at Philippi (Acts 16.29–34). God alone knows why one group is more receptive to the gospel than another but his Spirit prepares the harvest and his people are called to gather it in (Acts 16.6–10; Matt. 9.35–38; 1 Cor. 3.5–9).

Dr McGavran estimates that two thirds of all converts in Asia, Africa and Oceania have come to Christ through People Movements. He describes the phenomena and these 'multi-individual' decisions for Christ and gives the following examples from India, New Guinea and Indonesia.

'Near the city of Raichur in South India, about 120 Madigas were making up their mind to follow Christ. They had considered the step for many years. Many of their relatives were Christians. They believed becoming disciples of Christ was a good thing to do. During the year of decision, the question came up as to what they would do with their temple – a small dark room with an idol on a cylindrical stone. After weeks of discussion, all participated in the decision that on the day of baptism they would throw the idol into the village pond, make the cylindrical stone their pulpit, place the Bible on it, and hear what God really had to say. This was a multi-individual, mutually interdependent decision and part of their conversion. Had any of them decided to remain an idol worshipper, the rest could not have used the temple for Christian worship. but when the group acted as a unit, the change presented no problems.

'When the 8,000 Dani tribesmen in West New Guinea declared for Christ in a multi-divisional fashion, they resolved to burn their fetishes on a certain day. This symbolic act destroyed their former fears and allegiances and opened the way for them to learn biblical truth. Then, in one of the Indonesian islands recently, twenty Moslem communities decided to accept Christ and turn their mosques into churches. This very grave decision entailed participation by each person concerned. Each was saved, not by going along with the crowd, but by his participation in the decision. Multi-individual conversion is not a light matter. It, too, can result in persecution or death. Feared fetishes or remaining Moslems might make a terrible revenge. Participating in such a decision required genuine personal faith.'

(McGAVRAN 1980:341–2)

People movements that result in genuine conversions of large numbers of people must not be confused with mass movements to Christ for social and political reasons alone. There have been many 'conversions' for convenience or by force throughout Church history. Often kings or chieftains have been 'converted' in order to enter into politically advantageous marriages or to gain territory. They force their subjects to change their community religion and outwardly conform to a 'Christianity' which is nominal and grossly perverted by elements of the former religion.

When Charlemagne 'converted' the bulk of the pagan Saxons in the eighth century it was by the threat of the sword rather than the wind of the Spirit. This mass movement was the result of the extraordinary behaviour of a Christian King and not the extraordinary activity of God.

Could the British Church Grow Rapidly?

There is no doubt that the extraordinary activity of God in Revivals and People Movements is the greatest factor for rapid church growth. If we are praying and working for the rapid growth of the British Church today we would be wise to look for evidence of these two phenomena. Are there signs of Revival and People Movements in the British Isles in the 1980s?

There are many aspects of the charismatic movement that justify the classification of Revival. Thousands of Christians, from almost every Church tradition, have been revived and there is undoubtedly a 'repetition of the phenomena of the Acts of the Apostles'. The movement is now emerging from the early enthusiasm of the sixties and seventies to take a respected place in the life of most denominations. So far, sadly, there has been little evidence of this renewed spirituality being channelled into witness. We must hope, therefore, that during the eighties the Movement will wake up to the fact that demonstrations of the 'Spirit and power' are to convince and convict the sinner rather than the saved (1 Cor. 2.1–5). And 'signs and wonders' are to arouse interest and kindle faith in the unbeliever rather than the believer (Acts 2.22,43; 5.12; 8.13; 4.3, cf. Mark 16.20).

If the charismatic movement is to be a revival phenomena which will bring rapid church growth to the British Isles then it must correct this tendency to introversion. There is an over-emphasis upon worship and fellowship to the detriment of witness and service. When those within the movement correct this imbalance the renewal could be channelled into reaching the lost. 'Charismatic' Christians might then break out beyond the boundaries of their churches into joyous and spontaneous witness and service among unbelievers. The result could be rapid church growth through the networks of their relationships.

The search for a People Movement in Britain is incredibly difficult. Society is cosmopolitan and individualistic rather than local and tribal, and group consciousness is weak and transient. The established Churches are so distant from the masses of British people and so inept at effective evangelism that the majority of British Church leaders would not recognise a receptive group of people if they saw one. Traditionally the suggestion that the British Isles is a mission field has been resented and mission strategies are considered inappropriate. The Home Mission departments of the majority of our denominations do not know if British people are responsive to the gospel or not. If they ever ask the question they appear not to seek the answer. At least one exception is the Rev Jeffrey Harris of the Methodist Home Mission Division who has appealed to Methodism to recognise the People Movement phenomena in their history and present ministry. He writes:

'The reason why Methodism was able to grow in the mining communities in Durham or amongst the agricultural workers in South Humberside is that it became a people movement in McGavran's terms. The studies of Robert Moore ("Pitmen, Preachers and Politics") and Robert Colls ("The Colliers Rant") show that Methodism became a genuine working class culture to the inhabitants of the Durham mining villages. If Methodism is to penetrate significantly large sections of British society, it must assume in some places the characteristics of a people movement'

(HARRIS 1980:38)

Research into receptivity and openness to the gospel is in its infancy in Britain but preliminary results indicate that at least ten per cent of unchurched English adults are interested in the Christian faith. This suggests that approximately 3 million people would be prepared to listen to a sensitive presentation of the gospel. If five per cent of these people have been brought to the brink of decision by the Holy Spirit then about 150,000 people are ripe for harvest now and ready to be brought to Christ and into the churches. This could represent the first wave of millions who will be brought to Christ before the end of the century. That groups of people may be won for Christ in England today was demonstrated by fourteen members of one family who came to Christ in one month at a Pentecostal church in Nottingham. There is also a movement of the Spirit of God among British gypsies.

Prayer fellowships are flourishing. An estimated 100,000 house groups meet for prayer, Bible study and fellowship. New churches are being planted and existing churches renewed and restructured. Denominations are being formed and reformed and some of the mainline denominations are beginning to stress renewal and growth. Many parachurch agencies and inter-church activities are thriving. There are forces at work in the nation that have created a move towards the acceptance of a religious view of life and spiritual values. The Spirit of God is acting through all these factors and would appear to be working in extraordinary ways by sending revival to his people and openness to thousands who are lost.

While church growth is complex, all the evidence suggests that rapid church growth could come to Great Britain. This decade is therefore a period of great opportunity for the British Church.

THE VALUE OF THE BEHAVIOURAL SCIENCES

The fourth and final emphasis of the Church Growth movement that we want to introduce is the recognition of the value of the *contemporary social and behavioural sciences* of anthropology, psychology and sociology in understanding the growth of the Church. These academic disciplines provide innumerable insights into the practice of Christian missions, and the Church is able to profit from this growth of knowledge in the fields of human culture, thought and relationships. All truth is of God and all human knowledge should be in submission to and in service for Christ (2 Cor. 10.5). These contemporary advances in knowledge may therefore be *discerningly* used for the extension of the Kingdom, and the progress of the mission of God. Many illustrations of this conviction appear throughout this book but we will now give examples from each of the three disciplines.

The Contribution of Cultural Studies

Anthropology is concerned with the study of man, particularly the way one man or group of men differs from another. It is divided into two major spheres: physical anthropology is the study of man's biological characteristics, and cultural or social anthropology is the study of his various cultures. Cultural anthropology is especially helpful in Christian missions for every missionary is concerned to communicate the gospel across cultural barriers.

In *Communicating Christ Cross-Culturally*, Dr David Hesselgrave has identified a number of dimensions within cultures that have to be recognised by those wishing to evangelise a given group of people. He suggests that every culture should be examined through a seven-dimension framework that exposes cultural differences. These are different:

> ways of viewing the world
> ways of thinking
> ways of expressing ideas
> ways of acting
> ways of interacting
> ways of channelling the message
> ways of deciding

Those who want to communicate Christ effectively must be sensitive to these differences between groups of people. The following missionary experience illustrates the sort of problems encountered when we fail in just one dimension: *the different ways of acting*.

Two unmarried lady missionaries had a very disappointing ministry among a tribe of Mexican Indians. Their teaching and preaching had no effect and after several years of heartbreaking toil they moved to another area and handed over the mission to others. The new missionaries, a married couple, discovered that the ladies had frequently eaten breakfast in the open to take advantage of the cool morning air and with their breakfast they always dranks lots of limejuice. Unfortunately the ladies never knew that the Indian women also drank limejuice – to prevent pregnancy! The Indians were therefore convinced the missionaries had been visited by their lovers when they breakfasted in public. Their 'scandalous' lifestyle ruined their ministry. Some elementary cultural studies could have saved a great deal of personal heartache and mission resources.

British Churches may not face such dramatic misunderstandings in Great Britain but they repeatedly send 'Oxbridge' graduates without cross-cultural gifts or training to minister in working class parishes, with equally disastrous results. And middle class churches, with their great dependence upon books and related activities, continually fail to reach their 'non-book' neighbours. The insights of cultural studies could help us to see these errors and understand some of the reasons for our failure.

It is also important to appreciate the differences between cultures when planting new churches and evangelising new groups. Dr McGavran has said, '(People) like to become Christians without crossing racial, linguistic, or class barriers' (1970:198). A growing amount of mission research confirms this statement. It has been found that where cultural obstacles are recognised and new converts are nurtured in churches of their own culture, the evangelistic efforts are far more effective. This practice recognises the controversial Homogeneous Unit Principle (H.U.P.) of Church Growth. We consider its strengths and weaknesses in Appendix 3.

The Contribution of Psychology

Psychology is the science of the nature, function and phenomena of the human mind or soul. Psychologists investigate such processes as decision making, the reception of messages and attitudes to change. Christians who take advantage of the discoveries of psychology and apply them in their ministries are able to avoid the creation of *unnecessary* obstacles to Christian faith and growth. This is not an attempt to remove the 'offence' of the gospel for this is inevitable (Matt. 15.12; 1 Cor. 1.23), nor is it a failure to recognise the role and activity of the Holy Spirit. The use of psychological research helps us identify barriers to faith and growth that are *man-made and avoid any offence caused by our ignorance or insensitivity.*

Our example is taken from a field of research that is particularly relevant to contemporary church life – the introduction of change. A major study of the introduction of change is presented in *The Communication of Innovations* by E. M. Rogers and F. F. Shoemaker. Their studies of the process reveal that people responding to change pass through four basic stages *Knowledge, Persuasion, Decision* and *Confirmation* (see figure 11).

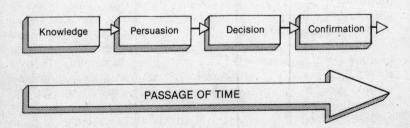

Figure 11. The Process of Change

Knowledge describes the stage where people are exposed to the nature of the change and the reasons why it is necessary. They need to be informed about the effects of the change.

The main responsibility of the person introducing the change, 'the change agent' at this stage of the process is education. The change agent must communicate with all who will have to accept and implement the change, paying particular attention to the leaders and influential people within the group.

If a minister is anxious to see the church buildings used for the benefit of the community, for service and outreach, he may want the premises used for example, by a playgroup. He will require the co-operation and in most cases the permission of church leaders and members. The playgroup will involve the church in a great deal of change. Playgroup leaders and helpers and extra facilities will be required. There will be increased costs for maintenance and repairs, and other activities and timetables will be disturbed.

The Minister's first task is to educate the church about the advantages (and disadvantages) of a playgroup on church premises.

It is interesting to trace these four stages in the experience of the apostle Peter. When Peter had to pioneer the evangelisation of the gentiles and break out of the confines of Jewish Christianity, the Lord used a vision and a gentile's messenger to prepare him for this radical change (Acts 10.1–21). Peter had to be educated.

Persuasion is the stage where the people who have to accept the change are forming favourable or unfavourable opinions about the proposed change. These opinions will be largely influenced by personal concerns – *how will it affect them*.

The main responsibility of the change agent at this stage is personal reassurance and explanation, which will involve him or his representatives in person-to-person communication. The benefits of the change should also be presented in personal terms.

The minister with the task of persuading the church to accept the playgroup will identify those who are hesitant and resistant and endeavour to allay their fears and objections. He or his representatives must be prepared to spend time with dissidents in order to reassure and explain. The value of the playgroup should be expressed in personal ways. The church must understand how the playgroup will help the lonely and depressed young mother or the single-parent family or the maladjusted child. The playgroup will become a tangible expression of Christian service and love for others.

When Peter was questioning the validity of gentile evangelisation he was being persuaded by the providential progress of events and the appeal of Cornelius' servants (Acts 10.22,23). That gentiles could become followers of Jesus was no longer an abstract or theoretical proposition. Peter was on his way to evangelise a God-fearing gentile named Cornelius and the whole thing had been arranged by God! Peter must have been deeply disturbed by this potential break with Jewish customs and tradition. He was probably very anxious about what would take place. Only his obedience to the Lord and the vision, and the personal request of Cornelius persuaded him to journey from Joppa to Caesarea.

Decision describes the stage where people are well informed about the change and are choosing to adopt or reject it. Time must be given for people to decide and change their minds on many informal occasions, before a formal decision is called for. The formal act of deciding must mark the *end* of this stage of Decision.

The church that is considering the possibility of a playgroup must be allowed time to weigh the proposal and prayerfully consider their decision. Every member should have sufficient opportunity to decide to accept or oppose it. Many will change their minds several times as they talk to friends and learn more details. When an agreed period of time has passed, the church should be called to formally decide about the change. They must accept or reject the playgroup.

On arrival at Caesarea Peter decided to enter the home of Cornelius and address the household. He explained why he had come but remained uncertain about the result of the visit (Acts 10.29). Any remaining doubts were dispelled by the testimony of Cornelius and the coming of the Holy Spirit (Acts 10.44–46). He was then so convinced that gentiles could become followers of Jesus and accepted by God, that he ordered them to be baptised and publicised his decision formally (Acts 10.47,48).

Confirmation is the final stage in the process of change. When the formal decision has been taken and the Decision stage completed people expect confirmation that their decision was correct. If they have accepted the change and their experience of the change is negative rather than positive they will become disenchanted and reverse their decision. Those who were opposed to the change but find it has proved beneficial may come to recognise its value and regret their opposition.

The church that decided to allow a playgroup on its premises must be constantly informed of its progress and achievements. If they only hears news of increased heating bills, spilled sandpits and flooded toilets, they will regret their decision and close the playgroup. There will be no point in appealing to the formal decision at the church meeting. All the evidence will have confirmed the church in the belief that the playgroup was a mistake and the change was not worthwhile.

Peter returned to Jerusalem joyful at the prospect of gentile evangelisation, but some were convinced he had done the wrong thing (Acts 11.1–3). Peter successfully defended his actions and even won over his critics (Acts 11.4–18). Unfortunately he later came under the influence of Jewish Christian extremists, the Judaisers, and began to question his original decision and actions. It took a confrontation with the apostle Paul to put him right again (Gal. 2.11–14).

These four stages in the process of accepting change provide a number of important insights into many problems within churches.

There are so many divisions caused by the introduction of change that could have been avoided if each stage had been recognised and passed. So many ministers demand major decisions for change without educating and persuading church leaders and members. They may have taken years to be convinced of the need for change themselves and yet they become disgruntled and impatient when others refuse to decide in an evening!

Further studies by E. M. Rogers and F. F. Shoemaker into the rate at which change is adopted by a group have produced a helpful model of group attitudes to change with approximate percentages of each attitude within the group. They suggest the following categories:

A. Innovators – 2.5 per cent of the group who are enthusiastic about the change and introduce it into the group.

B. Early Adopters – a further 13.5 per cent of the group who welcome the change and are quick to accept and promote it.

C. Early Majority – a further 34 per cent making a total of 50 per cent who accept the change. This group had some reservations about the change but have been won over and now persuade others.

D. Late majority – a further 34 per cent who were initially resistant to the change, some even actively opposing the change when introduced. They have been gradually persuaded by advocates for the change who are mainly from the early majority.

E. Laggards – the final 16 per cent who accept the change grudgingly. They were ready to leave the group when the change was first introduced and some will continue to resist when the change is tradition!

A graph may be plotted showing the number of adopters against the passage of time (see figure 12).

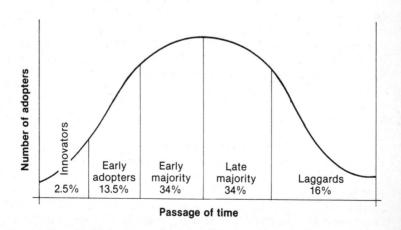

Figure 12. The Adoption of Change

If changes are introduced too rapidly the group cannot cope, and therefore fragments. Many churches have been split into groups, that have left to form or join other churches, because of the insensitive and impatient introduction of change. While this is not the only cause of division within churches, it is one cause that may be avoided. The process of introducing change is one insight from the behavioural sciences that contemporary churches struggling with change desperately need (see figure 13).

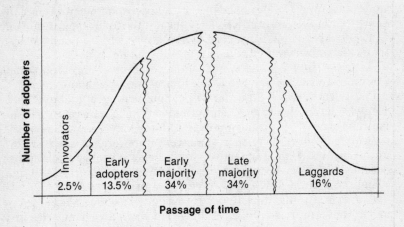

Figure 13. Introducing Change – Too fast!

The Contribution of Sociology

The contribution of sociology is well illustrated by the experience of a declining city-centre church. The church had once been full. Older members could remember the days when the pews were packed and chairs had to be placed down the aisles. Today the once great Tabernacle has only a handful of members and visiting preachers peer down from the pulpit at rows of empty pews. The dozen or so worshippers are scattered and separated.

The Tabernacle has been declining for years and even the most dedicated members realise they cannot keep going for much longer. Last winter the boiler broke down and they could not afford to repair it. They had the humiliation of huddling together in the deacon's vestry for the Sunday services.

Surprisingly, what had been a great tragedy actually became a blessing. They got to know each other, prayed for one another and discussed the Bible and their faith together. By accident (or was it providence?) they had stumbled upon a structure for renewal and growth. Forced to behave in a way that was appropriate to their size, they formed a 'primary group'.

Sociologists have identified three groups of different size and function in which people relate to each other. These groups exist in the Church as well as society and our failure to recognise the appropriate purpose and activity of each group is the unrecognised cause of many problems in contemporary churches. For growth, we need the right use of each group.

The sociologist talks of primary, secondary and tertiary groups, but we will follow Dr Peter Wagner and call them *Cell*, *Congregation* and *Celebration*. The actual size of each group varies according to circumstances but as a general rule the Cell numbers 3 to 12 people and the Congregation is ideally between 40 and 175. The Celebration group is larger than 175 – the bigger the better is the rule for this largest group (see figure 14).

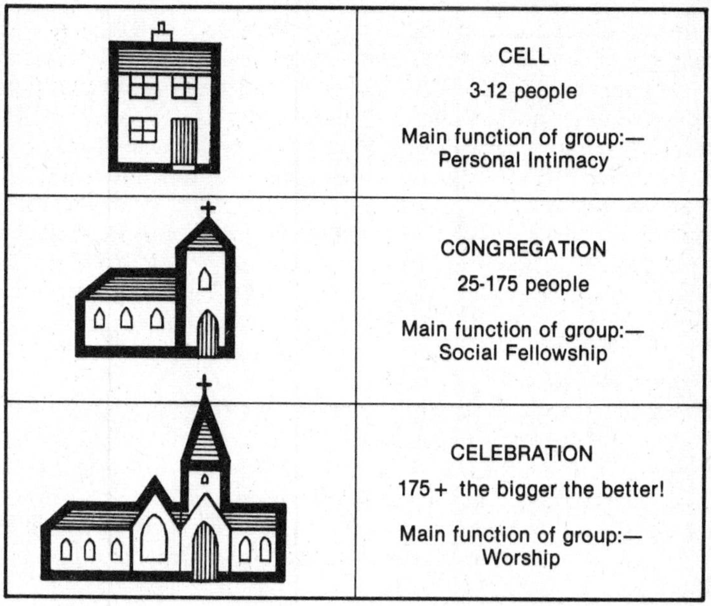

	CELL 3-12 people Main function of group:— Personal Intimacy
	CONGREGATION 25-175 people Main function of group:— Social Fellowship
	CELEBRATION 175+ the bigger the better! Main function of group:— Worship

Figure 14. Groups for Growth

Jesus related to people in these groups. He taught his disciples in the Cell-sized group (Mark 3.13,14); he shared in a Congregation at the Synagogue (Luke 4.16); and he participated in the Celebration activities of the Feasts and Temple from earliest childhood (Luke 2.41).

In his book, *Your Church Can Grow*, Dr Peter Wagner has suggested a formula for a healthy growing church:

Celebration + Congregation + Cell = Church

It is vitally important that we understand the main function and most appropriate activities of each group, so we will briefly examine each group in more detail.

Cell (3 to 12 people)

This primary and small group has the main function of providing *personal intimacy*. Every Christian needs those with whom he shares his feelings and unburdens his heart. Small groups also provide the structure for support and encouragement and an environment for personal development and growth.

Essential activities of the Cell include prayer, life-related Bible study, open sharing of life and faith, and a common desire to help each other grow to Christian maturity.

In many churches this Cell structure is provided by home Bible study groups. We estimate there are over 100,000 of these house groups of different denominations in the United Kingdom. In a recent study we discovered that ninety-four per cent of churches that are growing steadily had small groups, and there is no doubt that these were an important factor in their growth.

If house groups provide the formal structure for Cell-life they may succeed in involving sixty per cent of the active membership. This percentage could be increased if every gathering of small numbers of people incorporated the essential small group activities into their programme. The meetings of elders, deacons, sunday school teachers or youth leaders should function as a Cell before they act as a committee.

Congregation (40 to 175 people)

The main function of this secondary group is to provide *social fellowship*. People in a Congregation have a sense of belonging and identify with the group. When absent they are missed, for each member is recognised and usually known by name.

Congregations form around a particular interest or activity in the church. They may come together for systematic teaching, or to sing in the choir, or to engage in evangelistic visiting. These groups have leaders who are skilled at meeting the particular needs of the group and some will exercise pastoral oversight for the group. In larger churches a women's fellowship is a typical Congregation.

Though the majority of churches have a total membership below 175, they will still subdivide into numerous Congregations to perform certain tasks and provide fellowship circles that allow for flexible and variable relationships. When the Congregation ceases its activity or completes its task, informal small groups automatically form and the wise leader will encourage the development of Cell-life within this larger group.

Many Congregations develop their social fellowship by holding events such as outings, suppers and even barn dances. Many churches now follow the practice of regular Sunday lunches and picnics to provide opportunities for church members and adherents to get to know each other and form meaningful relationships. These occasions are particularly helpful to new and potential members of the church.

Celebration (175+ people)

Worship is the main function of the Celebration group. While it is possible to worship in a Cell or Congregation, the large numbers of the Celebration group produce a 'special' experience of worship. The ancient Israelite was called to participate in the worship of the Feasts and Tabernacle (Exod. 23.14; 25.8,9), and this worship of the tribe was significantly different from that of the clan or family.

Today, these Celebration groups and experiences are formed and found in a variety of contexts. The Salvationists finds it at the Albert Hall with the annual rally and massed bands. An Anglican will find it at the Easter Eucharist in the cathedral. The young people discover it at Greenbelt or Spring Harvest.

These large gatherings should be regularly provided at the Inter-Church level within denominations or ecumenical groups. Many of these gatherings are re-establishing the priority of worship over business and re-asserting the primary activity of this larger group. We will gain a greater understanding of our interdependence when our united worship provides the Celebration group and this essential experience becomes something we do not want to miss.

Large churches are able to enjoy the Celebration experience every week. When it is this size, the worship attracts many unbelievers who can participate anonymously and attend without feeling conspicuous. The drawing ability of a crowd is a well-known phenomena of which the Holy Spirit took full advantage at Pentecost, (Acts 2.6). When this occurs 'evangelism by attraction' takes place and many are drawn to Christ at the event.

Unfortunately there are some advocates of 'evangelism by attraction' whose group is little more than a Cell or barely a Congregation. They fail to realise that no group should rely solely on attraction and the small group should be particularly zealous in evangelising beyond its boundaries.

The tragedy of the Tabernacle was their failure to realise they had become a Cell and were no longer a Celebration group. By failing to do the appropriate things they had become grotesque. Visitors were appalled because they did not share the memories of the survivors and could not join in the re-enactment of past events.

The apostle Paul urged the Corinthians to be sensitive to the needs of outsiders (1 Cor. 14.23) and the task of the Tabernacle is to find a suitable gathering that will welcome the visitor.

These examples of helpful insights from cultural studies, psychology and sociology show the value of the behavioural sciences to the Church. Unfortunately many sincere Christians are suspicious and afraid of using them. They are believed to be unspiritual, compromising and superficial. The Church Growth Movement considers this is a hasty and unworthy judgement, and seeks to demonstrate that the 'related insights' may be used in a spiritual and sensitive manner that honours God and assists the fulfilment of the Great Commission.

SUMMARY

In this chapter we have seen that Church Growth is a technical term describing a school of missionary theory that has been formally defined.

Church Growth stresses the task and priority of evangelism within the mission of the Church. It believes that God desires the growth of the church, but the causes of growth and decline are complex. Church Growth also believes the insights of the behavioural sciences help the Church to understand this complexity and assist the Church in her fulfilment of the Great Commission.

3 Signs of Growth

THE GROWTH OF THE KINGDOM

In fulfilment of the promise of the Old Testament and following the preparatory ministry of John the Baptist, Jesus began his public ministry by preaching the Good News of the Kingdom of God (Mark 1.14,15). The Kingdom remained the constant theme of his preaching, during his ministry (Matt. 4.23) and after his death and resurrection (Acts 1.3).

Jesus taught that the Kingdom was a present reality (Luke 17.21) and a future event. It was in this world but would find its goal and fulfilment in the world to come (Matt. 1.7; 12.28; 16.28; 26.29). The present Kingdom as the reign and dominion of God in history and upon earth may be entered by all who are willing to humble themselves, repent and give life-long allegiance to Jesus Christ the King (Matt. 5–7; 18.31; Mark 1.15; Luke 9.60–62). Entrance to the Kingdom is free by the grace and mercy of God (Luke 12.32), for a place in the Kingdom is never earned and cannot be purchased (Matt. 19.16–26; 20.1–15; 22.1–14). Yet a place in the Kingdom is of such great value that men should be willing to pay any price to get in (Matt. 13.44,45). The principle blessings of the Kingdom that make it so precious, are eternal life, salvation and divine sonship by spiritual rebirth (Mark 10.17–26; John 3.3–8).

The life and ministry of Jesus confronts the individual with the presence of the King and the claims of the Kingdom (Mark 1. 14,15). Those who refuse to submit to his reign over their lives or who are insincere in their professed allegiance do not enter the Kingdom, even though they may appear to (Matt. 7.21; 13.47–50). The seekers and religious people, like the scribe, may be near but not in the Kingdom (Mark 12.32). The Jews, as a people, had every opportunity but failed to enter (Matt. 21.43), so the other nations are now privileged to go in and share its blessings (Matt. 8.11).

Those who enter the Kingdom should give the King and the Kingdom their first priority of loyalty and service (Matt 6.33) and should pray for the Kingdom to come (Matt. 6.10). The Kingdom will come, however, only when the Father decides (Matt. 24.36;

25.34) and then the true subjects of the Kingdom will be revealed (Matt. 13.24–30; 47–50; 25.31–46). Until the Kingdom comes from above the present Kingdom steadily and mysteriously advances (Matt. 13.31–33; Mark 4.26–29), and the reign of God upon the earth increases.

Jesus taught his disciples to expect this growth of the Kingdom:

1. He taught that his actions and their obedient service would spread the good news of the Kingdom throughout the earth in this present age. While not all mankind would receive it and respond, the dominion of God would extend world-wide (Matt. 5.5,20; 8.10–12; 26.13).

2. During his short earthly ministry Jesus gathered around him at least 500 devoted and loyal followers (1 Cor. 15.6). These disciples witnessed the signs and victories of the Kingdom of God and saw many people recruited into its service (Matt. 12.28; 13.11; Luke 9.62). Prior to Pentecost they may have mistaken the true nature of the Kingdom (Matt. 20.20–23; Acts 1.6) but when the Spirit came and they preached the Good News they were joined by thousands. Their expectation of growth was fully realised (Acts 2.41; 4.4; 21.20).

3. The agricultural motif of so many parables illustrates the expected growth of the Kingdom. The parables of the sower, weeds and mustard seed left them in no doubt that the Kingdom would grow, even if polluted and contaminated (Matt. 13.1–32).

4. As servants of the King and the Kingdom they were taught by direct statement and parable to be alert to the possibility of growth and understood that success would be rewarded (Matt. 19.27–30; 25.1–46).

5. The successful missions of the Twelve and Seventy (symbolic of the nations of mankind) were forerunners of the Great Commission (Matt. 10.5–15; Luke 10.1–20; Matt. 28.18–20; Mark 16.15–20). Though opposition, persecution and suffering would be encountered (Matt. 10.16–36), the increase and triumph of the Kingdom was assured (Matt. 25.31–40). When the disciples had recovered from the crisis of the crucifixion, when they were convinced of the truth of the Resurrection and had received the power of the Holy Spirit, they boldly and confidently preached the Good News of the Kingdom (Acts 8.12; 19.8; 20.25; 28.23,31).

There can be no doubt that the early disciples shared the faith of their Master that the present Kingdom would grow and the future Kingdom would come (1 Cor. 15.20–28). Most Christians have believed this through the ages, as the Creeds testify, and it is firmly believed by all within the Church Growth Movement.

AND THE GROWTH OF THE CHURCH?

If we believe in the growth of the Kingdom must we also believe in the growth of the Church?

To answer this question we must consider the relationship of the two and examine the teaching of the Scriptures. A most helpful analysis is found in *A Theology of the New Testament* by Dr George Eldon Ladd. He describes the relationship of the Kingdom and the Church under five headings (pp. 111–119):

1. The Church is not the Kingdom.
2. The Kingdom creates the Church.
3. The Church witnesses to the Kingdom.
4. The Church is the Instrument of the Kingdom.
5. The Church: The Custodian of the Kingdom.

Dr Ladd's summary of his analysis is the final paragraph of the section:

'In summary, while there is an inseparable relationship between the Kingdom and the church, they are not to be identified. The Kingdom takes its point of departure from God, the church from men. The Kingdom is God's reign and the realm in which the blessings of his reign are experienced; the church is the fellowship of those who have experienced God's reign and entered into the enjoyment of its blessings. The Kingdom creates the church, works through the church, and is proclaimed in the world by the church. There can be no Kingdom without a church – those who have acknowledged God's rule – and there can be no church without God's Kingdom; but they remain two distinguishable concepts: the rule of God and the fellowship of men.'

(LADD. 1974:119)

The inter-relationship of the two is so close and complex that the growth of the Kingdom must affect the growth of the Church. The growing Kingdom creates a growing Church for those who submit to God's rule join the ranks of the Church. And this growing Church is better able to serve and witness to the Kingdom. But what kind of Church? Obviously it must be the Church that meets the conditions of the Kingdom. It's membership must be made up of those, 'who have experienced God's reign and entered into the enjoyment of its blessings'. The growing Church must bear witness to the Kingdom and be its instrument to promote peace, justice and righteousness in the world. This means that a local church must be, in Markus Barth's phrase, 'a functional outpost of the Kingdom'. This local fellowship of people under God's rule, must proclaim the Good News of the Kingdom, heal the sick, destroy the works of the devil and manifest the King's presence. This is the kind of local church that grows as the Kingdom grows.

When Jesus responded to Peter's profession of faith and predicted the abiding presence and constant growth of the Church, he was speaking of the Church as an instrument of the Kingdom (Matt. 16.17–19). The church that does not meet these conditions of the Kingdom cannot presume upon Christ for growth or even survival

(Rev. 2.5). As Dr W. A. Visser 'T Hooft, former General Secretary of the World Council of Churches warned:

> 'The Promise that the gates of hell shall not overcome (the Church) is not given to every society which calls itself 'Church'. It is only given to the body which Jesus Christ calls '*my* Church'. And the great question which every part of the Church or every church-body must ask itself with fear and trembling is therefore: "Are we in truth in the Church of Jesus Christ?" '
>
> (VISSER 'T HOOFT 1956:69)

The tragedy of so many churches in Great Britain and Europe, with their long histories, established privileges and ancient organisation and buildings, is that they have ceased to meet the conditions of the Kingdom. They may have passed the test of time but do they pass the test of Christ? While we believe in the growth of the Kingdom this does not mean that we necessarily believe in the growth of these churches. The Church Growth Movement is not concerned to increase the efficiency of ageing and apostate ecclesiastical structures with management expertise. We do not want to apply cosmetics to the corpse of a dead denomination. And we certainly have no desire to provide a local church with promotional skills that will succeed only in adding nominal and unregenerate members to the congregation. The church growth we wish to promote fulfils the conditions of the Kingdom and the churches we long to see planted and established throughout the earth are 'communities of the King'.

Is it possible to recognise such churches? Are there 'signs of growth' in these outposts of the Kingdom in Great Britain?

TEN SIGNS OF GROWTH

The following list of *ten* 'signs of growth' is not exhaustive but I believe these are observable phenomena that accompany genuine church growth. I am not suggesting that growing churches have all of them but they generally have several, depending on their churchmanship and structure.

'Signs of Growth' are the evidence of spiritual vitality and life under the rule of God. They are discernible within the churches of the New Testament when these first 'communities of the King' were formed, and have reappeared throughout history whenever the Church has been renewed by the Spirit and Word of God. They cannot be manufactured or copied in isolation, for they are the product of prior submission to the Lordship of Jesus Christ. He is the head of the body and all genuine expressions of spiritual life within the Church are from his Spirit (1 Cor. 12.12–27; Eph. 2.21,22). 'Signs of growth' are therefore similar to the fruit and gifts of the Spirit. The former are the outward and recognisable manifestations of the presence and activity of the Holy Spirit within a community.

The latter are manifestations within an individual (1 Cor. 12.11; Gal. 5.22,23).

The Church on earth has never been perfect, therefore 'signs of growth' indicate health rather than perfection. The Church, like the Kingdom, awaits the end of history and the complete fulfilment of its destiny as the Bride of Christ (Eph. 5.27). It will not be 'without spot or wrinkle' until Christ returns and the Kingdom comes. The Church is complete and perfect before God in Christ (Col. 2.10) but in its present form on earth it strives for perfection under the ministry of the Holy Spirit (2 Cor. 13.11; 1 Thes. 5.23–28; Jude 24–25). These imperfections of the Church must be admitted but should never be passively accepted. The apostles did not hesitate to call the Church to holiness and health (Eph. 4.1; Phil 1.27; Heb. 6.1; 1 John 1.8–10; 1 Pet. 1.15–16).

The local church that is concerned to examine its health may use these 'signs of growth' for comparison and evaluation. (An exercise is provided in Appendix 4). When deficiencies and weaknesses are discovered they should be corrected. The first step, however, to an effective cure is always submission and rededication to the will and purpose of Christ for the Church (Eph. 5.24; Rev. 2.5,10,16; 3.3,19,20). The cause, rather than the symptom, of the sickness must be dealt with first.

When church leaders and members are prepared to undertake this 'diagnosis' of their church together a great deal may be learned about their churches. A valuable *subjective* assessment of church life is obtained which will supplement the *objective* analysis, about which we will consider in later chapters.

Constant Prayer

Constant corporate and personal prayer is an essential 'sign of growth' that is found in every growing church. The church that never prays does not grow. Jesus himself taught by word and deed that prayer is essential to life in the Kingdom of God. In the Sermon on the Mount he gave instruction about living under the rule of God and taught that prayer is a privilege and duty for every child of God (Matt. 6.5–13).

Jesus demonstrated the necessity of prayer in his own ministry. He prayed constantly throughout his life on earth: in public and alone (John 17; Luke 6.12); at great moments such as his baptism and transfiguration (Luke 3.21; 9.39); in the conflict of the wilderness and the anguish of Gethsemane (Matt. 4.1–11; Luke 22.39–46); in the conduct of his miraculous ministry and daily affairs (Matt. 7.34; 9.29; John 11.41,42); in the choice and defence of his disciples (Luke 6.12,13; 22.31,32; John 17.9–12); during the suffering and agony of his crucifixion (Luke 24.34; Mark 15.34) and at the moment of his death (Luke 24.46).

Jesus' life of prayer was an inspiration and example to his disciples

(Luke 11.1–4). They never forgot that they could and should pray constantly, earnestly and with great faith (Luke 11.5–13; 18.1; Mark 11.23,24). They saw extraordinary answers to their prayers, particularly when they prayed in agreement and gathered together (Matt. 18.19; Acts 1.14; 2.1–3; 4.31; 12.5). They learned from the Old Testament, the teaching of Jesus and experience, that their prayers could be hindered by unconfessed sin, an unforgiving attitude, unbelief, selfishness and bad relationships (Isa. 59.2; Mark 11.25; Jas. 1.5–7; 1 Pet. 3.7). But they also knew and continually proved that prayer based upon a right relationship with God had great power to effect the growth of the Church and the advancement of the Kingdom (Acts 4.23–33).

When the Church was first formed at Pentecost with the addition of about three thousand converts, the practice of prayer was one of the basic elements of their instruction (Acts 2.42). Constant prayer was a hallmark of the Early Church. In his introduction to the prayers recorded in Acts, Dr Donald Coggan, former Archbishop of Canterbury writes:

> In studying these prayers we overhear the Church at work – the Church in the sense of an ordinary cross-section of Christian disciples faced with a variety of situations and problems which drove them to their knees – It is the Church, in all its frailty, in all its perplexity, going to its Lord in prayer. It is the Church doing what it is made to do – having intercourse with its Lord.
>
> (COGGAN 1967:75)

Even a brief study of the prayer-life of the Early Church in Acts shows how prayer relates to every area of Christian life and service. The Christians prayed for such things as guidance and direction (1.24); boldness in witness (4.23–33); and forgiveness of murderers (7.59–60); that others might receive the Holy Spirit (8.15–17); that the dead might be raised (9.40–41); that prisoners might be freed (12.5); for the mission of Barnabas and Paul (13.3); and the welfare of the churches and their leaders (14.23; 20.36). In answer to these and other prayers God responded with many signs and wonders. He shook buildings; converted persecutors; poured out his Spirit; raised the dead; healed the sick; delivered demoniacs; thwarted the plans of Satan; equipped missionaries; converted individuals, households and peoples; and planted and strengthened churches.

Prayer is essential to the life and growth of the Church because it affects every dimension of growth. If Christians are to grow *conceptually* in the wisdom and knowledge of God they must pray (Eph. 1.15–19; Col. 1. 9,10; Jas. 1.5).

The *organic* growth of a local church takes place in the context of prayer. Church members pray for each other and their leaders (Rom. 15.30; Eph. 6.18,19; 1 Thess. 5.25), and against the devices of Satan (Matt. 6.13; Eph. 6.18). Church leaders pray for their churches. Paul prayed for a deepening of love and steadfastness in the church at Thessalonica (1 Thess. 3.12; 2 Thess. 3.5); for holiness and maturity among the Corinthians and Philippians (2 Cor. 13.7–9; Phil. 1.9–11); and that all the churches who read the Ephesian letter might be filled with the love of Christ (Eph. 3.14–19). Prayer is also an essential element within public worship and the ministry of the sacraments.

Jesus, himself, linked prayer to the *incarnational* growth of the church when he called for prayer for harvesters (Matt. 9.38). When the Church moves out into the world in service and witness it must always be accompanied by prayer. Paul knew that the progress of the church's mission depended on prayer (Rom. 1.8–10; 15.31), and he relied on the constant prayer support of the churches (2 Cor. 1.11; Col. 4.3; Phil. 1.19; 2 Thess. 3.1)

Prayer also affects the *numerical* growth of a church. Jesus prayed for the Twelve and lost only Judas who was destined to betray him (John 17.6–19). Paul prayed for the converts from his ministry and agonised over their ability to stand and grow in Christ (2 Cor. 11.28; Col. 1.29; 1 Thess. 3.1–10; 5.23). And John prayed for Gaius (3 John 1–4). Constant prayer for the lost and newly converted is a basic requirement in the task of evangelism and church growth. The evangelist or church planter who fails to pray and seek the prayer support of others, has forgotten the source of his power and effectiveness and will only experience failure. When 'making disciples', the Christian is only ever a co-worker with God and prayer is a mark of dependence and submission to the senior partnership of the Holy Spirit (1 Cor. 3.5–9).

Constant prayer is so obviously a 'sign of growth' that growing churches readily acknowledge this source of their power and blessing. Charles Spurgeon is alleged to have offered to show a visiting American the 'powerhouse' of the Metropolitan Tabernacle and took him to the prayer meeting!

The West Bridgford Full Gospel Church in Nottingham tripled its membership and planted a daughter church during the seventies. It is one of the fastest growing churches that our Bible Society research has found. When the Pastor, Leslie Bicknell, was asked to account for this remarkable growth, he described specific and constant prayer as the 'real reason'. He identified the regular persistent prayer at the weekly prayer meeting, a prayer group formed spontaneously by the ladies of the church, specific prayer related to personal requests at the fortnightly house groups, and, particularly, powerful and 'simple' prayers by groups of new converts associated with the daughter church.

Pastor Bicknell believes that these prayers have resulted in remarkable conversions among completely 'unchurched' people, manifestations of the Holy Spirit within the church and miracles of healing within the community. As in the Acts of the Apostles, God has moved mightily in response to the constant prayer of his people.

Respect for Biblical Authority

'The Bible,' said Emil Brunner, 'is the soil from which all Christian faith grows'. It is the source of Christian doctrine and the manual of Church practice. Throughout two thousand years of Church history the Bible has constantly reminded the Church of her distinctive message and mission. When the Bible is allowed to speak to the Church she is renewed and reformed. When the Bible addresses the world mankind is called by God to faith and obedience. Where peoples respond, churches are planted. The Bible, which is the Word of God, is therefore an instrument of the Holy Spirit for the growth of the Church and Kingdom. Recognition of the power and authority of the Bible within the Church is a universal 'sign of growth'.

After examining the place and effect of the Bible in evangelism and church growth since apostolic times Dr A. M. Chirgwin writes:

'Throughout its history the Christian Church has used the Bible as a main instrument of its evangelistic activity. The early Church used it not only to instruct the faithful, but also to evangelise the non-Christians. The Reformers translated it so that all men might read for themselves the message of God's grace. The Puritans and Pietists applied it to daily life and took it with them to the mission field as the means of winning converts to the faith. The Evangelicals founded societies to print it and to distribute it to all men everywhere. This evidence of history is impressive. There were, of course, some periods when the Church used the Bible less than at others, just as there were certain branches of the Church that used other tools beside the Bible. But no other tool has been in use always and in all sections of the Church. It is a fair summary that all through its history, whenever the Church has been engaged in trying to win the outsider and the non-Christian, it has used the Bible as its main instrument. What is more, the times when the Church has gone to its evangelistic task with the Bible open in its hands have been precisely the times when it has won many of its greatest conquests. The Bible has in fact been the cutting-edge of its advance.'

(CHIRGWIN 1954:64)

Contemporary examples from the world Church are so numerous that two illustrations will have to suffice. In Latin America one of the most influential movements for the renewal and growth of the Roman Catholic Church are the basic Christian communities. In 1979 it was reported that there were 150,000 throughout Latin America with about 80,000 in Brazil. This renewal movement among the working-class masses has been likened to the eighteenth-century Methodist awakening in England. These communities have become 'focal points' of evangelisation and the lessons learned have been passed around the world. Basic communities have become a major structure for renewal and growth within the Roman Catholic Church from East Asia to East Anglia. It is a significant fact that these communities respect the authority of the Bible. Typical descriptions of them contain such comments as, 'they are putting into practice the Word of God', 'they seek their nourishment in the Word of God', and 'the community opens itself to the power and judgement of the Word of God'.

In China, the Cultural Revolution, which began in 1966, closed the churches and outlawed the Bible, causing thousands of copies to be destroyed. Chinese Christians had to meet together secretly in groups of three or four to worship, pray and study the Scriptures. Surviving Bibles were torn into sections to be copied and shared with others. One young man from the eastern provinces who had a particularly good memory was commissioned to memorise the whole New Testament. He was sent from place to place to encourage the believers and dictate the Scriptures. By these and other means the Bible sustained the churches. When in 1979 the 'Bamboo Curtain' was lifted the value and importance of the Bible was demonstrated once again in the Chinese Church's survival and growth.

Unfortunately, in Great Britain, as in Europe generally, the Bible has been silent for decades in the mainline Churches. The negative school of biblical criticism discredited the Bible as the Word of God and ridiculed the traditional doctrines of the inspiration and authority of the Bible. This 'liberal' attitude to the Scriptures was believed to be the only reasonable and scholarly position and for two generations it has held sway in the majority of universities and theological colleges.

This has had disastrous consequences for twentieth century theology, the training of ministers, the ordinary Christian's knowledge and experience, and evangelism and church planting. Unbiblical and sub-biblical teaching has weakened the Church and affected every area of her life and witness. The effect of 'liberalism' has been felt in the university, the pulpit, the pew and in the street. The combined result has been an unremitting harvest of Church decline.

Dr Peter Beyerhaus, Professor of Missions at Tubingen University in West Germany, is so concerned with the present state of modern theology and the western Church that he calls for all theologians to recognise their position within the community of faith and under the Holy Spirit, and to submit to the authority of the Bible. He writes under the heading, 'Modernist Misery':

'The healing of our theology and our churches in Europe and America can only take place if we penitently subject our intellect in faith to the guidance of the Holy Spirit. This guidance can be gained only by a personal life in the Spirit and by listening to the continuous self explication of the divine Word within the fellowship of the Church of Jesus Christ. Theologians can never claim to be teachers of the Church as long as they act as autonomous interpreters of the Bible who respect only the thorough application of their "scientific" methods. They can become valid teachers of the Church only to the degree they enter the field where the Holy Spirit is displaying His energies. This means at the same time that they carefully study the living history of biblical interpretation which is the special field of the Holy Spirit's work. They must humbly join the chain of witnesses, not so much as historical critics, but rather as the faithful stewards of God's mysteries.'

(BEYERHAUS 1972:17)

The effect of 'liberal' theology upon the training of ministers, particularly within the Free Churches, has been devastating. Ministers have embraced 'liberalism' and the 'social gospel' in large numbers. Many have become hesitant about preaching the gospel, uncertain about teaching traditional and basic Christian truths, reactionary towards their evangelical heritage, and disparaging of the supernatural in Christian faith and experience.

This deadening effect of 'liberal' theological training upon ministers and the churches is typically illustrated by the personal testimony of Dr Clifford Hill, ex-President of the Congregational Church and former Director of Evangelism for the Evangelical Alliance. He writes:

'I, like thousands of other ministers over the past generation or so, left college with a good classical and theological education, but with no real living faith in God. Such faith as I once had having been systematically destroyed. Consequently, I lacked the power of the Holy Spirit in the early part of my ministry. It was not until some years later, when I came alive in Christ, that I rediscovered the Bible and it became precious to me as the word of God. Although I certainly did not react into a blind literalist view of scripture, my faith no longer depended upon the outcome of critical debate. I discovered a new basis of faith in my experience of the presence of the risen Lord in my life. It was from this certainty in Christ that I was able to come back and wrestle with the thorniest problems of Biblical criticism, without disturbing my peace in God. I have experienced the power of the Holy Spirit which has brought a new spiritual dimension, a new joy and peace into my life that was certainly not there before. I not only know that there is a difference in my own personal life, but that there is a difference in my ministry too. In the earlier years of my ministry I never saw anyone converted, and I didn't know what it meant to be alive in Christ, but since I have come alive myself I have seen the fruits in my ministry. I have seen people converted and I have seen many nominal and traditional Christians come alive in Christ, in the same way that I have done.'

(HILL 1980:129)

Fortunately the barrenness of 'liberalism' is now recognised. Its inability to hold the people in the pews or reach the people in the streets is generally acknowledged. Dr Rubert E. Davies describes the impact of 'liberal' theology upon Methodism after the First World War in the following terms:

'The gaps which appeared in once crowded churches were not all caused by the mass slaughter of the war. Becoming gradually conscious of the inadequacy of traditional evangelical theology, with its rigid plan of salvation and its literal adherence to the text of the Bible, Methodist preachers tended in the twenties to swing away to the newly discovered 'liberal' position, which discounted the theology of the Atonement in nearly all its forms, reduced the deity of Christ by heavy emphasis on the 'Jesus of History', treated the Bible as the record of man's progressive discovery of God, and put its hopes in the League of Nations as the harbinger of the Kingdom of God. This approach to the mysteries of the Christian religion certainly brought liberation to many thoughtful people who found the old dogmas hard to accept but it entirely failed to kindle the imagination or the faith of the multitudes now estranged from the Church.'

(DAVIES 1976:158)

Today the pendulum is swinging back and there are encouraging signs of a growing confidence in the Bible and its message. Biblical scholars and theologians of all traditions are returning to more 'orthodox' positions in Christian doctrine and the 'liberal' and radical theological colleges in the United Kingdom are closed or struggling to survive. Evangelical and Bible colleges are full and flourishing and the vast majority of ministers now being trained have confidence in the Bible for preaching and teaching in the churches.

A return to biblical preaching and teaching within established churches will undoubtedly stimulate renewal and growth. Biblical principles and patterns for church life and ministry will be discovered to challenge traditional and institutional practices that have become obstacles to growth. This has been graphically illustrated by the title and content of a little book on the biblical models for a church by an American Pastor, B. Smith. The book is called *When All Else Fails, Read the Directions*!

But a word of caution is required. The Bible is not merely the tool of men but an instrument of the Holy Spirit. Therefore an openness to the Holy Spirit is essential for all who seek to understand and communicate the Word of God. This is clearly seen in the earlier quotations from Professor Beyerhaus and Dr Hill. Without this submission to the Holy Spirit, biblical preaching and teaching is characterised by the pharisaic sin of 'dead orthodoxy' and produces decay and decline. The simple rhyme conveys the truth:

The Word without the Spirit – You dry up!
The Spirit without the Word – You blow up!
The Spirit and the Word   – You grow up!

When the Word and the Spirit of God are active together, Christians (even evangelicals) do not need to defend or battle for the Bible. As biblical truths are taught and obeyed, the Bible stamps its authority and authenticates its nature within the Church and the world. The Scriptures are dynamic and effective to fulfil the purpose God intends (Josh. 1.7–9; Ezra 8.5–12; Isa. 55.11; Matt. 5.17–20; Acts 17.10–12; Rom. 1.16; Col. 3.16; 2 Tim. 3.16; Heb. 4.12). When the Word of God is spread the Church grows (Acts 6.7; 12.24; 19.20).

In 1978 Dr Paul Beasley-Murray and Alan Wilkinson set out to assess the growth of Baptist churches in England. They were able to study 350 very detailed questionnaires from a representative sample of churches. The survey, which probed every area of church life, included one question about the theological position of the minister. The growing churches had conservative evangelical ministers and where there was the strongest bias toward growth, the ministers were also classified as charismatic. They were men who were consciously preachers and teachers of the Word and open to the Holy Spirit (see figure 15).

Bamford Chapel in Rochdale is one of the fastest growing churches within the United Reformed Church. If the whole denomination had been able to match their growth between 1973 and 1979 they would have added 130,000 new members! When the minister, the Rev Jeffrey Yates, was asked about the place of the Bible in his church he replied, 'The Bible is the source book of our faith and in various ways is becoming central to our life. It is our aim to make it ever more meaningful to all our fellowship. There is a new willingness to study the Bible.'

The evidence is overwhelming whether we examine Church history or study the Catholic, Orthodox or Protestant communions at home or overseas. Whenever or wherever the authority of the Bible is acknowledged, preached and taught in the Spirit and acted upon in faith, individuals are converted and churches are planted. The fact of the matter is that the Bible is essential for church growth.

Effective Leadership

Growing churches always have effective leadership. They have leaders who get the job done. Whatever leadership gift, skill or style is required for the healthy functioning of the local body of Christ, they possess and exercise it.

In his analysis of growing American churches, Dr Peter Wagner identified the role of the minister as 'the primary catalytic factor for growth'. Where the pastor has a vision for growth and a concern to

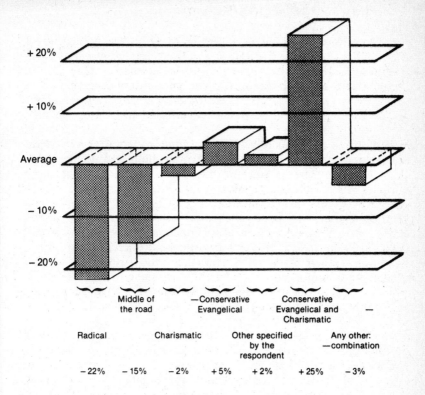

Figure 15. Theological Position of Baptist Ministers

(From *Turning the Tide* by P. Beasley-Murray and Alan Wilkinson. Published by Bible Society 1981.)

reach the lost he becomes the key to growth. When the minister has no vision for growth and little or no concern for evangelism he is an obstacle to growth. He is the proverbial cork in the bottle!

The role of the minister is so important that Dr Wagner places this at the top of his list of 'Seven Vital Signs' of growth:

'Vital Sign Number One of a healthy, growing church is a pastor who is a possibility thinker and whose dynamic leadership has been used to catalyze the entire church into action for growth.'
(WAGNER 1976:57)

It would appear that the rapidly growing Chilean Pentecostals have a similar belief in the role of the pastor for church growth.

They do not ordain pastors unless they are 'successful' and churches grow through their ministry:

> ' "We take the men who seem to us to be most suitable and we send them into the country; if the work produces results, then they are called to the ministry; if it has no results, they are not called and they go back home," explained a superintendent.'
>
> (Quoted in *Haven of the Masses*
> by C. L. d'EPINAY 1969:76)

This stress upon the role of the pastor for church growth raises penetrating and disturbing questions about the role of the clergy in Britain and Europe. It suggests they could be the greatest single cause of Church decline, a fact which has not gone unnoticed. Dr Ross Kinsler of the World Council of Churches, comparing the growing churches of the Third World with the declining churches of the West, writes, 'The historic denominations seem to develop dynamically in inverse proportion to the sophistication and professionalism of their leadership.' And the 1981 Partners in Mission Consultation Report on the Church of England, *To a Rebellious House*, repeatedly draws attention to the state of the Anglican clergy. One of the most disturbing comments refers to the absence of vision.

> 'In order to prepare clergy for the Church you must have a clear vision of what it means to be a believer in 1981, of the role of the Church community and of the function of the clergy within it. The quality of the Church depends upon the quality of its responsible pastors. In the Church of England such a clear vision seems to be absent; the laity, from whom the clergy are drawn, are confused when confronted with conflicting and contrasting lifestyles in neighbouring parishes and dioceses, and later also in contrasting (and perhaps conflicting) theological colleges. Post-ordination training, apparently without continuity, continues the absence of a clear vision of the role of the clergy within the Church.'
>
> (*To A Rebellious House*, page 23)

Does this mean that every pastor must be a success and a superstar? Must every minister be a dynamic 'go-getter' who, like the football manager, has to go if his team never scores? Not necessarily. The role of the pastor may be crucial for church growth but he cannot be held responsible for factors in the church or community over which he has no influence or control. But the pastor is the key to church growth when the following *seven* conditions have been realised:

1. *When the pastor sees* the possibility of growth and actively works for it. He has 'Church Growth eyes'. He sees people as lost yet loved (John 3.16). He knows that mankind is alienated and separated from God by sin, but may be reconciled and saved through the work of

Christ (2 Cor. 5.17–20). He is therefore deeply committed to the evangelistic mandate and is obedient to the Great Commission. As the faithful servant of the King, he seeks to save the lost (Luke 19.10) and see them enter the Kingdom.

Pastors of growing churches not only see mankind from God's perspective, they also see the potential for God's mission. They see what great things God has done in the past, is doing in the present and will do in the future. They have vision and faith for the growth of their churches. Like William Carey, they expect great things from God and attempt great things for God. Their vision is not bound by the pressures of the ministry or blurred by the problems in the church, but based upon the promises of Christ, who will build his Church (Matt. 16.18).

2. *When the pastor suits* the church because his gifts, talents, personality, experience and leadership style are appropriate to the situation. The pastor supplements the leadership gifts of others and matches the needs of the church. They are compatible and he makes it work.

This explains why some pastors of growing churches do not see growth when they move to other churches. They don't fit! It also explains why some ministers of ordinary ability and competence are pastors of growing churches. They don't have to be superstars, just suitable.

3. *When the pastor serves* the church and community as a representative of Christ. Jesus, as the Servant, is the supreme model of leadership. He calls his followers by word and deed to love and serve others too (Matt. 23.11; Mark 10.45; John 13.2–17).

All leaders, in society or the Church have three essential attributes. They have a *position* that is recognised, *power* that they exercise and *privileges* that distinguish them from those they lead.

In the church the pastor's position and status is quite simply that of a servant. Even the apostle Paul could claim no more (2 Cor. 4.5).

The pastor's power and authority is established by example and humble service (Matt. 23.8–12; Luke 22.26; 1 Pet. 5.1–4).

The pastor's privilege, as a servant of God and the Kingdom, is that he may suffer for Christ and the Good News (cf. Acts 5.41). Paul writes, 'We do not want anyone to find fault with our work, so we try not to put obstacles in anyone's way. Instead, in everything we do we show that we are God's servants by patiently enduring troubles, hardships, and difficulties' (2 Cor. 6.3,4).

Every genuine pastor shares the suffering of the Servant (2 Tim. 3.10–12) and the pastor of a growing church is no exception. He probably knows more than most the pain of Christian ministry.

4. *When the pastor shepherds* the flock and recognises this as his fundamental task. As his title suggests, his basic responsibility is to care for the flock of Christ. He is the guardian of the souls of his

congregation – an awesome responsibility and a joyful privilege (Acts 20.28; Heb. 13.17).

In the growing church the pastor must share the pastoral care with others or produce a self-limiting congregation. The pastor of a large and growing church cannot personally care for all his flock, so he must delegate the responsibility to other pastorally gifted leaders and members. However, he must never lose touch with his flock and should meet regularly with the pastoral workers to hear reports about the welfare of the members. He should offer personal care to everyone undergoing a crisis and be available for counsel. Whatever the size of the church, the pastor must always be known by his congregation as a shepherd.

5. *When the pastor steers*. Though the pastor exercises his authority from the 'inferior' position of a servant and the compassionate role of a shepherd, it is his responsibility to direct and guide the church.

When Paul explained the order of the body of Christ to the chaotic church at Corinth he listed a variety of gifts and ministries. The ministry of the 'director' or 'administrator' is included (1 Cor. 12.28) and literally describes the activity of a ship's pilot who steers a safe and steady course.

The pastor, as the presiding elder, must always keep his hand on the helm. Pastors of growing churches always know where they are going and confidently set the course for the church to follow. The author of Hebrews summarises the correct attitude of the crew, 'Obey your leaders and follow their orders' (Heb. 13.17). For the humility of the servant and the care of the shepherd must be matched by the submission and obedience of those who are served and loved.

6. *When the pastor stays* long enough to complete the task and fulfil his calling. Pastors of growing churches seldom change churches. They repeatedly start fresh chapters of ministry in the same church and stay for many years.

Lyle Schaller, an American Methodist minister, has been a church consultant for twenty-two years and currently advises two hundred churches annually. His observations suggest that a pastor requires five to seven years to reach maximum effectiveness in ministry to his congregation and within the community. Short-term pastors are not good for church growth and denominations like the Salvation Army that move pastors frequently actually encourage church decline.

7. *When the pastor shares* leadership with other leaders of the church. Pastors of growing churches recognise the biblical pattern of a plurality of elders (1 Tim. 5.17; Titus 1.5). They know that their gifts relate to specific areas and that other leaders are required to complement various leadership roles within the local church (2 Tim. 2.2).

At the Bible Society Church Growth Course we raise the issue of a church's expectation of its minister. Fourteen areas of church life are mentioned, ranging from visiting to burying the members. We point out that no minister can fulfil the total expectations of his church. I heard of a pastor who gave a questionnaire to his congregation and asked them to indicate how many hours he should spend on each activity. One member's total came to 200 hours per week!

The same exercise helps the pastor recognise his own limitations and face the challenge of sharing leadership in areas where he lacks gifts or resources to meet the church's needs.

When the pastor satisfies these seven conditions he becomes the key to church growth and a model for effective leadership that is an essential requirement if the church is to grow.

Mobilised Membership

Church growth studies from every continent and a great variety of cultures have confirmed a basic New Testament principle – that churches grow when they mobilise their total membership in the service of Christ.

The New Testament does not recognise the traditional and false distinction between the clergy and laity within the Church. It consistently states that every Christian belongs to the people of God and is called and equipped for active service within the body of Christ. Each member has a particular function to fulfil and a special contribution to make. This is expressed in many different ways within a local church or related itinerant ministries.

When the Holy Spirit came at Pentecost to form and empower the early Church, 'they saw what looked like tongues of fire which spread out and touched *each person* there' (Acts 2.3). That symbolic act confirms the Holy Spirit's desire to anoint every Christian for ministry.

The apostle Paul uses the universally applicable analogy of the human body to describe the essential part each member plays in the life of the church. He reminds the Corinthian Christians:

'There are different kinds of spiritual gifts, but the same Spirit gives them. There are different ways of serving, but the same Lord is served. There are different abilities to perform service, but the same God *gives ability to everyone* for their particular service. The Spirit's presence is shown in some way in *each person* for the good of all.

(1 Cor. 12.4–7)

There is some specialisation within the ministry of the Church. There are apostles, prophets, teachers, miracle-workers, healers and others (1 Cor. 12.27–31; Eph. 4.11). But even those 'specialists' have a specific task in relation to the other members of the church. They have to 'prepare all God's people for the work of Christian service, in order to build up the body of Christ' (Eph. 4.12). The leaders have the task of equipping the members for ministry.

This concept of every member ministry is reinforced by the fact that all who are in the 'community of the King' have been appointed to a 'royal priesthood'. They are eligible to participate in the worship (1 Cor. 14.26) and service (1 Pet. 2.9) of the Church and this is also their responsibility. There are no passengers or spectators, only participants.

In his study of the Church, the Roman Catholic theologian Hans Küng has affirmed this 'priesthood of all believers' and writes:

> 'The Church is *the people of God*, and we have seen that this means that the Church is never merely a particular class or caste within the fellowship of the faithful. On the contrary, *all* believers, in fundamental equality, are the Church, are members of the people of God. They are all 'elect', 'saints', 'disciples', 'brethren'. And hence they are precisely a royal priesthood.'
>
> (KÜNG 1967:473)

Of course this *doctrine* of the 'priesthood of all believers' was stressed at the Reformation. Unfortunately the *practice* did not develop. The clergy at the altar became the clergy in the pulpit and the laity remained locked in the pews. In the vast majority of British and European churches the position has remained unchanged.

The Partners in Mission Consultation identified this problem in the contemporary Church of England and placed it first in the list of recommendations in the 'Postscript: the Heart of the Message':

> 'We are still too dominated by the false view that the ministry of the Church is confined to bishops, priests and deacons. The whole pilgrim people of God share in ministry, and clergy and laity must be trained for this shared ministry, which is also an ecumenical ministry. Among related issues we must question the relevance of freehold and private patronage, face the challenge of equal partnership of men and women in ministry, and establish job descriptions for all ministers.'
>
> (*To a Rebellious House*, page 47)

It is one thing to acknowledge that a problem exists and quite another to solve it. If this problem is to be solved it has to begin with the clergy. Ministers must recognise the true nature of the church and their role within it. They have the task of equipping their congregation to minister and therefore of helping each member discover, develop and use their gifts.

Spiritual gifts are controversial. The emphasis upon them by the Pentecostal and charismatic movements has caused some to fear them or dismiss them as too divisive and contentious. They prefer the quiet life and would rather not face the subject at all. Unfortunately the issue cannot be resolved so simply. If the membership are going to be mobilised it can only happen as they understand how they have been personally equipped to serve in the body of Christ.

It is not possible to discuss the role of the laity apart from the gifts of the Holy Spirit. On October 31st, 1893, before the Pentecostal and Charismatic Movements began, Dr B. F. Westcott spoke on the subject of the 'Spiritual Work of Laymen'. This renowned Bible scholar and Bishop of Durham was addressing a Diocesan Conference at Gateshead. After challenging the traditional understanding of clergy and laity he went on to say, 'It is assumed in the Apostolic writings that in the rich variety of divine gifts no believer is left without provision: that in the manifold complexity of the body, no least part is left without its function.'

I hope that this word from the past, before all our controversies about spiritual gifts began, will help to allay the fears of those who are in danger of dismissing the subject and missing this vitally important truth. As Dr Peter Cotterell says:

'Churches which will not allow the gifts of the Spirit to be exercised are necessarily self-limiting churches. Not all that the Spirit *might* do is being done, because the tools that he has distributed to his workforce are never put to work. And it is sadly true that if the minister does not see this and if he will not allow the spiritual gifts to be used, then the Spirit *cannot* get to work. Unbelief is more than intellectual dissent; it is disobedience to teaching received. Ministers, above all others, *ought* to know the importance of mobilising all their congregation.'

(COTTERELL 1981:48)

For a comprehensive treatment of this subject and its relationship to church growth I would recommend Dr Peter Wagner's *Your Spiritual Gifts Can Help Your Church Grow*. He identifies and describes twenty-seven gifts and provides practical insights into their use within the church.

Eventful Worship

The Pentecostal denominations represent eighty per cent of Protestants in Latin America and they are probably the fastest growing section of the world Church today. In his analysis of their rapid growth Dr Peter Wagner has identified their worship as a key factor. The Pentecostals are also recognised as the most indigenous churches, so their worship is particularly strong in cultural relevance. They use the language, music and liturgy that suits the man in the street.

Another noticeable feature of Pentecostal worship is that everyone enjoys it! It is fun to go to church and therefore a good place to take an unconverted or newly converted friend. Wagner writes:

'One of the first things you notice when you go into a worship service in a Latin American Pentecostal Church is how much the people seem to enjoy themselves. The hardest thing to find in one of the Pentecostal services is a wide yawn. Unfortunately yawns are all too common in many other churches in Latin America . . . . But since Pentecostals have fun going to church, they do not hesitate to bring others along. They know ahead of time that when they lead another person to Christ, they can bring that new born babe to a spiritual home he will enjoy.'

(WAGNER 1974:106)

The contrast between Latin American Pentecostal worship and mainline British and European worship is so great that any comparison appears irrelevant. A Viennese Waltz is certainly not a Venezuelan Samba!

However, there are valid insights and many important lessons to learn about eventful worship from this Pentecostal experience. When the purely cultural elements are removed the general principles emerge and they may be applied throughout the world, even in Europe.

Dr Wagner has identified eight characteristics of Latin American Pentecostal worship and these help us discover the principles.

1. *The bigness*
The Pentecostals love to worship in large numbers. They enjoy 'Celebrations'. Thousands gather together in mammoth churches in such cities as Buenos Aires, Mexico City, and Santiago. In San Paulo, the Brazil for Christ Church seats 25,000 and has a specially strengthened roof to cope with the congregation clapping in unison! Worship in these churches is always an unforgettable experience – a memorable event.

We have already noted in chapter 2 the importance of the 'Celebration' size gathering. Of course it is possible to worship God in small groups or even alone, and Pentecostals do. But they worship in large groups whenever they can because it is good for the soul. It builds morale and confidence to witness. They know they are not alone in the Christian faith. They belong to a host on earth as well as in heaven.

In Britain today the opportunity to share in this type of worship is usually found at the Inter-Church level. Very few local churches are able to provide this dimension of worship every Sunday – not yet! The denominations which recognise the value of the large gathering are calling their churches to combine in united worship for special occasions, and the Christian festivals. Millions of Roman Catholics have worshipped together at services led by Pope Paul. The South West Province of the United Reformed Church held a provincial 'Celebration' and even composed a hymn for the occasion. And a group of Baptists packed Blackburn Cathedral for a festival of praise at the climax of a day's outing together.

These large gatherings help to make the worship memorable and eventful. This is just as true in Coventry as Caracas.

2. *The social opportunity*

Pentecostals love to relate to each other. Going to church is an occasion to renew friendships and share experiences. They arrive early and stay late because they like being together. They go to church not only to worship but also for fellowship.

Surely this is what one would expect of those who are in God's family. It is certainly more like the New Testament pattern than many British churches where greetings are never exchanged and it is possible to attend church for years with only a 'Goodbye' at the door to the minister.

Of course many churches are trying to overcome this problem by relational activities during the service. It is no longer unusual to be asked to introduce yourself to your neighbour or form a small group for prayer. Anglicans and many Methodists have introduced 'The Peace' at the Eucharist and greet each other with a warm handshake or embrace and such words as, 'The peace of the Lord be with you'.

Unfortunately some people believe that fellowship is optional, like the angry lady who stormed out of church complaining to the Vicar, 'When I come to church its to worship God, not to be friendly!' She obviously needed to learn from the Pentecostals that Christians are better able to love God when they learn to love each other (1 John 4.19–21).

When worship is shared with others in the context of true fellowship the size of the group is unimportant, for Jesus has promised, 'Where two or three come together in my name, I am there with them' (Matt. 18.20). It is *being together* in the presence of Christ that is essential for eventful worship.

3. *The noise level, participation and motion*

These three characteristics, identified by Dr Wagner, have cultural elements that are peculiar to Latin America, but collectively they demonstrate a fundamental principle of New Testament worship – *participation* (1 Cor. 14.6).

All Pentecostals believe they are free to participate in the worship of God and because they all have an opportunity to share, it becomes a meaningful event for each worshipper. When it's time to pray, they all pray. Their natural and spontaneous prayers encourage even the timid to pray. When it's time for personal testimonies, there is no shortage of volunteers. They feel free to contribute with exclamations of praise, or Bible verses, or hymns, as the service progresses. One researcher counted sixty-five individual contributions at a Pentecostal service in Colombia. They are also allowed to move. They can raise their hands or kneel or dance. When they worship God they become totally involved with body, mind and spirit.

All of this is in stark contrast to the deadly dull and monotonous services in so many churches in the United Kingdom. Any noise draws indignant and icy stares and any motion or speech is reserved for the minister! British Churches are plagued by 'one-man-band' worship which breeds 'mouth-and-bottom' congregations. The doctrine of the body of Christ and the practice of the priesthood of all believers is symbolically denied every Sunday. Sadly, the *Free* Churches, who should know better, are the worst offenders.

Christian worship has its roots in the Upper Room at Passover and Pentecost and is built on the 'twin pillars' of liturgy and liberty. Therefore the Pentecostals justify their practice from the New Testament. They are aware that spontaneity and freedom may degenerate into disorder and licence. Paul's caution to the Corinthians about excesses in worship is appropriate to them: '*Everything* must be done in a proper and orderly way' (1 Cor. 14.40). Paul's words are seldom appropriate for British churches where worship involves so few and so little.

4. Tongues

Speaking in tongues is recognised as the distinctive mark of Pentecostals, and it is freely expressed in their worship, especially at times of prayer. This gift, and other manifestations of the Spirit (1 Cor. 12.7–11), particularly the gift of healing, reveal an openness to the intervention of the Spirit during the services. Pentecostals believe the Lord will signify his presence by signs of his power. They have a sense of expectancy and faith. There is an anticipation that God will speak and act. Therefore worship is not only an event, it is an adventure! Pentecostals expect the sick to be healed, unbelievers to be converted, and the troubled to be comforted. They come in faith and expect something to happen.

I am not suggesting that 'sign gifts' are essential to worship or for growth. Many Pentecostal churches are not growing and many non-Pentecostal churches are. The important lesson to be learned from Pentecostal worship is that every service should be an adventure with Christ. And every worshipper should be filled with a sense of expectancy and faith that Christ will make his presence known. Eventful worship takes place when he does.

5. The music and the preaching

The cultural relevance of Latin American Pentecostal worship is most evident in the last two characteristics identified by Dr Wagner – the music and the preaching.

The music is contemporary and popular. Common and well-loved instruments like the guitar, mandolin and accordian are played to the accompaniment of clapping and percussion instruments. They use their own kind of music to express their praise and worship.

Pentecostal preaching is directed at the heart rather than the head. Though not without doctrinal content, it is emotional more than intellectual. Pentecostal preaching emerges from and relates to the life situation of the ordinary church member. Biblical truth is applied to everyday life. The preachers often exercise a 'tent-making' ministry and work alongside their congregations in field or factory. They belong to the people and share their joys and pains.

Far too much worship in Britain is culturally irrelevant. Music and preaching are so out of touch with the ordinary man in the street that attending church has become one of the most irrelevant activities imaginable. The music is chosen to satisfy the needs of a musical elite and the average preacher has lost the common touch. If he ever possessed it, the 'laundering' process of his theological training removed all traces.

Many Sunday services are so alienated from Britain in the 1980s, that church attendance has become an adventure in time travel – backwards! It is possible to join Medieval Anglicans, sixteenth century Independents, eighteenth century Methodists, Victorian Baptists or Salvationists, and pre-war Pentecostals. Their language and liturgies remain unchanged and they survive as cultural fossils in ecclesiastical strata. These relics of bygone ages appear insensitive to the spiritual needs of contemporary British people who need to hear the unchanging Good News of God's grace and salvation today.

However, one encouraging sign of growth in Britain today is a renewal of worship, spearheaded by the liturgical and charismatic movements. The liturgical movement has introduced contemporary language and forms of worship. The charismatic movement has brought freedom to many churches caught in the rut of tradition.

In 1980 the Church of England introduced the Alternative Services Book to supplement the Book of Common Prayer and has pioneered liturgical reform in England. Hundreds of Anglican churches are offering Family Services with modern music, drama, visual aids, music groups, bands and even orchestras. Thousands of young families are attracted to this bright and contemporary worship and many churches testify to the evangelistic potential of these services.

A typical testimony from the minister of a rapidly growing church in Yorkshire describes the conversion of a number of young couples originally contacted by the contemporary services. The vicar writes, 'Our main Sunday morning service regularly attracts a congregation of between 200–250 with a regular flow of newcomers. The service offers family worship in the context of Parish Communion. Music is led by organ and choir and a good music group of guitars and piano. Particular effort is made at a simple yet effective presentation of the Word.'

When a 'community of the King' worships, it celebrates the reign of God. This must always be eventful for those who participate or even watch (1 Cor. 14.22,25). Pentecostal experience from Latin America suggests that worship becomes eventful when manifestations of the Holy Spirit's activity are present and there is fellowship, liberty, faith and cultural sensitivity among the worshippers.

Continuous Evangelism

One of the signs of the coming Kingdom is world-wide evangelisation. When Jesus was asked what signs would 'show that it is the time of your coming and the end of the age', he mentioned, among other signs, 'this Good News about the Kingdom will be preached through all the world for a witness to all mankind, and then the end will come' (Matt. 24.3,14).

The Great Commission to evangelise the world by making disciples and planting churches is the mandate for every true 'community of the King' to engage in this task. Churches that fail to obey this command and do not continually evangelise have lost sight of their primary vocation to preach the Good News of the Kingdom. They not only fail to grow they also forfeit their right to exist.

Continuous evangelism should take place at two complementary levels. *Spontaneous evangelism* that involves every Christian in their daily affairs and *systematic evangelism* by individuals or groups who make new contacts and break fresh ground. Spontaneous evangelism takes place through the 'networks' or relationships of believers (John 1.40–45, Acts 8.1,4). Systematic evangelism uses planned missions, events, services etc. to discover new and responsive people (Luke 9.1–6; 10.1–20; Acts 8.5–8; 10.1–48).

1. Spontaneous Evangelism

Dr Max Warren, former General Secretary of the Church Missionary Society, attended a service of Holy Communion in a remote part of Nigeria at which over 600 communicants were present. He asked one of them how the gospel first came to the area and was told that two Christian market-women had gossipped about Christ to their customers and contacts. Their spontaneous evangelism had created a hunger for Christian instruction that eventually led to many conversions and the planting of the church. He comments on this incident of spontaneous evangelism:

'To a far greater extent than is commonly realised Africa has been evangelised by gossipping the gospel. . . . We could well seek to redeem the meaning of 'gossip'. It has proved one of the great methods of Christian witness.'

(WARREN 1976.66)

Spontaneous evangelism has been effective all over the world throughout church history. Dr Win Arn of the Institute of American Church Growth has estimated that between seventy-five per cent to ninety per cent of all Christians in areas of rapid church growth have been brought to Christ through the witness and influence of friends or relatives.

When Christians express their love and faith in committed relationships with unbelievers the Faith is shared and the Way is shown. The unbeliever learns by their example what to believe and how to behave and the Christian becomes God's medium for his message (Matt. 5.14–16).

The potential for spontaneous evangelism through the 'networks' of Christians is largely untapped in most churches. If every believer were taught how to tell the story of his Christian experience and share his faith in a simple manner (Luke 8.31; John 9.25), a tidal wave of witness would flood the neighbourhood. In addition, a simple apologetic sensitively taught and presented would equip the ordinary Christian to defend his faith when challenged or present his faith when called for. It is imperative that we try to 'open the mouths of the people in the pews' and encourage every believer to become an effective witness in his daily life.

2. Systematic Evangelism

When Christ gave the Church its evangelistic mandate, the *geographical and cultural* scope of the task was included. The disciples were to evangelise, 'all peoples everywhere', 'the whole world. . .to all mankind', 'to all nations, beginning in Jerusalem', and 'in Jerusalem, in all Judaea and Samaria, and to the ends of the earth' (Matt. 28.19; Mark 16.15; Luke 24.47; Acts 1.8). Systematic evangelism is particularly concerned with strategies and programmes that overcome these geographical and cultural barriers.

Geographically the Church had to begin evangelising where they were, in Jerusalem, in the midst of opposition and where rejection had reached its climax in the Cross. Judaea lay to the south and Samaria to the north and the ends of the earth were as far as the eye could see and man could travel. The world really was their parish.

Of course the world, at least the Jewish World, came to Jerusalem. When the Holy Spirit came at Pentecost, Luke was careful to note that the total sum of all known nations was represented in the crowd (Acts 2.5–11). Those who were converted by the apostolic preaching (Acts 2.41) would have returned home to evangelise and plant churches, probably in the context of the Diasporan synagogues. These later proved a fertile field for the missionary endeavours of Paul and others.

Culturally, the task was not so straightforward. The Jews of Jerusalem, Judaea and the Diaspora were at least Jews. Some were more Hebrew than others. Some, the Hellenists, had been influenced by the Graeco-Roman culture, but the cultural distance was closer than that between Jew and Samaritan. All Jews were culturally near neighbours, but the Samaritans and Jews, though related, were not on speaking terms (John 4.9). For historical and religious reasons, the divisions and barriers were wide. The task of evangelising the Samaritans required additional gifts and skills than those used to reach the Judaeans. Philip was an ideal man for the job and his cross-cultural gifts also proved invaluable in reaching the God-fearing nobleman from Ethiopia (Acts 6.4–8, 26–31).

Evangelising 'all peoples everywhere' included the dreaded gentiles, even Romans. It took a vision and much questioning to convince the Early Church that this too, was commissioned by Christ (Acts 10; 15.1–35). Once it had been accepted, however, the Church advanced to establish itself at 'the ends of the earth'. This commitment to continuous and world-wide evangelisation is an essential sign of growth.

Community Life

Lewin Road Baptist Church in Streatham is a large and growing church in the South West of London. With a membership of 400 and a regular worship attendance in excess of 500 it is one of the largest Baptist churches in the United Kingdom. There are many factors that contribute to its growth, but despite its size, a vital factor is the depth of fellowship and love openly expressed between the members. Visitors and newcomers often comment on the welcome received, 'I didn't think church would be as friendly as this!' They quickly discover that the church is a caring community. It is a fellowship of faith and love in Christ, and that, of course, is what every church should be.

Fellowship is one of the hallmarks of a church and characterises every true 'community of the King'. The new commandment that Jesus gave his disciples in the Upper Room on the night of his betrayal pointed to love and fellowship as the distinctive mark of Christian discipleship. 'If you have love for one another, *then everyone will know* that you are my disciples' (John 13.35).

If we examine the use of the Greek word for 'one another' in the New Testament, it reveals something of the community life of the Early Church. It is used fifty-eight times in the New Testament outside the Gospels, with forty references in the letters of Paul. Even a brief study of Paul's use of the word in his letter to the Romans is most revealing. Christians are to 'love *one another* warmly as Christian brothers' (12.10). Paul appeals for family love on the basis of their common spiritual parentage and adoption into God's family. Christians are related eternally to each other because of their common relationship to the Father, through the Son and by the Holy Spirit. The local church must therefore be a visible expression on earth of that divine community. Those who are not 'God's people' should be aware of a distinct group who are. They should recognise God's family and want to join it! Contemporary western society longs for community and the witness of Christian community is as powerful a commendation of Christ as ever.

Paul goes on in the same verse to counsel the Christians at Rome to, 'show respect for *one another*' (12.10). He stresses humility in relationships within the community. 'A willingness to let the other man have the credit', is J. B. Phillips' pungent paraphrase. They must also 'live in harmony with *one another*' (12.16 RSV). The only obligation they have 'is to love *one another*' (13.8). In fact it is a perpetual debt of love (JBP).

'Stop judging *one another*,' commands Paul. Rather they should build up and 'strengthen *one another*' (14.19). And because they have been accepted by Christ they must 'accept *one another*', too (15.7).

It is assumed that the Roman Christians have reached sufficient maturity in the Faith to be able to 'teach *one another*' (15.14) and keep each other 'on the right road' (JBP). Finally, says Paul, don't forget to 'Greet *one another* with a brotherly kiss' (16.16). The kiss may be cultural, but the greeting has universal application. At the very least, the cross-cultural smile is always appropriate!

Even this brief study demonstrates the commitment to Christ and each other that is the hallmark of Christian community. We have already seen that it is essential for the maintenance and maturity of the Christian faith. Which is why the communal life has always been stressed in times of ecclesiastical lukewarmness, heresy or worldliness.

That Christianity is meant to be lived in the context of loving and caring relationships, was seen at the birth of the Church at Pentecost. The first Christians had 'a religious communism of love' (Acts 2.45; 4.32–37) and shared whatever they possessed with each other, so that no one lacked or had need. Private property could be kept (Acts 5.4; 12.12), but many sold and shared all (Acts 4.32). Whether or not this proved economically foolish and led to the impoverishment of the Jerusalem church is unclear. What is clear, is that their love for each other in Christ was freely and practically expressed in community life. Growing churches usually do the same. A word of caution however, is required. There are historical and current examples of an over-emphasis on fellowship leading to *fellowshipitis*. The church or group becomes pre-occupied with itself and the members only have 'eyes' for each other. They become insensitive and oblivious to the needs of outsiders. The fellowship in the church may be wonderful but unbelievers outside remain lost and unsaved.

An extreme form of *fellowshipitis* is *remnantitis*. This describes the group that has degenerated into a 'holy huddle'. So holy and huddled are they that they become suspicious of the outsider and even justify their exclusiveness and isolation by quoting the Bible! Hans Küng exposes the extraordinary behaviour of these groups by contrasting them with the example of Jesus:

'It is striking that Jesus, while aware, even painfully aware of the decisive and divisive effect of his message and the fact that it was rejected by the majority of his people, never bases his preaching on the idea of the remnant, as the other select groups of his time did. He stresses a public ministry and rejects withdrawal from the world; his love for sinners, which excludes no one and is a source of scandal, is an urgent protest against any religious separatism and exclusiveness.'   (KÜNG 1967:105)

There can be no doubt that the local church is a community and fellowship within a boundary of faith – 'a crowd of men and women who believed in the Lord' (Acts 5.14). But the boundary must never become a barricade against the unbeliever seeking Christ or a barracks providing security from the battle raging in the world. A church exists to serve its Master, not satisfy its members. It is a community that must always be ready to serve and grow.

Compassionate Service

The pattern for Christian mission has been laid down in the ministry of Jesus. 'As the Father sent me, so I send you', Jesus said to his disciples (John 20.21). There could be no doubting the cost of obedience to this command. The hand that bid them go bore the scars of Calvary.

The disciples also knew that Jesus, 'did not come to be served; he came to serve and to give his life to redeem many people' (Mark 10.45). As the suffering Servant he fulfilled all the prophecies and expectations of the Old Testament and accomplished his mission to Israel and for the nations. The Apostles seized upon this example of Christ as the Servant, to explain and justify their own suffering for the sake of the gospel (1 Pet. 2.18–21). As servants of Christ (2 Cor. 4.5), sent into the world, they must also be willing to serve and to suffer (Rom. 8.16ff.) A servant is therefore the appropriate model for the status and role of the Church (Col. 1.24,25) and Christian (Phil. 3.10) in the world. The servant Church must follow the example of its Servant Master.

The service of Jesus was motivated by love for all men. It was often manifested in surges of strong compassion (Matt. 9.36; 14.14; 15.32; 20.24; Mark 1.41; Lk 7.13) and always found expression in deeds of love and mercy. He gave sight to the blind; comfort to the bereaved; hearing to the deaf; food to the hungry; healing to the crippled; and deliverance to the demonised. He touched the leper and raised the dead. He had the reputation of 'doing good' (Acts 10.38).

Likewise, a local church must be motivated by love to reach out and serve its neighbourhood. The love within the community of believers should spill over to embrace all men (Gal. 6.10). Good works are meant to characterise the life of all Christians (Eph. 2.8–10) and are the fruit of the faith they profess (Jas. 2.14–18). These good deeds are also an essential foundation for the Good News (Matt. 5.16).

Gladys Aylward was a remarkable missionary among the Chinese and showed great courage in caring for orphaned children during the Second World War. She declared that 'love is seen in what it does'. Her example is typical of countless similar deeds throughout Church history. In the battle against the barbarism and cruelty of the Roman Empire the early Christians offered solace to slaves, homes to abandoned children, care for the sick and comfort for the dying. Many of the great reforms in human society have been motivated by compassionate service in the name of Christ. Mother Theresa of Calcutta is within a long tradition of Christian service to the destitute, deprived and diseased.

Preaching the Good News of the Kingdom is always accompanied by deeds of compassion and acts of mercy, as Jesus and the apostles clearly show (Matt. 4.23; Acts 5.12–16; 8.5–8 etc.) If a 'community of the King' is genuinely concerned to preach this Good News it cannot ignore this call to serve others. Growing churches never do, and personal and corporate acts of love and compassion are legion in stories of church growth.

Two members of a rapidly growing Baptist church in Kent were enjoying a Sunday afternoon stroll across a common when they saw a heap of old clothes. To their surprise it turned out to be a homeless, destitute and depressed man, sleeping rough. The couple took the man home, befriended him and offered a room. Six months later he was converted to Christ and has fully recovered. This act of compassion led the couple to sell their house and buy a former nursing home. They now offer residential care to the depressed and emotionally disturbed. Over the years a number have been converted and joined the church.

The Newcourt Pentecostal Church at Finsbury Park in North London is vigorously evangelistic. Its desire to grow is expressed in continuous programmes of door-to-door visitation, special services and events, and regular missions. However, that the church has not lost sight of the need to serve its deprived multi-racial and inner-city community is evident in this notice outside the church:

'This Church is vitally interested in the following activities. . .
- Telling people that Jesus Christ can better their lives
- Old age pensioners luncheon clubs
- Providing accommodation for single young people locally
- Providing a lounge for old age pensioners to relax in
- Providing jobs for the unemployed
- Financing missionaries all over the world
- Meeting places for the local housing and tenants co-operatives
- Meeting young people in the local schools
- Providing cassettes for those who cannot attend services
- Providing good Christian books to feed the soul
- Visiting the homes of those in need
- Meeting people from all races and classes
- Keeping three ministers very, very busy
BUT MOST OF ALL WE ARE VITALLY INTERESTED IN YOU!'

The pastors and members of this Elim Church know that they have been called to serve in the name of Christ. They also realise that their service may be rejected and will often fail to bring those helped to profess faith in Christ. Just as lepers failed to thank Jesus for their healing (Luke 17.11–19), so many people remain unmoved by the love shown to them. The servant is not greater than his master and the rejection that characterised the ministry of Jesus will also be found by his followers.

Openness to Change

The plight of mankind required change within the Godhead – 'the Word became a human being' (John 1.1–14; 3.16; Phil. 2.5–8).

The plight of the first century world demanded a remarkable degree of openness to change on the part of the apostles and the Early Church. Paul was prepared to adapt his message and his methods to preach Christ in the multicultural Roman Empire (1 Cor. 9.19–23). Even the Galilean fisherman Peter changed sufficiently to become an effective advocate for the Gospel beyond his native land and outside his traditions.

The vast majority of Christians want their churches to grow. Unfortunately many are unwilling to pay the price for growth. Especially the price of constant openness to the changes required by growth in all dimensions.

Growing churches are not only open to change but have successfully managed all the changes that they believed the Holy Spirit required. This is not change for change's sake, but for Christ's sake. Life in the Kingdom of God is life with new dimensions (Matt. 19.17; John 3.3; 2 Cor. 5.17) and the coming of Jesus inaugurated a new age in the Spirit (1 Cor. 4.20; Rom. 14.17). Therefore life in the Kingdom of God is for changed and changeable people (1 Cor. 6.9–11; Eph. 5.5; 2 Thess. 1.5; 2 Pet. 1.11), who are open to changes at three fundamental levels (see figure 16).

(i) To the Individual

Those who enter the Kingdom and join the Church experience the most radical change of all. They become new creatures (1 Cor. 5.17)! They have been regenerated by the Holy Spirit and recreated as children of God (John 1.11,12; 3.3–14). As they continue to follow Christ they are being changed in order to become more like Christ (2 Cor. 3.18). So Christians should be open to the process of sanctification and the goal of Christian maturity. This calls for constant openness to change (Col. 1.28,29).

(ii) In the Church

The goal of maturity for the Christian is also put before the Church. She should be a perfect Church, like a chaste bride, awaiting the coming of the bridegroom (Eph. 5.27; 2 Cor. 11.2). All the changes necessary to reach this goal of perfection should be accepted by the local church that wishes to please Christ. While the attainment

	**TO THE INDIVIDUAL** '. . . in order to bring each one into God's presence as a mature individual in union with Christ' (Col. 1.28).
	**IN THE CHURCH** '. . . so we shall all come together . . . we shall become mature people, reaching to the very height of Christ's full stature' (Eph. 4.13).
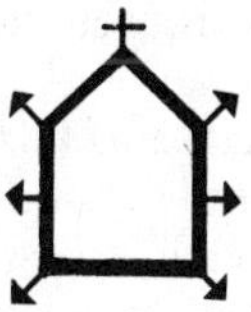	**FOR THE WORLD** '. . . I make myself everybody's slave in order to win as many people as possible' (1 Cor 9.19).

Figure 16. Levels of Change in the Church

of the goal must await the coming of the King and the Kingdom, the call to aim for maturity is constantly given by Christ and the Apostles (Eph. 4.11–16; Heb. 13.22; James 1.4; 1 Pet. 1.13–15; 1 John 3.2,3; Rev. 2.1–3.22).

(iii) For the World

The Christian and the Church have a ministry of reconciliation in the world and appeal to men and society on behalf of God (2 Cor. 5.11–6.10; Eph. 1.9,10). Individuals are called to repentance and faith (Acts 17.30–31) and society is challenged to conform to the righteousness, justice and peace of the Kingdom of God (Matt. 5.1–16).

One of the great questions facing the contemporary Church is whether or not it is prepared to change in order to communicate God's offer of reconciliation to modern man.

In his book *The Church at the End of the Twentieth Century*, Francis Schaeffer describes resistance to change as 'An old-fashioned *spiritual* problem'. He writes:

'There is a place for the Church until Jesus comes. But there must be the balance of form and freedom in regard to the policy and the practising community within that Church. And there must be freedom under the leadership of the Holy Spirit to change what needs to be changed, to meet the changing situation in the place and in the moment of that situation. Otherwise, I do not believe there will be a place for the Church as a living Church. We will be ossified and we will shut Christ out of the church. His Lordship and the leadership of the Holy Spirit will become only words.'

(SHAEFFER 1970:96)

Growing churches have learned to accept change as a condition of life in the Kingdom of God.

Released Resources

Many candidates for believers' baptism keep some money in their baptismal clothes. This practice symbolises for them the Lordship of Christ over their material resources. All they have and indeed all they are belong to Christ (1 Cor. 6.19,20) and in that solemn moment of baptism they want to acknowledge it.

This truth is valid for all Christians. Tithes and offerings to further the mission of God must be given thoughtfully, cheerfully, faithfully and regularly (Matt. 6.2; 1 Cor. 16.2).

One of the most common signs of growth is a zealous commitment to this responsibility. Members of growing churches love to give. One independent Pentecostal church in Essex has rapidly grown to eighty members. They are not wealthy people but their annual budget already exceeds £40,000.

In the early 1960s St Philip and St Jacob's ('Pip and Jay'), an Anglican church in Bristol, was scheduled for closure. In 1965 the congregation, who were beginning to experience renewal and growth, claimed God's promise that if they put his Kingdom first, he would meet all their material needs. They decided that despite large financial commitments within the church, each year they would first give money to Christian missions outside the parish. In 1965 they gave £187. In 1970 they gave £3,000 in 1975 over £20,000 and in 1980 almost £50,000. Even allowing for inflation this is a remarkable growth in giving and a sign of an equally remarkable growth of the church.

Of course, money is not the only resource the people of God possess. They have time. When this is released for the work of God through the local church, especially when directed to reaching non-Christians, growth follows. If church members give time as well as money and exercise their respective ministries, the church is released for action.

Dr Donald McGavran has identified five 'classes' of church workers. Class 1 workers are those who serve the needs of the existing local church. They are the sunday school teachers, deacons, choir members, flower-arrangers, and all the other workers who enable the church to function. They are generally all volunteers and unpaid.

Class 2 workers are those who are also voluntary and unpaid but they actively reach out from the church into the community in service and witness. These workers evangelise from door-to-door; or hold open-air services; or visit the elderly and sick. They are concerned to see non-Christians brought to Christ. Class 2 workers are essential for church growth.

Class 3 workers are the leaders of small churches or groups. They may be paid or partially paid by their churches. These workers are pastors or lay-pastors of small or newly established churches.

Class 4 workers are the paid, professional ministers of large and well-established churches.

Class 5 workers are the denominational executives; the Inter-Church leaders such as bishops, moderators, superintendents; and church leaders of international repute and influence.

By analysing the number of hours people spend in each activity McGavran is able to assess a church's potential for growth. When these workers are identified and placed alongside the number of members who merely attend the following comparisons emerge:

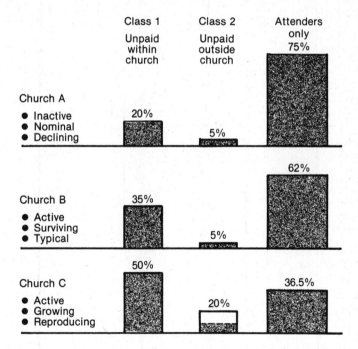

Figure 17. McGavrans 'Classes' of Workers

McGavran has shown that growing churches release the resources of leadership and ministry of a large proportion of their membership, for service not only in the church but in the world.

SUMMARY

This chapter has attempted to show that the promises of Christ regarding the growth of the Kingdom may only be applied to the true Church and its local expression in 'communities of the King'.

These outposts of the Kingdom of God have certain characteristics or 'Signs of growth' and ten have been identified.

Churches grow when they pray constantly; respect the authority of the Bible; appoint effective leaders; mobilise their membership; worship God in eventful services; engage in continuous evangelism and compassionate service; develop genuine community life; are open to Spirit-directed change and release the resources of the church for the mission of God.

4 Laying a Foundation for Growth

When Dr Donald McGavran began his foundational research into Church Growth, he was motivated by a desire to examine the effectiveness of Christian Missions in India. He was determined to face the facts and put the missionary enterprise to the test. He believed the task of evangelisation was too important to be frustrated by ignorance or inefficiency. This demand for honest analysis and appraisal of the life and work of churches remains a fundamental characteristic of the Church Growth Movement. We believe that before many churches and denominations experience the growth that God desires for them, they must face the facts of their situation and emerge from the fog that envelops their ministry and blurs their vision.

It is, of course, essential to face facts in order to learn from the past, understand the present and plan for the future. However, not all Christians are convinced of the value of analysis. They believe the whole exercise is *unspiritual* and stress the mysterious and sovereign activity of God (John 3:8; 1 Cor. 3.6). They resist attempts to assess the life and growth of the Church. Analysis is considered impious.

There are also Christians who resist analysis, especially the use of statistics, because they believe it is contrary to the scriptures and dismiss the exercise as *unbiblical*. An incident that is often quoted is David's census of Israel (1 Chr. 21.1–2). There is no question that the counting of the people of Israel was sinful on this occasion, but the sin was David's motive. His pride prompted the poll!

In Numbers 1.1–3, Moses and Aaron are actually commanded to take a census to prepare God's people for their role in his mission. This remains the legitimate and primary motive for all surveys and analyses in the Church – *to make the people of God more effective in the mission of God*.

I respect the piety and appreciate the motives of Christians who are suspicious of surveys. However, I am convinced that they would be among the first to acknowledge their stewardship and servanthood in the Kingdom of God. As co-workers with God they would also recognise their accountability in his service (1 Cor. 3.9–15) and as faithful and wise servants would want to be on their guard and about their master's business when he comes (Matt. 24 and 25). If modern analytical tools, including statistics, help them in this task of assessment and keep them in the plan and purpose of God, then surely these are to be welcomed rather than scorned and feared.

At the Bible Society Church Growth Courses we ask participants to complete a form with a few basic statistics of their churches. It is obviously a difficult and unpopular exercise for only 16 per cent of the churches actually return the form! Those who do often testify to the value of even this simple exercise. One church leader wrote, 'Researching the statistics has been an interesting but extremely revealing exercise. In some cases the figures have backed up our "feel" for the situation but in other cases shed new light on it. One of the more alarming facts is that we really didn't realise that the decline in membership and attendance over twenty years had been so pronounced. The general view had been that we were "holding our own" with perhaps admitted slight losses.'

Do you know if your church is growing or not? Have new members come from other churches or joined because they are new Christians? Have you any idea how many people attend church in your parish or community? Or do you know how effective your Sunday School and youth work are at winning children and young people for Christ? This chapter should help you answer these and many more related questions. It will attempt to demonstrate the value and use of simple statistical insights to establish the facts needed to answer such questions. Hopefully these analytical tools will encourage you to face the facts in your church and lay a foundation for future growth. It assumes you are not afraid to be honest!

MEASUREMENT FOR MISSION

The purpose of Church Growth surveys is very *specific*. It is the advancement of the mission of God. Therefore sufficient information to make the Church more effective in its mission is all that is required. It is possible to gather so much information that it defies interpretation and 'analysis paralysis' sets in!

When William Carey, the 'Father of Modern Missions' published his *Enquiry* in 1792 he marshalled the facts of world evangelisation to the best of his knowledge. A large section of the book contained the name of each country, its size, estimated population and religious condition. It was an amazing piece of research when one realises the resources available to this Baptist pastor and shoemaker. Carey used this foundation of careful research and a biblical refutation of the Reformers' thesis that the Great Commission was limited to the apostles, to awaken his hyper-Calvinistic colleagues and form the Baptist Missionary Society. Carey did not have all the facts and many were obviously inadequate, but he had sufficient to begin formulating plans to take the Christian message to those who had never heard.

The information that is collected and the facts that are discovered provide an *objective* foundation for future plans and decisions. Fact-facing is the first step in good planning and is essential if wise stewardship of the Church's resources is to be achieved. Only a fool makes plans and take decisions on the basis of assumptions and guesswork.

'Why is a clever person wise? Because he knows what to do. Why is a stupid person foolish? Because he only thinks he knows.'

Proverbs 14.8

Church Growth surveys should lead to problem solving. They are intended to identify obstacles to growth and discover new opportunities and areas for mission. They are *corrective*, for surveys expose what is lacking in the Church and reveal needs in the world. Then the Church is able to examine its life and witness in the light of the facts and use its resources more effectively. Jesus himself invited his disciples to look at the harvest in preparation for the prayer and action that would gather it in (Luke 10.1–3). When surveys are undertaken with humility that is willing to face the facts no matter how painful; with honesty that admits to failure and sin and leads to repentance, and with courage that embraces the lessons learned in faith, they become the prelude to prayer and more effective mission.

Surveys should lead to action, and have *practical* application constantly in view. The lessons learned must be acted on if the analysis is to have any real and lasting value for the Church. When Nehemiah returned to Jerusalem to rebuild the city, particularly the wall, he began with a secret night inspection (Neh. 2.11–18). When the time came to rebuild and repair he knew exactly what action to take and how to proceed. This is precisely what a Church Growth survey should do.

Finally, a survey must be *prayerful*. Measurement for God's mission requires the additional discernment of spiritual factors in data-gathering, analysis, evaluation and action. Christ knows what his churches do and he would have them listen to the Spirit. The ideal Church Growth survey should provide the Church with a fresh opportunity to hear his voice.

FACING FACTS IN THE CHURCH

Today every missionary who intends to evangelise a region and develop an effective strategy for his mission begins with research. Firstly, he requires data about the Church in the area. He needs to know the quantity and quality of the Christians and churches. He must find out the resources of people, premises, finances, equipment, etc. that are available for the mission. He faces facts in the church and undertakes a thorough *ecclesiological survey*.

Secondly, he requires data about the people or peoples who have to be reached in the region. Some groups may have been thoroughly evangelised while others have never had an opportunity to hear the gospel and become Christians. He faces facts in the community using sociological and anthropological insights and conducts an *ethnological survey*.

Only when the research is completed can he produce his *missiological strategy* and commence his work. This is the normal procedure expected by missionaries sent overseas and they could be justly criticised for failing to do 'field work' in advance of and in the course of missionary work.

Today the United Kingdom and Europe are mission fields with millions of nominal or non-Christian peoples. Therefore Churches and ministers must look at their work in missiological terms and follow their missionary colleagues by doing 'field work' at home. This must begin by facing facts in the Church.

The present state of British denominations have been described elsewhere and the ski-slope graphs of the mainline denominations are recorded in a variety of British national surveys. For example:

Churches and Churchgoing by Currie R., Gilbert A., and Horsley L., (OUP, London, 1977)
Prospects for the Eighties Vol I (Bible Society, 1980) and Vol II (MARC 1983)
I believe in Church Growth by Eddie Gibbs (Hodder and Stoughton, 1981)

In this chapter I propose to concentrate on an analysis of the local church rather than a denomination or group of churches.

Membership and Attendance

The basic data required is the number of church members for each of the past eleven years. While it may be helpful to examine membership figures for longer or shorter periods the span of a decade provides sufficient perspective for evaluation and the calculation of decadal rates of growth or decline if required, (see Appendix 5, *Understanding Your Church*).

If a simple graph of the membership is drawn then a 'picture' of the church's past begins to emerge. While it will not reveal the whole story it provides an opportunity to discuss the history of the church and gain some idea of its present progress in terms of numerical growth. As leaders and church members discuss the 'ups and downs', many of the causes of growth and decline come under review and can be openly discussed. The effect of changes such as new worship services or the introduction of evangelistic training programmes often becomes apparent, although it must be remembered that their effects will take at least twelve months to register on a linear graph.

A membership graph similar to the one below of a Baptist church in the Midlands would produce a lively discussion at any church meeting! (See figure 18)

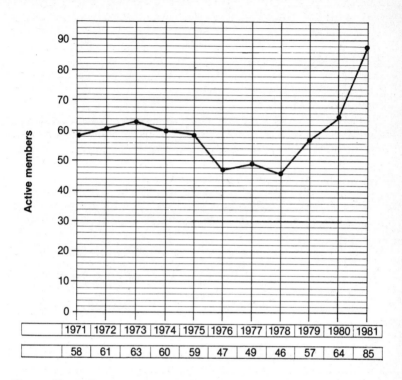

	1971	1972	1973	1974	1975	1976	1977	1978	1979	1980	1981
	58	61	63	60	59	47	49	46	57	64	85

Figure 18. A Growing Baptist Church

Local church membership is a difficult category for many churches. For example, the Anglican Church has several degrees of affiliation and membership is difficult to define (see figure 19). In such cases the average normal Sunday attendance or number of communicants may prove a more useful equivalent.

Some churches may prefer to take a composite attendance figure for a normal Sunday by adding the totals of all services. Special festival or family services should be recorded separately. As long as you are comparing 'like with like' the graph will be just as revealing.

Five useful classifications of churches can be made from linear graphs of membership or attendance. *Growing steadily* describes a church that has shown consistent growth throughout a decade. *Growing erratically* describes a church that has had its 'ups and downs' but is larger at the end of the decade. A church that is at a *Plateau* has remained at the same level of membership throughout the decade. Churches that are *Declining erratically* have lost members over the decade but have had their years of growth. *Decli-*

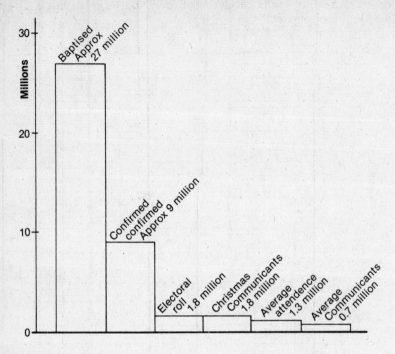

Figure 19. The Church of England: Degrees of Affiliation

ning steadily describes those churches who have experienced unremitting decline throughout the decade.

In churches where attendance and membership may be plotted on the same graph, interesting comparisons may be drawn and a variety of issues are revealed. For example, a United Reformed in the north of England (figure 21) is a 'picture' of renewal and growth. In 1969 only half of the members attended worship, indicating nominality, or aged and infirmed members or inefficient roll-keeping. In this case the main problem was nominality. A new minister joined the church in the early seventies. He had been greatly influenced by the charismatic movement and introduced contemporary and inspiring worship, Biblical preaching and teaching, and a variety of new programmes and activities. Many of the old members were renewed in their faith and experience, lapsed Christians were restored to active membership, Christians moving into the area were attracted to this 'lively' church and new converts were continually being added to the fellowship. By 1976 the attendance had exceeded the official membership which began to grow rapidly. This church had 'come alive' and was growing and the graph confirms the story at a glance!

A Methodist Church in the north of England had reached a plateau of attendance mainly because of overcrowding (figure 22). The mini-

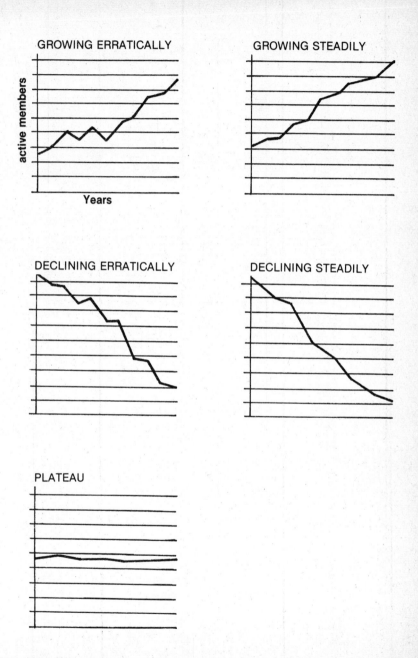

Figure 20. Five classes of churches

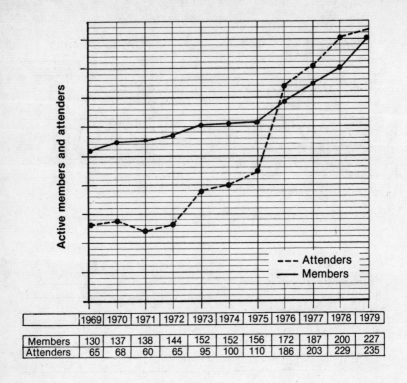

	1969	1970	1971	1972	1973	1974	1975	1976	1977	1978	1979
Members	130	137	138	144	152	152	156	172	187	200	227
Attenders	65	68	60	65	95	100	110	186	203	229	235

Figure 21. 'Renewal and Growth'

ster was very evangelistic and had been planning a major outreach into the community. When the graph of his church was drawn showing attendance and membership (which indicated commitment to Christ and active discipleship) he suddenly realised he had a mission field in the church building each Sunday!

While a linear graph 'tells a story' it does not tell the whole story and its limitations should be recognised. A standard graph will show *how much* a church has grown or declined but it cannot tell *how fast* or *how*.

If a linear graph is drawn on standard graph paper of a church which adds a hundred members in its first year and a hundred members annually thereafter, it would appear as a straight line (see figure 23).

This church is growing steadily but its rate of growth is not apparent on this type of graph. To discover *how fast* this church is growing we can plot the graph on 'semi-logarithmic' paper, which is designed to reveal rates of growth and decline. The resulting graph shows consistent growth but at a decreasing annual rate and the slowing rate of growth becomes obvious (see figure 24).

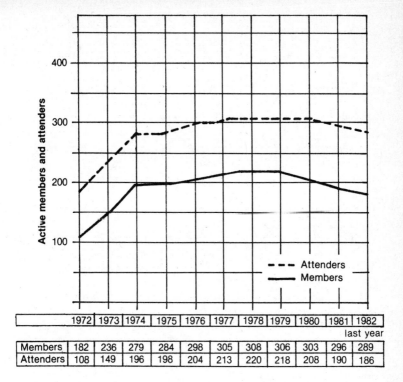

	1972	1973	1974	1975	1976	1977	1978	1979	1980	1981	1982
											last year
Members	182	236	279	284	298	305	308	306	303	296	289
Attenders	108	149	196	198	204	213	220	218	208	190	186

Figure 22. A 'Mission Field' Church

To discover *how* a church has grown or declined, an analysis of the way members have joined or left the church is necessary. We have already noted the essential categories of gains and losses in Chapter 2 under the heading of Numerical Growth. In the next section we will examine the value of these categories.

Gains and losses
Members are added to the local church in *four* ways.
1. BIOLOGICAL GROWTH – when the children of committed Christian parents come to personal faith in Jesus Christ as Saviour and Lord and join the church, usually by a rite or ceremony that recognises their status as responsible members.
2. TRANSFER GROWTH – the recruitment of members who are already committed Christians, by transfer from other churches.
3. RESTORATION GROWTH – describes the recruitment of lapsed Christians (of at least two years' duration) to active membership in regular worship and service.
4. CONVERSION GROWTH – takes place when those outside the

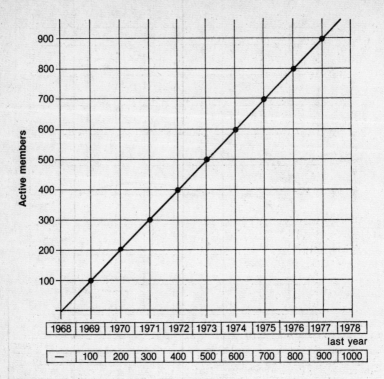

Figure 23. The Standard Graph

Church are brought to repentance and faith in Christ and join a local church as responsible members.

A local church loses members in *three* ways:
1. DEATH – members die and become members of the Church Triumphant!
2. TRANSFER – members transfer to other churches.
3. REVERSION – members lapse, cease to worship and apparently no longer follow Christ.

These categories of gain and loss in church membership probably provide the *greatest assistance* in evaluating the life and health of the local church. Insights to be gained will be found by examining two churches (see figure 25).

Church A is a suburban church that has a net annual increase of eight members. Obviously it would appear as a growing church on a linear graph.

Church B is an inner-city church with no net increase in membership over the past year. It would be drawn as a 'plateau' on a linear graph.

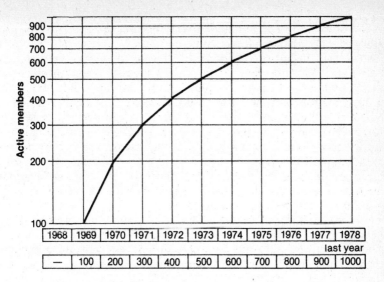

Figure 24. The Semi-log Graph

Church A is apparently the 'successful' church whose minister is likely to be invited to speak to other ministers at conferences about evangelism and 'church growth'.

Church B attracts little attention and often the minister and leaders are dispirited and even despairing. They have a busy and exhausting programme but appear to be getting nowhere.

An analysis of the gains and losses of each church which uses these categories will throw new light on the situation and challenge these presuppositions.

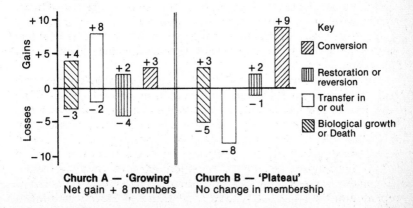

Figure 25. Gains and Losses

Lessons from Church A

Biological Growth has added four new members who are the children of Christian parents. Where did they come to faith in Jesus Christ and become convinced of the need to become church members? Was it in the context of the Christian home, through the sunday school or at a youth camp? As we ask questions about the biological growth or lack of it, issues related to the quality of Christian family life, sunday schools and youth programmes are raised. A surprising number of churches exhaust themselves with 'children's work' that produces very few Christians who become church members and this fact should be faced. Most churches also fail to differentiate between the children of Christian and non-Christian parents. They are usually taught together without regard to their different needs in Christian education.

Many mainline and long established denominations use biological growth as the *main* source of recruitment for the 'future church'. Their structures and procedures are almost solely based upon this form of numerical growth with consequent weaknesses when recruiting members in other ways.

Transfer Growth has resulted from eight new members transferring from other churches, but how many could have joined during the past year? If Church A is a suburban Methodist church and thirty Methodists moved into the area and worshipped once or twice, but only eight remained, then twenty-two decided the church was unsuitable, possibly even unwelcoming and uninspiring. If those twenty-two Methodists are now active in the local Anglican church then the Methodist church should get the message! If visiting Christians tend to settle in a church it indicates that their needs are being met and is a commendation of the quality and vitality of the church.

Many charismatic and House Churches recruit the majority of their members by transfer from other churches. One prominent House Church leader has suggested as many as ninety per cent. Sadly, this usually results in the neglect of evangelistic responsibilities as new members are mistaken for new converts.

Restoration Growth has accounted for two new members who had lapsed or 'backslidden' and are now actively involved in the life of the church again.

This is a particularly difficult and delicate ministry as lapsed Christians usually justify their condition by criticising the Church. Many have had bad or unfortunate experiences and great wisdom and tact is needed in counselling. The need for this ministry is obvious when the hundreds of thousands of lapsed Christians in the United Kingdom are counted. If the mainline denominations were able to restore their lapsed members they would enjoy very rapid growth!

Conversion Growth has produced three new members. These have repented of their sins and trusted Jesus Christ as Saviour and Lord. They have been converted to Christ and from the world, so conversion describes the spiritual and social change that has taken place.

It is important to know how this happened. Were these three converted through a student mission when tracts were scattered like confetti? Or were they won by their Christian neighbours who cared about them and shared their faith with them over a period of months or even years?

It may also be necessary to find out so that the church does not stop doing what God is blessing. A zealous but foolish new minister resolutely defied his membership and closed the sunday school and youth programmes of his new church. Had he faced the facts and analysed the main means of Conversion Growth in the church he would have discovered conversions came through the contacts made by these programmes in the predominantly multi-racial and working-class community. It is important to ask the question because Christians should do what God blesses rather than ask him to bless what they do!

Conversion growth is essentially the Church's primary form of numerical growth. In the United Kingdom and Europe millions need to be converted to Christ. The Church must therefore discover effective evangelistic methods rather than constantly use those that are obviously ineffective. The church that is complacent when no new converts join its ranks has lost sight of its essential and primary task.

Death has reduced the membership by three. Ageing congregations lose larger proportions of their membership by death and, as has often been said, the Church is only one generation away from extinction. Each subsequent generation must be won for Christ, to pass the gospel on to the next.

Two more members have been lost by *Transfer*. If they have moved from the area then they need to be followed up by referral procedures that link them with another church. If they have become disenchanted and joined another local church the reasons for their disenchantment should be faced. One free church pastor told me a harrowing story of two young leaders in his church. They were undoubtedly deeply committed and anxious to serve. Unfortunately the pastor felt threatened and eventually drove them from the church. He came to the end of his story with eyes narrowed and through gritted teeth muttered, 'I got rid of them in the end!' They are much happier serving the Lord in a neighbouring church, and the pastor is happy with his dwindling one-man band!

Four members have lapsed and been lost by *Reversion*. If the church had been able to hold them their growth would have increased by fifty per cent.

When local churches discover a constant stream of lapsed members they must 'plug the hole' and deal with the causes. The problem may be caused by such things as self-limiting structures, inadequate pastoral care, poor Christian education, bad relationships or closed fellowship groups. Some churches may discover how members join the church with great ceremony at the 'front door', bounce off all the closed and unwelcoming groups and fellowship circles for a few months, and quietly leave by the 'back door'!

Lessons from Church B

Recruitment by *Biological and Restoration Growth* has been similar to Church A. There has been no *Transfer Growth*. Christians seldom move to the inner-city!

Conversion Growth has added nine members. A remarkable fact in the light of Church A's performance. If churches want to know about effective evangelism then the minister and leaders of Church B rather than Church A need to be heard: *a fact that would never have been known from a linear graph.*

Of course Church B loses as many members as it gains. Five by *Death*, due to an ageing church and community, where even new converts are often elderly.

Eight new members were lost by *Transfer*, mainly caused by 'Redemption and Lift' that takes place when people become Christians. Poor inner-city converts change their lifestyle and spend less on 'booze' and 'baccy' and put their savings in a building society. They begin to lift socio-economically. Their values change, they become more middle-class and eventually move to suburbia! A vicar near Leeds graphically illustrated the problem from his experience. His parish is totally made up of local government housing and is noted for its debtors as the local Council send all those who fail to pay their rent to live there. When someone is converted they begin paying their rent so the Council move them out of the parish!

Another cause of loss by Transfer is the general mobility of the population. Inner-city areas are notorious for the large numbers of transient residents. A fifty per cent turnover every five years would not be unusual. As one pastor commented, 'It's like hatching eggs on an escalator!'

Only one member has been lost from Church B by *Reversion* which suggests that it probably takes better care of its members than Church A. Perhaps the minister and leaders of Church B can take heart after all!

There are obviously many more variables that need to be explored in a thorough evaluation of each church, for every church is unique and must face these issues for itself.

I believe an *honest* appraisal of how a church has gained and lost members over a decade is the most revealing exercise it can undertake. When facts are discovered, frankly discussed and the lessons learned are applied, a church can take a major step forward. This happens as presuppositions and myths are exposed and future planning and decision-making is based upon fact rather than fantasy.

Church Finances

Churches seldom have difficulty recording their finances; raising them is more likely to be a problem.

If the finances are plotted on a linear graph, once again a 'story' is told. Most graphs will appear to grow but the growth is mainly due to inflation. Therefore inflation corrected figures should be plotted too. (A correction table based upon the Department of Employment's Cost of Living Index is provided in figure 26.)

Year	Correction Factor	Year	Correction Factor
1970	0.708	1977	0.288
1971	0.654	1978	0.263
1972	0.605	1979	0.231
1973	0.551	1980	0.200
1974	0.474	1981	0.177
1975	0.389	1982	0.164
1976	0.326		

Figure 26. An Inflation Correction Table

An inflation-corrected graph depicts the true situation for the decade and normally corrects false assumptions about the financial health of the church. The Anglican Church finances used in figure 27 appear to be very healthy at first glance, as their income has trebled in the decade. The true picture, however, is that they are only just keeping abreast of inflation. If the membership has also grown in the decade, then the annual giving by each member is actually down, for by dividing the corrected income by the number of members for each year a comparable sum of annual giving per member is found. This calculation may be used when measuring financial stewardship over a period of time.

When graphs of income and expenditure are presented to church members financial issues become much clearer and even a very simple graphic presentation can enliven the Annual Treasurer's report.

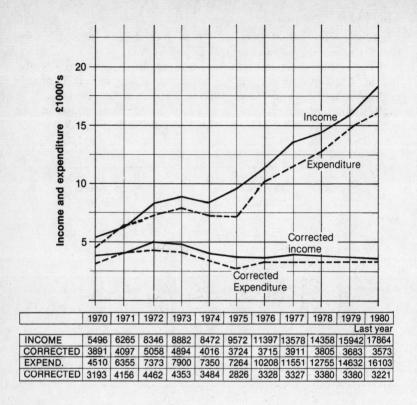

	1970	1971	1972	1973	1974	1975	1976	1977	1978	1979	1980
											Last year
INCOME	5496	6265	8346	8882	8472	9572	11397	13578	14358	15942	17864
CORRECTED	3891	4097	5058	4894	4016	3724	3715	3911	3805	3683	3573
EXPEND.	4510	6355	7373	7900	7350	7264	10208	11551	12755	14632	16103
CORRECTED	3193	4156	4462	4353	3484	2826	3328	3327	3380	3380	3221

Figure 27. Church Finances

Age and Sex of Membership

Using a simple bar graph it is possible to draw an age/sex profile of a congregation (see figure 28). This is helpful for identifying areas of strength and weakness in ministry, especially when compared to the profile for the community.

The profile may be used to identify areas where priorities for programmes and activities should be established. It may also reveal neglected or pampered groups who are disproportionately represented in leadership or resources.

The proportions of male and female may also be represented by a pie chart. The percentages of male and female in figure 28 of thirty-six per cent male and sixty-four per cent female could therefore be represented as in figure 29.

There proportions of about one-third male and two-thirds female are typical of most churches that have been established long enough to span the generations. There are a variety of reasons for this dominance of women in the church:

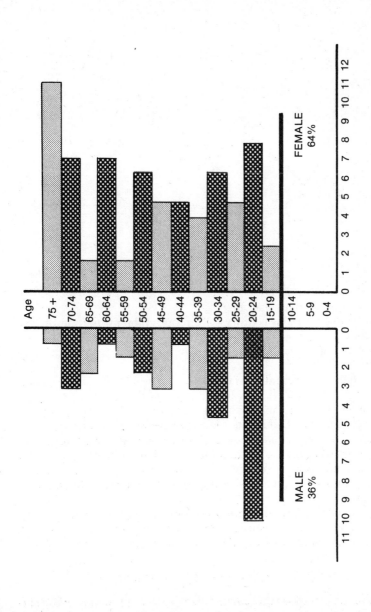

Figure 28. Age/Sex Profile of a Congregation

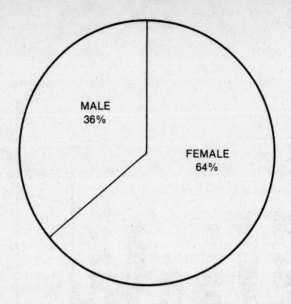

Figure 29. Age/Sex Pie Chart

1. Women live longer than men.
2. Two world wars this century have reduced the proportion of men in Europe.
3. Women meet and mix more easily and share their faith more readily.
4. Christianity is presented as unmanly and 'wet'. Effeminate clergy, whether real or of media invention, confirm the caricature.
5. Women take the main role in the 'rites of passage' – birth, marriage, death etc, when people are open to spiritual issues.
6. British churches have stressed 'children's work' which suggests to the average man that religion is for the 'wife and kids'.
7. Many ministers have little experience of the ordinary man's working life so their preaching and teaching seldom relate to his life experiences.

Further analysis of the congregation that seeks to identify the social, ethnic and economic identity of the members will also help to relate the church to its task of reaching the community.

FACING FACTS IN THE COMMUNITY

A church must know the community in which it serves and bears witness. Christ has commanded that disciples be made of all peoples everywhere and the task of discovering lost and hidden peoples is the continuing task of each church.

When a community survey is conducted new opportunities for mission emerge and fresh insights into church problems are found. A large number of difficulties in churches have their origin in community factors and they will never be overcome or successfully resolved without detailed knowledge of the community. But before a community survey can be conducted the community has to be defined.

Anglican and other established churches have their parish boundaries and therefore their community is already mapped out. Free churches generally consider the 'world' as their parish, but should define a local community that is the focus of their ministry. Usually Anglican parishes are consistent with local government boundaries, and ideally all churches ought to use local administrative areas such as wards, boroughs or districts for which statistical information is already collated and readily available. This information is compiled from the National Census (the most recent in the United Kingdom is 1981) and local government research and is known as Small Area Statistics. Copies are available for study at central libraries and local government offices. Additional plans and projections are often freely available to churches from local government planning departments.

Rural churches in areas with small and scattered populations may need to define their community on the basis of driving time from the church. A Sunday morning car journey of about 15 minutes in every direction from the church will provide the perimeter points and where these roughly coincide with local boundaries will establish the 'parish' boundary (see figure 30). A mission strategy that embraced the outlying hamlets would be needed by this rural town church.

Once the community has been defined there are a number of facts that need to be discovered.

Population

There are a surprising number of churches that have no idea how many people live in their communities and need to be reached with the gospel. They are afflicted with '*people blindness*' and are insensitive to the spiritual needs of multitudes of people who remain lost and unsaved and outside their churches. They are ignorant of thousands who have never had an opportunity to hear the Good News of salvation through faith in Jesus Christ.

Church Attendance

A salutary exercise is to compare the population of a community with its churchgoing population. When the total attendance at all the churches in a community is added together the actual proportion of churchgoers is often alarming. A 1975 survey discovered that in East London less than 0.5 per cent attend church; many other Euro-

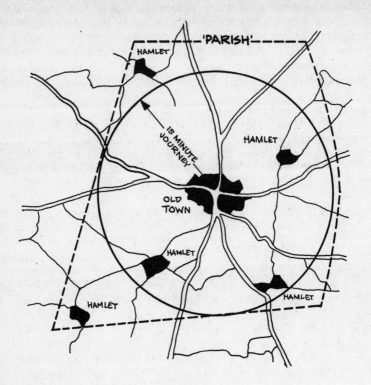

Figure 30. A Rural Church's 'Parish'

pean cities would not consider one per cent unusual for vast urban areas.

Even in areas of higher percentages of church attendance, Christian practice is so minimal that gross nominality grips most of Western Europe.

The Lausanne Strategy Group for World Evangelisation uses the following classifications for nations:

> 1%   practising Christians – initially reached
> up to 10%   practising Christians – minimally reached
> 10 – 20%   practising Christians – possibly reached

Nations with less than ten per cent are considered dependent on the assistance of others from outside to effectively reach the rest of the nation.

If similar classifications were applied to regions and cities of the United Kingdom and Europe, priorities could be established and strategies prayerfully developed for major re-evangelisation. The facts would expose the dreadful spiritual plight of many neglected areas, make the churches more zealous to evangelise and more open to the assistance of missionaries and evangelists from overseas, many of whom are eager to come.

Race and Class

The task of evangelisation may be further clarified by exploring the ethnic and social make-up of a community. New ethnic groups may move into an area and eventually predominate. If local churches have failed to reach the new groups they will have suffered decline as their actual and potential membership have moved away. This loss of membership due to change of community is called '*ethnicitis*'. Where this is 'terminal' it may be necessary to rent or sell the church property to Christians from the new ethnic group.

Where ethnic groups remain a minority and unreached it may be necessary to develop cross-cultural strategies of evangelism and church planting.

Social distinctions between peoples produce many obstacles to effective evangelism and church growth. These distinctions may not be obvious to the casual observer but careful research will reveal the facts, so that solutions may be sought. When the social make-up of the church is compared with the community, issues become clear.

An Anglican city parish church decided to identify the houses of its 150 members on a map of the parish. The church existed to serve all 10,000 people in the parish. The map of members, however, revealed that those who lived in the parish were all middle-class and owned their own homes in the 'nicer' part of the parish around the church. Three vast council and working-class estates were totally unrepresented (see figure 31).

Another disturbing fact about the membership of this Anglican church was discovered by the analysis – only forty-one per cent of the members actually lived in the parish (see figure 32). The rest travelled to church each Sunday from outside the parish, some from many miles away. Many members had moved home but failed to change church.

When the facts were faced in this Anglican church, the parish could hardly be described as reached! The neglect and need of evangelism was obvious to all. While that may not have been news to the church, the specific neglect of the working-class that the survey revealed should challenge them to consider new methods and programmes – even the planting of new churches – that recognise the needs of working-class culture, and function in working-class ways. As Roy Joslin states in his excellent and challenging book *Urban Harvest*:

'. . . if a church in a working-class area is composed of people who are largely unrepresentative of the local community, there

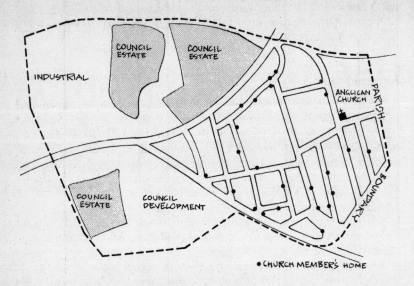

Figure 31. A City Parish of 10,000 People

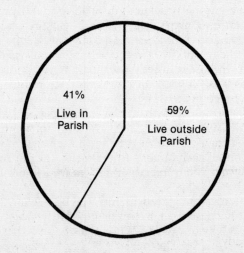

Figure 32. Percentage of Members Living in the Parish

will be great difficulty in integrating working-class Christians into the life of that church.'

(JOSLIN 1982:96)

Only a careful community survey will reveal the sort of problems faced by this Anglican church. Of course they could have remained oblivious to the facts and continued to minister in ignorance, many churches still do!

Age and Sex

An age and sex profile of a community that is drawn from data obtained from the Small Area Statistics provides models for comparison with that of the church. Figure 33 illustrates the comparison of ages between church and community.

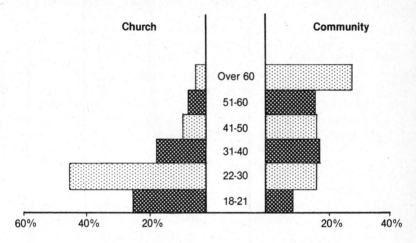

Figure 33. Age Proportions in Church and Community

This predominantly 'young' church where eighty-five per cent of the members are under forty is clearly unrepresentative of the community. If other churches in that community are also failing to minister to the elderly these are neglected peoples and need to be reached.

Geography

We have already seen how a simple plot on where church members live exposed social distinctions between people. It may also reveal geographical obstacles related to the site of the church in its parish or community. If church buildings and boundaries have been established for centuries or even decades in a rapidly changing environment, the construction of roads, railways, shops, etc. may obscure or prevent access to a church.

A community may 'move' as a town develops and expands. If a church intends to continue its ministry it must move too! Tonbridge Baptist Church in Kent recognised this phenomena and saw it as an opportunity to move from its town centre site to new and larger premises in the expanding part of the town. The rapid and continuing growth of the church confirms the wisdom of the move.

EMERGE FROM THE FOG

The survey examples in this chapter are basic and limited in scope. They have been chosen to demonstrate the value of using very simple analytical tools to try to understand a local church and its context. It is possible to probe more deeply into areas of church and community life as facts emerge. See Appendix 5. 'Understanding Your Church'.

It may be helpful to investigate the length of attendance, married status, educational standards, occupation, income, etc. of church members to better understand a congregation. Community needs and receptivity to the gospel must also be assessed but the *objective of the survey* must be constantly kept in mind – *to make the people of God more effective in the mission of God*. Remember that all analysis is also intended to assist problem-solving by identifying the purely cultural and environmental obstacles that prevent people become disciples of Jesus Christ. It is as much our task to overcome man-made obstacles as it is to preach the gospel in the unfettered power of the Holy Spirit.

Many church leaders would value a Church Growth survey but do not know where or how to begin with limited resources of time and manpower. An often untapped resource are church members who regularly compile data and draw graphs. Planners, statisticians, research officers and people in allied occupations are found among members of churches. I even know an Anglican lay reader who is a professor of statistics – but his Vicar refuses to let him examine the church roll!

If a small group of members are assigned the task of data-gathering the Church Growth survey can become a cause for support and prayer by the church. If the right atmosphere is created for the research and proper attitudes maintained throughout, the information can be selectively shared among the leaders and members. Some information will undoubtedly be useful only to the leaders for their planning and decision-making, but goal-setting exercises on the basis of data gathered should be shared at all levels of the church.

When the facts are discovered an objective foundation for future planning for growth can be established. Practical steps to overcome problems and grasp new opportunities may be taken and a prayerful advance of the church's mission be made. Only when the facts are faced is it possible to emerge from the fog into more effective ministry. Those who refuse to face facts are not merely fools who 'think they know' – they are also unfaithful to God for not finding out!

5 Organised for Growth

The first chapter contrasted the growth of the World Church with the decline of the British Church and described the development of the Church Growth Movement from the study of church growth in the Bible, Church History and the contemporary World Church.

In the second chapter we identified the main emphases of the Movement, and suggested that British Churches need to give priority to evangelism. They need to believe once more in the *possibility* of growth and recognise the complexity of factors that help or hinder it. British churches should also face the awkward issues raised when social sciences are applied to their institutional form and to the enormous and complex missionary task that now confronts them.

The 'signs of growth', described in chapter 3, that characterise growing churches provide criteria for evaluating a church's strengths and weaknesses.

The analysis of the local church and community using the basic statistical tools described in chapter four, give a church additional ways of understanding its history, performance and mission. As obstacles and opportunities are discovered, strategies for mission can be drawn up from facts rather than fantasy. When the actual situation is understood, specific prayer and faith may be channelled into effective evangelism.

In this and the final chapter we will attempt to apply the lessons learned and introduce Church Growth principles to the church. This chapter will describe how to organise your church for growth.

IS THERE AN IDEAL CHURCH?

The contemporary Church has an enormous variety of structures, forms of ministry, types of government, order, liturgy, etc. Dr David Barrett has identified 22,189 denominations in the world Church (1985), each one justifying its separate existence on the basis of particular emphases in doctrine or practice.

This denominational diversity can be traced to differences in biblical interpretation, in historical development, in mission strategy, cultural perspective or simply personal preference. But whatever its cause, this variety offers a rich choice of local church 'models' and raises the question, 'Is there an ideal model for a local church?'

In 1954 Dr Paul S. Minear was commissioned by the Faith and Order Department of the World Council of Churches to undertake a study of the Church in the New Testament. The purpose of the study was to provide a biblical contribution to the continuing debate within the Faith and Order Movement. Dr Minear identified 96 'images' of the Church (see Appendix 6) and published his study under the title *Images of the Church in the New Testament*.

This great variety of images constantly challenges those who accept narrow definitions of the Church and adopt inflexible forms of the local church. Dr Minear writes:

'For many moderns who crave an exact calculation of the New Testament ecclesiological images. Those images are too elusive, too elastic, too ambiguous to satisfy their need. Often the recourse is to select one image, to concentrate upon it, to force it into a non-imagistic mould, and then to rely upon it for a definition of boundaries.'

(MINEAR 1961:225)

There have been numerous attempts to define the nature of the Church and its visible form and theologians have debated the tests or 'marks' of the visible Church for centuries. There are the traditional four marks of the Apostles' Creed – one, holy, apostolic and catholic (universal). The Reformers looked for the two or three marks of the preached Word, two sacraments of baptism and the Lord's Supper, and discipline. Others have identified a variety of marks and preferred to use such terms as 'attributes', 'symbols', 'landmarks', 'credal marks' and Karl Barth even used the term 'pointers'!

The order and practice of your church may be influenced by one or more of these definitions and the interpretation of your denominational scholars. If you add the influence of history and tradition; the peculiarities of culture, both ancient and modern; and the foibles of the men and women who found and lead our churches, then we have a recipe for local church life that is far from 'ideal'. In fact, it is probably true to say that an ideal form of local church does not exist.

In his book *The Church at the end of the Twentieth Century* Dr Francis Shaeffer argues for 'form and freedom' in the visible church, and identifies eight 'biblical norms' or marks to govern the form:
1. There existed local congregations, made up of Christians.
2. They met together in a special way on the first day of the week.
3. There were church officers (elders) who had responsibility for the local churches.
4. There were deacons responsible for the community of the church in the area of material things.
5. The church took discipline seriously.

6. There were specific qualifications for elders and deacons.
7. There was place for forms on a wider basis than the local church.
8. The two sacraments of baptism and the Lord's Supper were practised.

Dr Shaeffer recognises that other 'norms' may be added or even subtracted from his list but concludes his argument:

'My primary point as we prepare for the end of the twentieth century is, on the one hand, that there is a place for the institutional church and that it should maintain the form commanded by God, but, on the other hand, that this also leaves vast areas of freedom for change . . . *anything the New Testament does not command in regard to church form is a freedom to be exercised under the leadership of the Holy Spirit for that particular time and place.*'

(SHAEFFER 1970:84)

If we admit our need for change because our church is less than 'ideal', and adopt change in order to follow the Holy Spirit into effective mission today, then we require a pattern or model of a local church that identifies the areas requiring change and guides the process of change. The model should also be 'functional' in the sense that it describes the activities of a local church seeking to obey the Great Commission and 'make disciples'.

A FUNCTIONAL MODEL

I originally developed this 'Functional Model' for the Advanced Course of the Bible Society. The inspiration for the model is Ephesians 4.1–16; it has many limitations but the following advantages:
1. The Headship of Jesus Christ is acknowledged.
2. Leadership issues are raised.
3. Relational groups are identified.
4. Evangelistic tasks are defined.
5. Members' ministries may be categorised.
6. Areas of weakness and omission become apparent.

This model may be used to prepare any local church for effective evangelism, regardless of denomination, churchmanship or size. It is therefore a valuable tool with which to organise a church for growth. (see figure 34).

1. Jesus Christ is the Head

'Jesus is Lord' (Rom. 10.9) is the fundamental Christian confession and a local church is basically a community of believers living together under the Lordship of Jesus Christ. In a church, therefore, Christ has supreme authority and is its Head (Eph. 1.22). In this sense he is the chief, ruler, or leader of the church and his commands

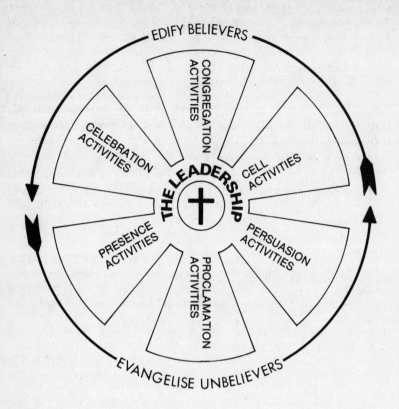

EDIFY BELIEVERS

CONGREGATION ACTIVITIES

CELEBRATION ACTIVITIES

CELL ACTIVITIES

THE LEADERSHIP

PRESENCE ACTIVITIES

PERSUASION ACTIVITIES

PROCLAMATION ACTIVITIES

EVANGELISE UNBELIEVERS

Figure 34. A Functional Model for a Growing Church

are binding upon all true believers (1 Cor. 14.37) who are his slaves (Rom. 1.1; Eph. 6.6).

Jesus Christ is also Head of the body of Christ (Eph. 4.15–16). In this sense, the Spirit of Christ empowers its members, co-ordinates its activities, directs its mission, sustains its life and produces growth:

'Under Christ's control the whole body is nourished and held together by its joints and ligaments, and it grows as God wants it to grow.'

Col. 2.19

Therefore the first step for any local church that wants to grow is a conscious acknowledgement by all that Jesus Christ is Lord and Head. Every church must want the will of Christ to direct its affairs and the Spirit of Christ to empower its activities. This united confession and desire is essential for genuine growth.

A church constantly needs to be reminded of Christ's position and power lest it degenerates into a mere human institution. Ideally every act of worship (1 Cor. 11.17–12.3) is an opportunity to recognise and confess the Lordship of Christ. As the people of God submit themselves to God's Word and open themselves to his Spirit so the will of Christ is made known (John 14.15–24; Acts 13.2; 1 Cor. 11.27–32; 14.26–32).

Many churches find it helpful to write this clearly into their constitution and regularly remind themselves of its implications. Sale Baptist Church, near Manchester, has the following statement in their church membership course:

'At the heart of our fellowship's life is a desire and determination to live under the lordship (the kingly, authoritative, decisive rule) of Jesus Christ, both in our individual and corporate walk with Him. Jesus wants disciples, and He has the right to disciple us, if we are His, in every area of our life – our home, family, money, work, plans, hopes – and even our church!

'We are resolved to walk the path of radical discipleship with Jesus, believing that anything less is a denial of His lordship. This means a readiness to change *anything* within our life, or within our church that He points out to us.'

As the church has endeavoured to follow this resolution, they have experienced remarkable renewal and growth. During the past five years the membership has almost doubled and new converts are being added to the church month by month.

Unfortunately churches are often ruled by other authorities than Christ, so this area of the Lordship of Christ is where the battle for renewal and growth rages in the institutionalised church. It may be represented by a vicar wrestling on behalf of Christ with a nominal Parochial Church Council. Or a Free church pastor struggling with an influential but ungodly church family. Other churches have entrenched and unspiritual leaders who frustrate the genuine Christian aspirations of the membership, or leaders of church organisations who determinedly resist any change that threatens *their* will and power.

It is at this point that many who long for the renewal and growth of their churches face the cost of church growth. It is significant that when Jesus trained the twelve apostles for their first experience of Christian mission (Matt. 10) they were taught about suffering (16–28) and conflict (34–36) as well as commitment (37–39). Suffering and sacrifice have always marked the mission of the Church and this price still has to be paid. Nominal and unspiritual leaders and members have to be challenged and their opposition overcome and it is particularly sad when this conflict and consequent suffering has to be encountered within a church in order to prepare it for mission. Those who seek the renewal and growth of their churches have to be resolute because this issue of the Headship of Christ must be resolved or there will be little, if any, progress towards growth.

The Church's foundation is Christ and unless a local church is firmly grounded and built in him any growth is worthless (1 Cor. 3.11–15). A church must belong to Christ before it can become an effective outpost of the Kingdom.

2. Leadership for Growth

When the Headship of Christ is established as a fundamental principle in a church, the next issue to be faced is leadership. Christ appoints and equips leaders who in turn equip the members for the ministry of the church (Eph. 4.11–16). A church will only reach the goal of growth when it follows the pattern and order given by God – Christ appoints its leaders who prepare God's people for his mission.

'It was he (Christ) who "gave gifts to mankind"; he appointed some to be apostles, others to be prophets, others to be evangelists, others to be pastors and teachers. He did this to prepare all God's people for the work of Christian service, in order to build up the body of Christ.'

(Eph. 4.11–12)

Leadership in the Kingdom of God, under the reign of Christ, may be defined as the *God-given ability to govern the people of God in such a way that they voluntarily follow God's will and fulfill his plans*. (Rom. 12.8; 1 Thess. 5.12; 1 Tim. 5.17).

When Christ is Head of a church no one else can reign, so leaders must not 'Lord' it over the members. Indeed their authority is derived from Christ and is based on servanthood. Domineering leaders are denounced by Jesus (Matt. 20.25–28; 23.1–12) and rebuked by Peter (1 Pet. 5.1–5) for following a pattern that belongs to the world.

Historically, God's people have not always struggled to find models of leadership that are true to God and the Scriptures rather than the world with its cultural models. Israel chose a king to be like other nations and thereby rejected God's reign over them (1 Sam. 8.4–9). Today we face a similar problem in the Church.

The Church constantly seeks models of leadership from society or scripture, from the prevailing culture or the primitive Church, and has opted for one or the other or a permutation of both. Some contemporary Churches confuse the issue even further by holding on to forms of leadership that are neither biblical nor contemporary but from ancient and even foreign cultures that are several centuries old! The pagan priestly hierarchy of ancient Rome that continues to dominate the Roman Catholic Church is a typical example (see *The Church* by Hans Küng p. 526f). The question the Church must constantly ask is, 'Where do our models of leadership come from?'

Leaders in Society

Leaders within contemporary English society generally hold their position or status in an hierarchical manner. The leader is above or superior to his followers. There is a ladder of leadership to climb and promotion is aimed for. The leader may have ascended the ladder by achievement, because he is wiser or stronger or better educated or more articulate. On the other hand, he may have reached the top of the ladder, or at least started several rungs up, because of his class, family, school, age, race, or even sex. As Anthony Sampson shows in *The Changing Anatomy of Britain* (1982), in England it is a great advantage to be white and male, to have been to the right public school, to have attended Oxbridge and if at all possible to have served as an officer in the Guards!

Leaders in our society always have privileges that separate them from their followers. They usually wear different clothes, have better homes, live in nicer areas and are excused mundane duties. Leaders are generally aloof and elite.

Even this very brief summary of leadership in English society provides us with a great variety of models. But are they appropriate for the English Church? To answer that question we must turn to the Scriptures and particularly the leadership of the Early Church as portrayed in the New Testament.

Leadership in the Church

A study of the New Testament churches reveals that various models of leadership existed simultaneously. There appears to be no single or simple model. Leadership needs and roles changed as churches become established and models of local church leadership, and possibly government, were greatly influenced by the cultural setting. For example, the overseers in Jewish churches were called *elders* and followed the synagogue pattern, (Acts 11.30; 16.4; 21.18). The same officer in a gentile church was called a *bishop*, after the pattern of local town government (Tit. 1.6,7). Among their many duties overseers exercised loving care, showed concern for sound doctrine and gave guidance on ethics, and usually worked in teams in a single local church (Acts 20.28; Phil. 1.1). The Pastoral Epistles describe their qualities and it would appear that they were all mature married men (1 Tim. 3.1–7).

This brief study of only one leader in the Early Church raises a number of controversial issues in the contemporary debate about Christian ministry. While almost all churches recognise the need for reform there is very little agreement about the nature and relevance of the biblical data. Some, like the Roman Catholics, would argue that their present form of ministry is a legitimate *development* from the Early Church. Others, such as most Baptists, see their present form as a *decline* from the Early Church and constantly struggle to recover a New Testament pattern. Dr Charles Kraft, Professor of Anthropology and African Studies at the School of World Mission, argues for a *dynamic equivalent* leadership in the Church. The leadership model for a church must be biblically based but also culturally valid (see *Christianity in Culture* by Charles H. Kraft [Paternoster, 1979] pages 323–327).

Dr Kraft argues that the contemporary Church, especially when engaged in mission and church planting, should be less concerned with the *form* of leadership (what they are, e.g. Bishop, priest, deacon, elder, etc.) and concentrate upon the *functions* of leadership (what they do). This pragmatic approach to leadership is the characteristic of growing churches. The leaders, whatever the form (Anglican vicars, Presbyterian elders, Baptist deacons, Catholic priests, Pentecostal pastors or House Church apostles) fulfil the functions of church leadership in a culturally valid manner. But what are the functions of leaders?

Functions of Church Leaders

The responsibilities of church leaders in the New Testament are not precisely defined and there appears to have been a great deal of flexibility in terms of the ministries they exercised, but at least five inter-related functions are clearly discernable among them all (see figure 35.). All leaders, regardless of their special gifts and ministries, had to fulfil them and excel in them.

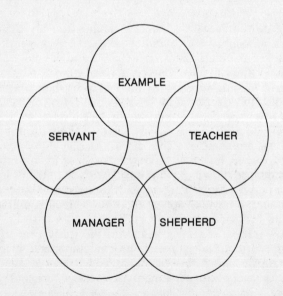

Figure 35. Five Essential Functions of Leaders

(a) A Leader was an Example   Every Christian leader had to be an

example to others (1 Tim. 4.12; 1 Pet. 5.3). He (or she) had been converted to Christ, though ideally not a new convert (1 Tim. 3.6), and was growing in Christ. The leader had to demonstrate Christian spirituality, morality and virtues (Acts 6.3; 1 Tim. 3.1–13) and was followed as long as he followed the Lord (1 Cor. 11.1).

As leaders were models of growth to maturity they were not afraid to share their own struggles and pilgrimage (Rom. 7.21–25; 2 Cor. 1.8–11; Gal. 2.11–21; 2 Pet. 3.15–18).

(b) A Leader was a Teacher Leaders had the function of equipping or preparing 'all God's people for Christian service' (Eph. 4.12). Paul's list of apostles, prophets, evangelists, pastors and teachers (Eph. 4.11) suggests that this was mainly through 'the ministry of the Word', by inspired utterance and the exposition of Scripture. A leader must therefore know the Scriptures and 'be able to teach' sound doctrine and refute error (1 Tim. 3.2,9; 2 Tim. 3.16; Tit. 1.9).

Teaching, however, was more than telling or even forthtelling! Jesus prepared the selected group of his twelve disciples in the context of an 'apprenticeship' relationship, so that they might learn by seeing and doing as well as hearing. Paul did the same (2 Tim. 3.10). When selected people were taught in this personal and pastoral context leaders reproduced the next generation of leaders (2 Tim. 2.2). Teaching was not limited to 'up-front' public ministry but also took place in small groups and 'one-to-one' situations. All leaders could therefore function as teachers.

(c) A Leader was a Shepherd When Paul addressed *all the leaders* at Ephesus he called them to 'keep watch over yourselves and over all the flock which the Holy Spirit has placed in your care. Be shepherds of the church of God' (Acts 20.28). So pastoral care was not the sole responsibility of one leader but all of them.

Of course, to some degree, pastoral care is the responsibility of all church members (Heb. 12.15; 1 Cor. 12.25), but it is the special function of leaders to guard and guide the flock (1 Tim. 3.5, 1 Pet. 5.2) and exercise discipline when necessary.

Leaders had particular responsibility to care for the weaker and needy members of the fellowship and their prayers and loving ministry were to be especially sought by the sick (Jas. 5.14,15).

(d) A Leader was a Manager All leaders had to be able to manage the affairs of the church as good stewards of resources that belonged to God, and 'rule well', (1 Tim. 5.17). Leaders had to prove themselves capable managers by being successful at managing their homes and families (1 Tim. 3.4,12). (No hint of celibacy here!)

The need for the seven additional leaders in Jerusalem (Acts 6.1–6) was mainly caused by poor administration and the consequent neglect of the Greek-speaking widows (Acts 6.1). The apostles showed wisdom and cultural sensitivity by allowing the neglected group to choose their leaders (Acts 6.3,5,6). The qualifications for leadership are worth noting, they were 'men among you *who are known* to be full of the Holy Spirit and wisdom'. Leadership qualities were noticeable and readily identified by the fellowship of believers.

(e) A Leader was a Servant   This was a mandatory function of leadership according to the example and teaching of Jesus (Matt. 20.25–28; 23.9–12; Jn 13.1–17). A leader who was not a servant was not a Christian leader.

This function of a servant formed the basis of the authority of leaders in the local church while their gifts and special ministries further established their positions.

Whether the synagogue or town council pattern was followed, it is probable that one leader presided over the team of leaders but he was not elevated above the other leaders or members. Markus Barth summarises Paul's teaching and says of the leaders in Ephesians 4.11:

> 'The task of the special ministers mentioned in Eph 4.11 is to be servants in that ministry which is entrusted to the whole church. Their place is not above but below the great number of Saints who are not adorned by resounding titles.'
>
> (BARTH 1974:481)

If all church leaders in the New Testament had to fulfil at least these five functions then their selection was primarily based upon the *qualities* they possessed. Their specific ministries would be governed by their gifts but biological characteristics such as age, sex and race, educational accomplishments or social standing were either unimportant or only culturally significant. It was the quality of the leaders that counted most and Jesus and the Early Church were quite revolutionary within their cultures in choosing and appointing some leaders who had the necessary qualities but would normally have been disqualified because they were women or uneducated or slaves (Acts 4.13; 21.9; Rom. 16.1,3).

Organisation of Leadership
If we apply these New Testament principles to the leadership of a church today then the five essential functions become *the main criteria for selecting leaders*. These should be given priority over cultural criteria, such as the ability to pass formal educational exams, or conformity to social class values. Cultural criteria may be complementary to the biblical criteria but they may not! Dr David Sheppard, Bishop of Liverpool, has recently drawn attention to this problem in churches among the urban poor. In *Bias to the Poor* he writes:

> 'The Church's insistence on particular styles of training and qualifications has prevented some much-needed gifts from being used in God's service. This wastes the gifts of some who would help to

bridge the long-standing gap between urban working-class people and the Church.'

(SHEPPARD 1983:212)

This perception is not new: Roland Allen, the renowned Anglican missionary in China at the turn of the century, criticised similar practices on the mission field. He identified 'four very serious consequences' of using the wrong criteria (in this case, the ability to pass formal examinations) for selecting leaders. I have summarised these from his book, *'Missionary Methods: St. Paul's or Ours'* (p 105f) which makes interesting and relevant reading even today:
1. The churches were deprived of the sacraments.
2. The young men, so educated, were sometimes by that very education placed out of touch with their congregations.
3. The natural leaders of the church were silenced.
4. The natural teacher and the divinely gifted preacher (prophet) was silenced or seceded.

When biblical criteria are used to select leaders the leadership of a church is open to all suitable members and not just those who are already leaders in society, many of whom are ill-equipped to lead a church. Far too many British churches are dominated by 'the Squire and mill owner' and far too high a proportion of British clergy are selected and trained as if they were leaders in society, rather than the Church. Therefore many pastors themselves fail to fulfil the biblical functions of church leadership and must begin the organisation of leadership by closely examining the quality of their own lives and leadership.

The pastor, as the presiding elder, is the key to effective church leadership and it is vitally important that he (or she?) set the standard of leadership by fulfilling the essential functions. He must endeavour to be what he wants the other leaders to become, and play his part in the organisation of a leadership which will require the following elements:
1. *Existing leaders should be challenged* to fulfil the functions of leadership lest they hinder the renewal and reformation of the church. The quality of a church cannot rise above the quality of its leaders, so unspiritual and unsuitable leaders are a major obstacle to growth.
2. *New leaders should be recruited* on the basis of the quality of their lives and the evidence of the essential functions of leadership. Some may be undeveloped but once these qualities are discerned in a potential leader he should be selected in the confidence that the Holy Spirit will develop his qualities and gifts. Note Paul's appointment of elders in new churches (Acts 14.21–23).
3. *Leaders should be trained* in an 'apprenticeship' relationship, as Jesus trained his disciples. Selected potential leaders should work alongside existing leaders, so that their confidence may grow, and gifts and ministries develop.

4. *Leaders should be deployed* on the basis of their gifts. The Functional Model (See figure 34) identifies activities of edification and evangelism where leadership in support of members' ministries is required. No leader has all the gifts so he should not attempt to be a 'jack-of-all-trades'.

5. *Leaders should be supported* by each other by means of affirming relationships. Differences and problems should be overcome in the context of commitment to Christ, to each other and to the ministry of Christ through his Church. Leaders should share common goals, be united in their vision for the church and act as a team.

3. Edifying Believers

The New Testament uses the verb *oikodomeo* to describe the building up of the Church. Older translations use the verb *to edify* and call the process *edification*.

Oikodomeo is used literally of building with bricks and mortar (e.g. Mark 13.1.2; Luke 4.29) and metaphorically (thirty-six times in various forms) of the moral, spiritual and numerical growth of the Church (Rom. 14.19; 15.2; Acts 9.31). Individual believers are pictured as 'living stones' or building blocks for the construction of God's temple (1 Pet. 2.5) in which the Holy Spirit dwells (Eph. 2.20–22) and of which Christ is the foundation and cornerstone (1 Cor. 3.11; 1 Pet. 2.4–8).

The actual builder of the Church is God (1 Cor. 3.9; cf Matt. 16.18) by means to the Word and the Spirit (Acts 9.31;20.32) and the process continues as each new believer is added and grows morally and spiritually (Eph. 2.21–22). However, Christians have to play their part by building upon their faith to the best of their gifts and abilities (Jude 20; 1 Cor. 3.10–14). The apostles and prophets have shown the way (Eph. 2.20) but all believers are involved (Eph. 4.12) and build each other up in the Christian life (1 Thes. 5.11).

The goal of individual and corporate edification is Christian maturity that glorifies God (Col. 1.28; Eph. 4.13; cf. Matt. 5.13–16). Therefore *two essential tests for all church activities and ministries is whether or not they glorify God and edify believers.* (1 Cor. 14.26; Eph. 2.19–22; 4.4–13; 1 Pet. 4.7–11).

The Church is built up in the context of love (Eph. 4.16) which is why the apostles constantly called churches to manifest it. (1 Cor. 8.1; Col. 3.12–14; Phil. 1.9–10; 1 Thess. 3.11–12; 1 Pet. 4.8; 1 John 3.11,23). Love is so important, the 'greatest' says Paul, that it is not surprising to find that *right relationships are the key to edification.*

A right relationship with God results 'in reverence for the Lord' (Acts 9.31), and right relationships with one another produce a community at peace and in harmony with itself (Acts 9.31; Rom. 14.19). We have already seen that people relate to each other in Cells, Congregations and Celebrations. Therefore a helpful way of organising the edification of the church is to link activities with the appropriate groups. The social organisation of people provides us with useful categories in our Functional Model and identifies the structures required for edification (see figure 36, Structures for Edification).

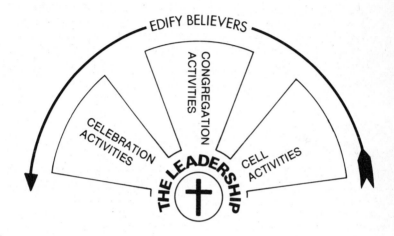

Figure 36. Structures for Edification

Cell Activities

The Cell is the primary group and basic structure that provides the church with a face-to-face context for personal and intimate relationships and lifestyle formation. This small group numbers approximately three to twelve people and its main function and essential activities have been discussed in relation to other groups in chapter 2 (page 52, see figure 14).

Dr Howard A. Snyder lists the following advantages of small groups in his book *New Wineskins* p. 130ff:

(a) 'It is flexible' – can be used for a variety of purposes.
(b) 'It is mobile' – can meet anywhere.
(c) 'It is inclusive' – open to all kinds of people.
(d) 'It is personal' – people really get to know each other.
(e) 'It can grow by division' – it can multiply like living cells.
(f) 'It can be an effective means of evangelism' – especially in urban contexts.
(g) 'It requires a minimum of professional leadership' – excellent for lay training.
(h) 'It is adaptable to the institutional church' – does not replace the church but is an essential structure.

The small group is not the answer to all the Church's difficulties, as some imagine, and it often generates a new set of problems, but our research into growing churches does show that small groups make an important contribution to growth. Churches that fail to offer small group experiences to their members are withholding a vital element for their edification.

The commonly held fear that small groups undermine the church and are likely to break away can be overcome by the careful selection and training of leaders, an efficiently-run programme and the wise choice of discussion and study materials.

A wide range of literature on the small group and a growing selection of materials are now available in Britain and no church can be excused for failing to use them at some point in its programme.

When the Lord's Supper or Holy Communion was instituted (Matt. 26.26–29; Mark 14.27–31; Luke 22.31–34; see John 13–17; 1 Cor. 11.17–34) and celebrated by the primitive Church, it was usually in a small group. The passover meal origins of the Last Supper (Luke 22.8) also point to family-sized groups as the most likely social context. I am unaware of any studies into the effect upon the theology and practice of celebrating the Eucharist in other sized groups but there are a growing number of churches and groups who are attempting to recapture the original New Testament practice (Acts 2.46) and family feeling by using homes for the celebration of the Lord's Supper.

Of course it is not just the small numbers in a cell that are the secret of renewal. The small numbers are conducive to close fellowship and the creation of an atmosphere of acceptance, openness, frankness and freedom that the Holy Spirit is able to use for edification. Renewal and growth must be personal and the small group provides an environment for the sharing of personal needs and experiences that is impossible in larger groups.

It has been suggested that great renewal movements have been incubated in the small group. Augustine described the 'little church within the church'. A great variety of orders such as the Benedictines and Franciscans restored the Church's spirituality by using them. Luther and other Reformers commended the use of the home for prayer, Bible reading, the sacraments and 'other Christian exercises'. The Moravian 'bands' helped John Wesley to form the concept of the 'class' system which eventually consolidated Methodism's revival. Small groups are therefore not new and as Elton Trueblood has said, 'No one has a copyright on the small group movement.' So if your church does not have any, start them and take advantage of this vitally important structure for renewal and growth.

Here are some 'do's and don'ts' to help you avoid some of the most common pitfalls when introducing small groups to your church.

Ten 'Do's' for Small Groups

1. Do have a clear covenant or contract of purpose for a group that is accepted by all members. Agree why the group is meeting and what you want to achieve in the lives of its members.

2. Do invite the Holy Spirit into the group!
3. Do agree how the group will function: expected regular attendance; how many weeks it will meet; periods for prayer; methods of Bible study; refreshments, etc.
4. Do select and train leaders who promote and encourage the participation and development of all group members, even the timid and uneducated.
5. Do foster love and care in order to create an atmosphere of openness, trust and acceptance – it will take time, so be patient.
6. Do insist on life-related Bible study and discussions and allow the truth of God's Word to fashion the lifestyles of the members.
7. Do encourage prayer for people and circumstances outside the immediate prayer concerns of the group – a few church prayer topics can be given to all the groups.
8. Do encourage the discovery and exercise of gifts in this ideal context of the small group – look out for potential small group leaders for new groups.
9. Do select people with a ministry of hospitality to host the groups.
10. Do assess the groups regularly and be prepared to close, divide or re-structure as necessary.

Ten 'Don'ts' for Small Groups

1. Don't insist that every church member join a small group – some cannot cope emotionally or relationally.
2. Don't over-organise!
3. Don't be inflexible when allocating people to groups. Some prefer to meet with those they already know, others are happy to get together with any members who live nearby.
4. Don't allow the programme to become more important than the people in it.
5. Don't permit groups to become cliques and get introverted – a rhythm of isolation and involvement, 'inwards and outwards', is required.
6. Don't allow leaders to dominate the group: it is not a Bible class.
7. Don't insist on conformity of opinion on non-essentials of belief and behaviour.
8. Don't allow opinions to have more authority than the Word of God – not so much 'What do you think?' but more 'What does the Bible say?'
9. Don't allow insensitive and rebellious individuals to destroy the peace and happiness of a group.
10. Don't allow the group to become a substitute for personal piety or corporate worship and other essential activities within the church.

The importance of the small group for the growth and development of a church has been dramatically demonstrated by the Full Gospel Church in Seoul, South Korea. This is considered to be the largest church in the world with 341,000 members in 1983 and a faith projection of 500,000 by 1984!

The church was founded in 1958 and met originally in a tent. Dr Paul Yonggi Cho, the Pastor, has developed a 'web of love' throughout the church with over 20,000 small groups which are centres of spiritual growth, pastoral care and evangelism. These groups are constantly recruiting new members and multiplying.

When asked to explain the phenomenal growth of his church, Pastor Cho explained, 'Just as the physical body grows by the division of cells, so this church body grows by the division of cells.' He also believes the same principles would be effective in other cultures throughout the world and has described his use of small groups in his book *Successful House Cell Groups* (Logos International, 1981). A very full and thrilling description of the church has been written by Eileen Vincent in *God Can Do It Here* (Marshalls, 1982).

Of course, many churches are little more than small groups when all their members come together. In England, thirty per cent of the churches have less than twenty-five adult attenders! While the small church is prone to a number of serious and often terminal problems, it does have three very important strengths. *The small church has to concentrate on basics* – the ministry of the Word and sacraments, the fellowship of its members, and the ministry of the laity. Small churches can be greatly helped by ministries that focus on these areas and which offer inter-church support to provide Congregation and Celebration relationships and experiences.

Congregational Activities

The Congregational group has about 25 – 175 members depending on the task or interest that brings them together. A choir of thirty or a women's meeting of eighty are both Congregational groups. The primary function of this structure is social fellowship which produces a sense of common identity and purpose (see chapter 2).

Approximately sixty per cent of English churches have practising memberships within this sized group and are often unable to grow beyond it because of self-limiting patterns of ministry and inappropriate structures (see the research of the Rev David Wasdell of the Urban Church Project, St Matthias' Vicarage, Poplar High Street, London E14 0AE). Obviously, almost all the activities within these churches take place within the Congregational group so the value of identifying this social structure on the Functional Model lies in seeing its position in group dynamics. Most churches are unaware of the effects of these various groups on their members and fail to appreciate the value of activities that are peculiar to each group.

The Congregational Group provides a sense of belonging and clannishness. The group is large enough to offer a wide range of relationships and activities that meet members' needs and interests but not so large that people cannot be recognised and participate if they wish. A 'fellowship circle' is created where everyone is known by sight and it is possible to know everyone by name.

Leaders of Congregational groups require special gifts and abilities that meet the particular needs of the group, for example, musical gifts to lead choirs, or preaching and teaching gifts to occupy a pulpit. In addition they have to be able to organise this larger group and maintain its activities and identity.

The fact that the majority of British churches are of Congregational group size means Cell and Celebration activities have to be introduced into the church programme. The Functional Model provides a framework for evaluating the need of such activities and establishing the priorities of introduction.

Celebration Activities

The main function of worship and other activities related to the Celebration group have been described earlier (chapter 2, p. 000; chapter 3, p. 000).

In his book *I Believe in Church Growth* (p. 290f), the Rev Eddie Gibbs identifies five benefits associated with this sized group.

1. Celebration expresses identity – a great sense of belonging is created when the whole 'tribe' gathers.
2. Celebration provides inspiration – for the individual and subgroups.
3. Celebration crystallises intention – an occasion when the 'tribe' re-affirms its common identity and purpose.
4. Celebration restores confidence – participants realise they are not alone.
5. Celebration establishes visibility – crowds attract attention.

Celebration groups require a sense of occasion and eventfulness to justify their gathering. A Papal visit or Annual Assembly or evangelistic Crusade will draw the crowds. In addition, the programme and leadership at such meetings must be exceptional to fulfil the expectations of the group.

Very few British churches are large enough to offer Celebration experiences every week, so most churches have to join with others for that 'special' event and should plan to do so regularly. The main Christian festivals are ideal occasions.

There is a growing awareness of the importance of Celebration events in the Church and many are taking place at local and national levels. The success of set programmes such as 'Come Together' and Bible Society's 'Sing Good News' and the explosion of Christian praise associated with the charismatic movement, have encouraged local initiatives to sponsor well-attended rallies for united worship. Mission England and Mission to London have been promoted through 'Prepare the Way' meetings and the House Churches regularly call together their groups in large worship events.

These manifestations of Celebration groups to build up God's people today are the product of the same needs that gave rise to

Canterbury Cathedral, the Methodist Conference and the Assembly of God's week at Butlins! While Celebration events may lose sight of their main function and sometimes degenerate, at their best God's people always need them.

4. Evangelising Unbelievers

The 'Functional Model' uses three essential *elements* of evangelism to identify and categorise the evangelistic tasks of a local church (see figure 37, Three Essential Elements of Evangelism). The failure to recognise the activities associated with these tasks often leads to serious weaknesses in evangelism with disastrous consequences for the local church.

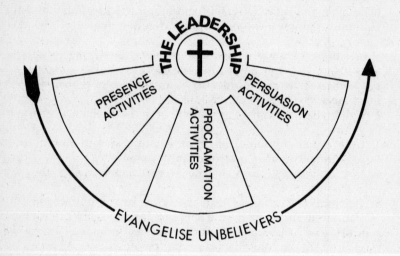

Figure 37. Three Essential Elements of Evangelism

The '3P' Definition of Evangelism
The Lausanne Committee for World Evangelisation has drawn up the following definition:

Nature The nature of evangelisation is the communication of the Good News of Jesus Christ.
Purpose To give individuals and groups a valid opportunity to accept Jesus Christ.
Goal The persuading of men and women to accept Jesus Christ as Lord and Saviour and serve him in the fellowship of his Church.

This definition embraces the '3P' definition advocated by Church

Growth and presented by Dr Peter Wagner in his book *Frontiers of Missionary Strategy'* (p. 124ff).

The '3Ps' stand for Presence, Proclamation and Persuasion. These are considered to be three essential elements in effective evangelism.

Presence describes the witness of works that are part of God's purpose in saving his people and forming the Church (Eph. 2.8–10). The Church, like her Lord, must be known for doing good (Acts 10.38). These good works glorify the Father and attract an inattentive world (Matt. 5.16) and there are occasions when actions speak louder than words (1 Pet. 2.12).

Christian presence reduces moral evil, dispels ignorance and demonstrates the love and righteousness of God through an alternative lifestyle (Matt. 5.6.7). Christians have the potential of being 'salt' and 'light' wherever they are, so long as they maintain their distinctive character as citizens of the Kingdom when at home, at school or college, in the office or on the factory floor. Christians do not have to be sent out into the world – they are already there – but they do have to become radiant witnesses in word and deed, unlike the President of McDonald's Hamburgers who is alleged to have said, 'I believe in God, the family and McDonald's Hamburgers, and when I go to the office I reverse the order!'

Presence includes the 'signs and wonders' that signify the Lord is with his people and demonstrate his victory and reign over the powers of darkness (Mark 16.20; Acts 3.1–16; 4.30; 2 Cor. 12.12). One of the most remarkable and popular courses on offer in 1982 at the School of World Mission was the 'experimental course' MC510: 'Signs, Wonders and Church Growth'. The lecturer was Pastor John Wimber whose church 'The Vineyard Christian Fellowship' had grown from a home Bible study group to 3,000 members in five years. John Wimber had become convinced from exposure to Third World church leaders, studies at the School of World Mission and several years as a consultant with the Fuller Institute of Evangelism and Church Growth, that the 'power encounter' was missing from most Western evangelism.

Recognising that 'no miracles now' and 'miracles whenever we want them' represent unbiblical positions, John Wimber prayed and studied the Scriptures in search of principles that would release God's power in mission. He writes:

'We believe that Jesus ministered in power to the total man. His message was not for mind alone; it also was for the spirit and body. Jesus preached, taught *and* healed. We believe this kind of balanced ministry is needed today if the Church is to minister as Jesus intends.

'*People in our culture need to see* that God is more powerful than the lifestyles that they are serving. We are discovering that scripturally defined signs and wonders are playing a major role in getting the Gospel message out to a nation that needs help and spiritual direction.'

He baptised 700 new converts within two months of the first outpouring of the Holy Spirit!

Presence embraces every good deed done in Jesus' name. *People are helped* and glimpse the goodness of God through his people. Christians have rightly been to the fore in alleviating human suffering and deprivation, in calling for justice and righteousness, and this has involved them in a deep penetration and interaction with society. Mother Theresa, Bonhoeffer, Martin Luther King are names that immediately come to mind. Often such involvement is costly, even to the point of martyrdom. But this is God's world and his people have a *Cultural Mandate* that requires them to bring the social order into conformity with his will. The liberal and the more contemporary liberation theologians are undoubtedly right in calling the Church to recognise the social and political implications of the gospel (Luke 4.18,19). While many Christians may be nervous about the extent of the response called for, especially the violent option advocated by some liberation theologians, active social concern is always an essential requirement for the people of God.

There is a growing awareness among conservative evangelicals of this need to face up to social responsibilities. This found expression in the Lausanne Covenant which states:

'We affirm that God is both the Creator and Judge of all men. We therefore should share in his concern for justice and reconciliation throughout human society and for the liberation of men from every kind of oppression. Because mankind is made in the image of God, every person, regardless of race, religion, colour, culture, class, sex or age, has an intrinsic dignity because of which he should be respected and served, not exploited. Here too we express penitence both for our neglect and for having sometimes regarded evangelism and social concern as mutually exclusive.'
[LAUSANNE 1975.25]

This commitment to Presence by a local church raises the issue of resources to meet the needs of the local community. The advice of a sympathetic social worker from the local government often reveals needs that the church can meet. Perhaps church premises could be used by the elderly, or for a day nursery or for the unemployed. Church members with gifts and abilities to serve the community should be encouraged and supported, even if they are local and national politicians! Gifts of money or goods may be a tangible expression of Christ's love in certain situations. 'Find a need and fill it; find a hurt and heal it', has been the philosophy of at least one rapidly growing church.

Among the urban poor of Britain's cities Dr David Sheppard

believes this is primarily seen in a willingness to stay. He calls for a believing and worshipping presence and writes:

'First we need to be the kind of Church which stays present in the neediest areas and continues to believe and worship. Sheer survival takes much courage in areas where the rate of collapse of community projects is extremely high.'

[SHEPPARD 1983.201]

There are some advocates of Christian Presence who equate it with evangelism and maintain that the witness of works is sufficient *alone*. But there can be no evangelism without the proclamation or the evangel – the Good News. As the Bishop of Liverpool goes on to say:

'Effective evangelism includes naming the name of Christ. The right moment for that may be ten years down the road, when neighbours have had the chance to see signs in the life of the Christian community. At the right moment Christians should be ready to give their witness by lip as well as by life.'

[SHEPPARD 1983.217]

Here the Liberal and Radical churches are grossly at fault. Sir Alan Walker, Director of World Evangelism for the World Methodist Council, addresses this error in his book *The New Evangelism* when he writes:

'On the other hand, let it be stated bluntly that social agitation which has lost touch with an evangelical base is largely beating the air. The old statement that there can not be a new world without new men and women is fundamentally true. An older evangelism neglected the bodies of men and women and over-emphasised the soul, but today there is the peril of seeing people only in their physical dimension.'

[WALKER 1975.41]

Proclamation Activities
Proclamation is concerned with the content and communication of the gospel message. It is the *witness of words* that arises out of the witness of works.

A grave distortion of modern evangelism, especially among evangelical churches, is that Proclamation is not based upon Presence. While it is not legitimate to describe all Presence activity as evangelism, the foundation of the witness of works is essential for effective Proclamation. The Church, like Christ himself, has to become incarnate before she can speak.

When Presence is neglected and Proclamation stands alone, the evangelising church is seen to break out of its ghetto and behave, as

Hans-Ruedi Weber so graphically suggests, like Red Indians on a raid. Unfortunately they are easily satisfied with a scalp or two!

1. The Content of the Gospel

Ever since C. H. Dodd wrote *The Apostolic Preaching and its Developments* (1936) a great deal of study has focused on the basic gospel message, the *kerygma* (1 Cor. 1.21), that was preached by the primitive Church.

Dodd saw a clear distinction in the New Testament between the message preached as 'the public proclamation of Christianity to the non-Christian world' and the preaching of doctrinal and ethical instruction for believers (*didaskein*).

In his book *Evangelism and the Early Church* Dr Michael Green discusses the work of Dodd and the contribution of numerous scholars and asks the question, 'Was there a fixed *kerygma*?' He concludes his discussion:

'But although Dodd claimed too much, his work is of lasting value in working out in considerable detail the hint given in Mark and Paul that the gospel had recognisable shape and content. Christians had a common approach to evangelism, however much they might differ in details and transpose some of the thought forms into other keys: and they did plenty of that as we shall see. There was some sort of "pattern of sound words" and this proved a useful springboard for the memories of the evangelists: it did not serve as a strait-jacket, inhibiting all imagination and initiative on their part.' (GREEN 1970.70)

What was this 'pattern of sound words' (2 Tim. 1.13) and the so-called 'foolish message' (1 Cor. 1.21) Paul preached?

There have been many analyses of the apostolic preaching but one of the most helpful is the Rev. John Stott's in his book *Christian Mission in the Modern World* (Falcon, 1975). I have summarised his analysis in my *Tell What God Has Done* booklet published by Bible Society (1982) as follows:

1. *What Jesus Did* – Gospel events – the facts about Jesus Christ especially his death and resurrection.
2. *Why Jesus Came* – Gospel witnesses – the Old Testament witness to Jesus Christ plus the apostolic witness that became the New Testament.
3. *Who Jesus Is* – Gospel affirmations – Jesus Christ is Lord and the only Saviour of mankind.
4. *What Jesus Offers* – Gospel promises – the forgiveness of sins and the gift of the Holy Spirit.
5. *What Jesus Requires* – Gospel demands – repentance, faith and public baptism.

Once this, or a similar outline, is recognised as the bare bones or skeleton of the gospel message, then the local church has the task of communicating it.

2. The Communication of the Gospel

Communication is complex and communication theory is an expanding discipline which offers the Christian communicator many valuable insights. A growing body of research and an increasing vocabulary of terms attempt to clarify issues and solve problems in communication.

This is not the place for a detailed discussion of the theory of Christian communication for we are concerned to identify activities and therefore need to focus on methods. As a general principle, I want to follow Dr Charles Kraft who wrote in the Ashland Theological Bulletin (Spring 1979) under the heading *Communicating the Gospel God's Way*:

> 'For generations, we who seek to communicate God's Word have looked to the Bible for our *message*. I am afraid, though, that we have seldom looked to the Bible for our *method*.'
>
> (KRAFT 1979.3)

As we look to the Bible for the way to develop our Proclamation activities we need to keep in mind the three basic evangelistic agencies (see figure 38) and how they relate to each other and the unbeliever.

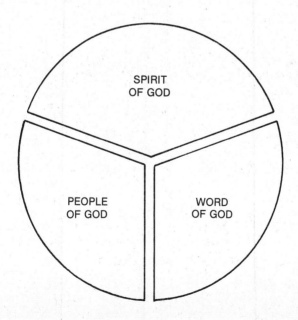

Figure 38. The Three Evangelistic Agencies

When communicating the gospel the role of the *Spirit of God* is of paramount importance, so all *our activities must be subordinate to his*. Awe and mystery will always remain, for the gospel is God's message and the Holy Spirit takes and holds the initiative in its communication (Luke 10.21–22; John 3.3–8; 16.7–11; Rom. 1.16). Dr Michael Green identifies the following activities of the Spirit in mission in his book *I Believe in the Holy Spirit*:

1. The Spirit initiates Mission.
2. The Spirit universalises Mission.
3. The Spirit uses testimony.
4. The Spirit enlivens the Word.
5. The Spirit convicts and attracts.
6. The Spirit brings repentance and faith.

The *Word of God* is the message being communicated and *activities will be fashioned by the media used*. The written word has little relevant to illiterates and the spoken word cannot reach the deaf! Fortunately there are many imaginative uses of media in the church today with films, slides, flannelgraphs, overhead transparencies, video, drama, music, etc. all helping to get the message across.

Dr Charles Kraft makes six preliminary observations concerning God's communication and they help us evaluate our use of media and activities:

1. God seeks to communicate, not simply to impress.
2. God wants to be understood, not simply admired.
3. God seeks a response, not simply passive listening.
4. God has revealed not only what to communicate but how.
5. God is 'receptor orientated' (he focuses on the hearer).
6. God's basic method of communication is incarnational (he uses his people to get alongside other people).

So the *People of God* are the key agents for communicating the gospel according to Dr Kraft. This may seem an obvious statement to make but if acted upon would mean a major re-evaluation of the evangelistic activity of most churches. Far too many rely on the impersonal scattering of Scripture or keyspeakers or come-visit-us events.

Priority will have to be given to activities that equip and use the ordinary church members where they are in society for Spontaneous Evangelism (see chapter 3, p. 78) *among the network of their relationships* (see figure 39). While some Christians are evangelists (Eph. 4.11) every believer has the role of witness and requires training in how to tell his story and share his faith (Luke 8.39).

Training programmes, such as those offered by 'Evangelism Explosion' and 'Campus Crusade', which offer basic training to ordinary Christians, are among the most effective proclamation activities

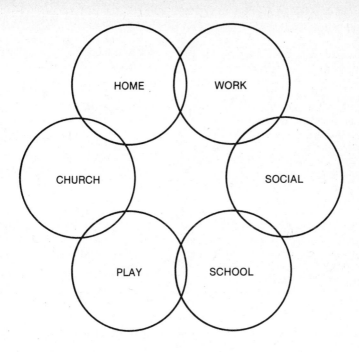

Figure 39. The Network of Relationships

available to British churches today for this very reason. If their contact procedures could be further directed into the networks of those they train and who are converted I believe they could be even more effective.

When priority is given to *Spontaneous Evangelism* other evangelistic activities become complementary and ought to be supported as resources allow. Well-prepared Crusade evangelism, student missions, guest services, Scripture distribution, etc., all have their place in the continuous proclamation of the gospel by the Church.

Persuasion Activities

It is now generally agreed that the *goal* of evangelism is 'making disciples'.

In order to stress this element in modern missions Dr McGavran proposed a 'Theology of Harvest', which focuses on the purpose of mission, and Dr Wagner suggested the concept of 'Persuasion'. (For a full discussion of the issues, debate and implications see *The Growth of the True Church* by Charles Van Engen, pp 454–507.)

Van Engen concludes that the Church Growth emphasis is valid when interpreted in terms of intention and a 'yearning' for numerical growth, but invalid when related to consequence and the actual numerical growth achieved. The Church's faithfulness to the Great Commission cannot be measured by results and the true church is not necessarily found where numerical growth is greatest. 'Yearning' for numerical growth is the essential test and he elevates it to a mark of the true Church.

It is undoubtedly true that the Church's faithfulness cannot be tested by the number of converts resulting from evangelism, for this is dependent upon the activity of the Holy Spirit. However, a 'yearning' church will strive to bring about the conversion of people by inviting them to follow Jesus Christ as Saviour and Lord and by helping those who respond to join its fellowship. This is Persuasion (2 Cor. 5.11, 18–20) and a willingness to engage in it may be tested!

The concern of McGavran and Wagner and the Church Growth Movement is that far too many churches, missions and evangelistic agencies pay scant attention to Persuasion activities and consequently see little, if any, numerical growth.

Persuasion describes the Church's participation in what is essentially God's activity – the finding of the lost and their incorporation into the fellowship of the Church. Christians act as co-workers with God in bringing home His harvest (Luke 10.2; 1 Cor. 3.5–9). There are at least *five elements* in Persuasion:

1. Personal Relationships   We have already seen that God's people are the key agents for Proclamation. When Christians also commit themselves to meaningful relationships with responsive people, unbelievers encounter the love and reality of Christ and gain an understanding of life in the Kingdom (Luke 9.4,5; 10.5–11). The Christian becomes a model and counsellor to answer questions and explain the way.

Personal relationships are essential to the well-being of the unbeliever throughout the Persuasion stage as he comes to faith and joins the Church. Long-term commitments to people are costly, which is one reason why 'hit and run' evangelism is so popular. This also reinforces the importance of the 'network', where relationships already exist.

Apart from personal contact, relationships can be maintained and strengthened by prayer, personal representatives and correspondence; all are found in the New Testament.

Dr Win Arn of the Institute for American Church Growth has conducted research into Crusade Evangelism and discovered that eighty-three per cent of new converts who are in the churches after a crusade have friends or relatives already attending the church, so the importance of the network and personal relationships cannot be over-emphasised in evangelistic programmes today.

2. Call to Commitment   The apostle Paul declared that all men should have an opportunity to decide for Christ through repentance and faith (Acts 17.39–31). Jesus, himself, with all the apostles preached for a verdict and did not hesitate to call for a turning from sin and commitment to discipleship (Mark 1.14–20; Acts 2.38–42).

Of course, this call to commitment is an essential part of the *kerygma* itself and therefore an element of Proclamation. It is included in Persuasion because the actual response to the call is usually expressed verbally by the unbeliever as he comes to faith, and the church needs to identify activities which will help him.

The Holy Spirit convicts of sin and convinces of the truth. When he is at work in the mind and heart of the unbeliever, the call to commitment provides an opportunity to exercise the will in a personal profession of faith (Rom. 10.8–10). It may be presented in a number of ways and the method used must always respect the integrity of the person and avoid manipulation or pressure.

Churches need to develop ways of calling for commitment that are appropriate to their ethos and churchmanship, always remembering that people require help to make a decision for Christ that will lead to a life of discipleship.

The reality of the profession of faith and the new birth will become evident in changed beliefs and behaviour (Acts 9.21; 2 Cor. 5.17).

3. Elementary Instruction   Those who came to Christ require basic instruction in the fundamentals of the faith (Acts 2.41,42; Heb. 6.1–3). The following programme identifies three phases of instruction and is described in detail as a possible model:

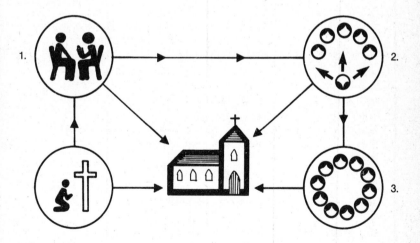

Figure 40. Phases of Elementary Instruction

Phase 1 is a personal 'one-to-one' brief period of instruction to clarify issues to the profession of faith and to prepare the new convert for *Phase 2*. The counsellor or 'sponsor' meets at the convert's convenience, offers to accompany the convert to church or the *Phase 2* classes if necessary, and continues to help as required.

Phase 2 is a longer period of 'Discipleship' or 'Beginners' classes usually taught by the minister, which might cover such subjects as:

(a) Christian assurance
(b) The practice of prayer – the devotional life
(c) The Bible – nature, contents and methods of study
(d) The Holy Spirit – with emphasis upon the 'fruit' and 'gifts'
(e) The nature of the Church (including procedures for joining)
(f) The sacrament of the Lord's Supper (including grounds for participation)
(g) The sacrament of baptism (including an invitation to receive this or another rite of initiation)
(h) Christian witness – evangelism and service
(i) The history of the Church – introducing the denomination and its particular beliefs.
(j) Christian stewardship
(k) The Christian hope
(l) Balanced discipleship – the 'three priorities' of Worship, Fellowship and Service

These studies should be very informal and simple and assume no prior understanding, not even of chapters and verses of the Bible. New converts may want to attend the series more than once as a great deal of evaluation and re-orientation is taking place. If the flow of new converts is sufficient, the series may run continuously with people joining any class and leaving when all are completed.

As non-churchgoing habits may have to be broken *Phase 2* instruction should take place at the same time as *Phase 3*.

Phase 3 is the usual cell-group used for edification to which new converts are introduced once they possess a basic understanding of the Christian faith. If converts have formed friendships in *Phase 2* small numbers of them should be introduced into the cell-groups together to reduce the tensions of joining the new group.

4. Early Incorporation   This describes the welcoming of the new convert to the fellowship of the church. Every new member, and especially the new convert, needs the embrace of the local family of God.

While the convert will have developed relationships with his 'sponsor', minister and cell, he still needs to be introduced to other church members so that he may form meaningful relationships of his own choice. A conscious attempt to build a supportive Christian network around the new convert will establish new relationships and strengthen old ones, and build a sense of belonging that will complete the early stages of incorporation.

This practice must be encouraged at every level of the church structure and within every organisation or the new convert will 'pass through' the church in a few months.

The new convert is particularly vulnerable during the period of Elementary Instruction and Early Incorporation and prayerful and sensitive support is required to overcome any disillusionment or misunderstanding.

5. *An Initiation Rite*   New converts should join the church through an initiation rite which will mark their entry into the local community and the people of God. The rite of the New Testament is baptism. Dr George Beasley-Murray summarises the evidence of the New Testament:

> . . . by baptism a man that was formerly not a member of the people of God is identified with the Lord and his people, and in an open, visible, public fashion he is admitted to the church.
> (BEASLEY-MURRAY 1972:284)

Denominational practices now vary considerably but the value and importance of an initiation rite as graphic and memorable as believers' baptism cannot be overstressed. While this rite will be consistent with the practice of the welcoming church and the previous experience of the convert it must be unforgettable.

With the initiation and incorporation of the new convert the process of persuasion is complete. He has joined a community living under the headship of Christ and taken his place, according to his gifts, in the edification and evangelistic activities of the church. Hopefully he becomes an active part of the Functional Model of a growing church!

SUMMARY

We have rejected the concept of an Ideal Church and suggested a Functional Model to organise and overhaul any church.

The Model seeks to establish the headship of Christ, the basic functions of leadership, the social structures in which edification takes place and the activities associated with the three essential elements of evangelism.

6 Planning For Growth

God has a plan for the universe (Eph. 1.5–12) and expects his people to play an active part in its fulfilment (Eph. 2.10).

God has determined to use the Church as a chosen instrument to accomplish his purposes. He does not want his people to be uncertain about his will or confused about their mission, so has made them known (1 Pet. 1.10–12). God wants the lost found and saved (Luke 19.10) and 'all to turn away from their sins' (2 Pet. 3.9). He loves mankind so much that he sent his Son to die for their sins (John 3.16) and decreed that 'the message about repentence and the forgiveness of sins must be preached to all nations' (Luke 24.27). Therefore there can be no doubt that evangelism and church growth are part of God's eternal plan and purpose, and to stay in the centre of God's will a church must plan to evangelise and grow.

Many Christians are reluctant to plan because they believe planning is unspiritual or unnecessary. However, the fact that they are free to choose and obey God's will requires right rather than wrong decisions and good rather than bad management. This involves wise and prayerful planning.

The apostle Paul sums up God's plan in his sublime description of the 'cosmic' Christ in Ephesians 1.10:

'This plan, which God will complete when the time is right, is to bring all creation together, everything in heaven and on earth, with Christ as head.'

In anticipation and preparation for that great day when the Kingdom comes and God's plan is fulfilled, the Church has to obey the Great Commission. Each church and every Christian has the privilege of participating in this part of God's plan – the bringing of people to conscious and personal submissiom to the Lordship of Jesus Christ and under the reign of God.

Because God has a plan that is as yet unfulfilled, he wants his people to be involved in the process of changing things from the way they are now to the way he wants them to be.

At the present time 36 million British people are unchurched and

God wants them to be made disciples of Christ. This is consistent with God's desire and Christ's command, so the British Church should plan accordingly (see figure 41, Plans for Growth in the United Kingdom).

Figure 41. Plans for Growth in the United Kingdom

The concept of a national plan for evangelism and growth may appear extremely bold and even presumptuous but it has been considered before. In 1945 the Church of England published a booklet entitled *'Towards the Conversion of England – a* plan *dedicated to the memory of Archbishop William Temple'*.

The booklet concludes with 'Recommendations and Findings' which begin with the following statements:

'The state of the Christian religion in this country urgently calls for definite action. That definite action is *no less* than the conversion of England to the Christian faith.'

If these statements were true in 1945, how much more true must they be today? Nothing less than the grand task of the re-evangelisation of the British Isles by the British Church will do!

This book is not the place to develop a strategy for 'Discipling the Nation', for we have deliberately limited our application of Church Growth principles to the local church. Even so, we shall not be far amiss, for the local church is the primary centre for effective evangelism and as we have already noted, *if every church in the United Kingdom experienced a net increase of two members per year the decline would be arrested and the British Church would grow again.*

PLANNING STEPS

The local church which wants to grow must plan for it and develop effective planning procedures. Five simple and basic planning steps are described below:

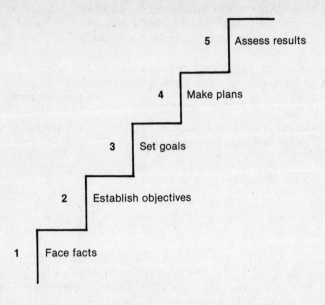

Figure 42. Five Basic Planning Steps

1. Face Facts

In chapter 4 we stressed the importance of basing decisions upon facts rather than fantasy. A foundation of facts that represents an accurate understanding of a church's true situation is essential for good planning. Every local church ought to undertake a thorough survey of itself and its community as a first step to planning for growth.

A surprising amount of fervent prayer, openness to change and zealous activity is generated when a church discovers, as one on the south coast of England did, that if present trends continued it would cease to exist in a few years' time!

Fact-facing will also include accepting God's will for the church as revealed in Scripture – it often comes as a great surprise to many that God wants their church to grow.

As a general rule fact-facing attempts to answer the questions, *'Where are we now?'* and *'How did we get here?'* It is not an easy exercise, as many people feel threatened by the questioning of the status quo, especially if facts prove unpalatable, but it is better to face facts sooner than later.

God's people are always given opportunities for self-examination and repentence but often leave it too late, as before the overthrow and destruction of Jerusalem in 586 BC. The prophetic ministry of Jeremiah and others went unheeded by the king, aristocracy, religious establishment and people. Their failure to face facts, repent and change their ways brought God's judgement and exile. In the midst of carnage and desolation the poet lamented:

'Let us examine our ways and turn back to the Lord.
Let us open our hearts to God in heaven and pray.'
Lamentations 3.40–41

Fact-facing is the initial stage in bringing God's people to repentance for the past and to faith in the future.

2. Establish Objectives

This stage of planning seeks to answer the questions *'What are we here for?'* Answers will establish the broad *'philosophy of ministry'* of the church and express, in general terms, the purposes for which the local church exists.

An Anglican Church in Kent has the following on its letterhead:

> THIS ANGLICAN CHURCH IS HERE
> * To Proclaim the Good News of Jesus Christ
> * To Build Human Community
> * To Help those in Need

These statements of purpose indicate the main objectives of this church and they provide a framework for planning and guidelines for developing their various programmes for growth.

Every church should establish objectives that are consistent with its own churchmanship, theological position and present resources and opportunities. Ideally every philosophy of ministry will be sufficiently comprehensive to provide a balanced ministry for the church. At the same time it needs to be condensed into a brief statement for easy communication to all church members. When the whole church is seeking to fulfil the established objectives, this *'Agreed Agenda'* harnesses the resources of the church for effective mission.

3. Set Goals

God-given goals are those that satisfy the general objectives of the church in specific ways. If the Anglican Church referred to above believes that, after prayer, one way of proclaiming the Good News of Jesus Christ is through a series of special Guest Services it could set a goal of six such services every year. A goal answers the question *'What do we do?'* – to achieve our objective.

A church which established the worship of God as one of its main objectives, yet discovered its worship services were uninspiring and unhelpful, might set the goal of services led by a group of musicians and singers. The main objective is to improve the worship of God and the set goal to achieve it is the formation of a group to lead the worship.

At this point we need to distinguish between good and bad goals! A good goal has the following qualities:

(a) *It is relevant*. It is consistent with the main objective and fulfils this overall purpose. Its relevance has been confirmed by research.
(b) *It is measurable*. It is set in time and quantity so that it will be known if the goal is achieved or not. For example, the group will have six musicians and singers and will be leading the services within four months.
(c) *It is achievable*. The goal must be within reach but not so easily accomplished that it does not require faith. The church would need at least six members who could sing and play musical instruments. Faith may be required when you hear them sing and play!
(d) *It is significant*. A good goal really makes a difference and produces the desired changes. This new group will improve the quality of the church's worship.
(e) *It is personal*. A good goal has the endorsement of the church. Members own the goal and work and pray for its fulfilment.

Goal-setting is frowned upon in most churches in the United Kingdom, yet it has tremendous potential for giving a church a sense of direction and purpose and, when achieved, celebration. Even when not reached, goals provide reference points for evaluation and new planning. As someone has said, 'If you aim at nothing you will certainly hit it!'

When goals are set after prayer and in faith they become the focus of God-honouring planning and progress.

In 1970 the Conservative Baptists were a relatively new and small denomination in the Philippines with twenty-one local churches and 1,500 members. In 1972 they launched an 'Operation 200' with the goals of two hundred churches and 10,000 members by 1981. Backed by prayer, dedicated workers at every level of the denomination and William Carey's conviction that they were to 'Expect great things from God' and 'Attempt great things for God' the denomination had reached eighty-one churches and 8,000 members by 1978 (see figure 43, Philippine Conservative Baptists).

While the goal of two hundred churches was not reached the membership goal was exceeded and the resulting growth is a vivid testimony for Christian mission. A fuller account of 'Operation 200' is recorded in *The Discipling of a Nation* by James H. Montgomery and Donald A. McGavran, published by Global Church Growth Bulletin, 1980 (pages 81–89).

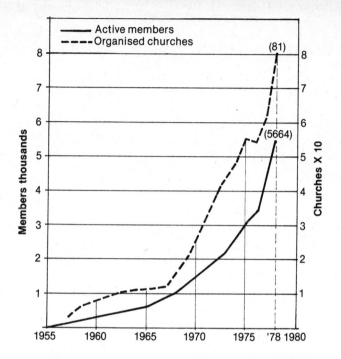

Figure 43. Philippine Conservative Baptists 1955–78

4. Make Plans

When facts have been faced, general objectives prayerfully established and specific goals set in faith, the next step is to make plans
to reach them. Plans answer the question, *'How do we achieve our
goals?'* Making plans is essential:

> After all, you must make careful plans before you fight a battle,
> and the more good advice you get, the more likely you are to win.
> Proverbs 24.6

One of the most simple planning tools available is PERT –
Programme Evaluation Review Technique. It was originally developed by the Office of US Naval Research in 1958 and helped to
place the first man on the moon! The merit of the tool is that it helps
the planner to constantly evaluate and review the plan.

PERT enables the planner to graphically present the plan and
identify each event and activity that must take place to reach the set
goal. The sequence of events and the time required for their comple-

tion may also be inserted. The PERT diagram is easily understood and is therefore excellent for communicating a plan to others, as well as monitoring progress and marshalling and allocating resources.

If we take our example of improving the worship service, we may draw up a simple plan for introducing the group and we could produce the following PERT diagram:

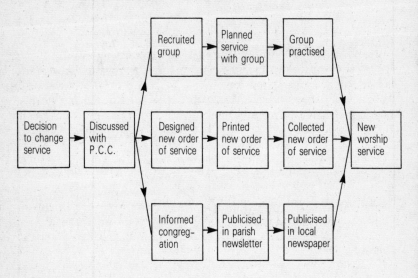

Figure 44. Planning with PERT

There are numerous planning and management programmes available to Christian leaders in the United Kingdom today and they all help to improve the use of the vast resources of the British Church that are available for Christian mission. Hopefully the theological colleges will add training in management to their curricula for ministers. So many are ill-equipped to manage their churches and are therefore constantly frustrated by their inability to achieve success in even the most simple projects. God is not glorified by bungling inefficiency that wastes resources, and basic management skills are easily learned.

If PERT appeals, there is a thorough treatment of its use in the Church, particularly for developing evangelistic strategies, in *God's Purpose/Man's Plan*, a Workbook by Edward R Dayton published by World Vision/MARC (146, Queen Victoria Street, London EC4V 4BX).

5. Assess Results

All Christian planning is an attempt to follow God's plan and is therefore done in an attitude of humble dependence upon the guid-

ance of the Holy Spirit. The Book of Proverbs states the fundamental
principles:

> We may make our plans, but God has the last word. You may
> think everything you do is right, but the LORD judges your
> motives. Ask the LORD to bless your plans, and you will be
> successful in carrying them out.
>
> Proverbs 16.1–3

When plans are constantly under evaluation and review it is
possible to learn from mistakes and solve problems as they arise.
The question asked at this stage is *'What is the Lord teaching us?'*
Plans need to be revised as necessary and must never be seen as
ends in themselves. They are merely tools and a means of achieving
the end results desired by God. Church planning tries to think God's
thoughts after him and discover his strategy for growth.

Dr Leonard Tuggy, of the Conservative Baptist Foreign Mission
Society, concludes his report on 'Operation 200' in the Philippines:

> 'We are profoundly grateful to God for this growth we have experi-
> enced, especially the thousands who have come to personal faith
> in Christ. *We are also thankful for the lessons learned*. Here are
> some:
> 1. Goal setting is absolutely essential for effective strategy
>   planning.
> 2. Goal setting is best done in the light of past performances. The
>   goals should be both challenging and attainable.
> 3. Long-range over-all goals are most meaningful when they are
>   broken down to year-to-year, area-by-area goals.
> 4. Goal setting must be followed immediately by formulating a
>   practical plan by which goals can be reached.
> 5. Goal ownership by the churches as well as by the mission is
>   essential to motivate everyone to work towards reaching goals.
> 6. A movement adopting a challenging church multiplication
>   strategy should anticipate the appearance of the "church devel-
>   opment syndrome". Concrete steps should be taken to help the
>   existing churches, but the original thrust must not be subverted.
> 7. New strategies often necessitate new structures. Existing organ-
>   izational structures may be too bulky or too inflexible to accom-
>   modate the new programme.
> 8. Dedicated, hard-working, goal-orientated leaders are essential
>   for any church growth programme. People, not plans, produce
>   results.'

The 'Operation 200' plan for growth became the means by which
the Conservative Baptists, under God, harnessed their resources for
evangelism and church planting. It produced the greatest advance in

their ministry to date and, like so many others, has affirmed the Church Growth maxim, *The church that plans to grow, will.*

IDENTIFY THE EVANGELISTIC TASK

Dr Ralph Winter, Director of the Center for World Mission, has developed a useful categorisation for identifying the various evangelistic tasks. Dr Winter uses a code with E for evangelism followed by various numbers to differentiate between the form of evangelism required to reach different cultural groups. He also relates the codes to four *Phases of Growth*.

The phases of growth identify the cultural obstacles to effective evangelism in response to the contemporary challenge to preach the Gospel, 'in Jerusalem in all Judaea and Samaria and the ends of the earth' (Acts 1.8).

1. Internal Growth

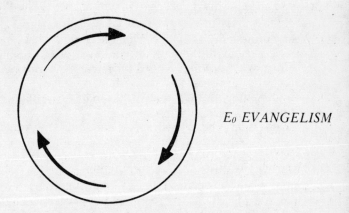

E_0 *EVANGELISM*

Figure 45. Internal Growth

Internal Growth includes the processes of Conceptual and Organic Growth that we have already defined in chapter 2, but focuses on the task of *evangelising nominal Christians* within the membership of the church.

The apostolic exhortation to the Roman Catholic Church by Pope Paul VI, *On Evangelization in the Modern World*, laments the multitudes of baptised but non-practising Catholics who need to be evangelised.

Anglican Bishop Stephen Neill also identified this task and considered the Church's evangelisation of itself as the primary and easiest form of evangelism. Writing more than a generation ago he points out that the Church is always one generation away from extinction:

' . . . it remains the fact that every human being is an individual, that to be a Christian is to have made an individual, personal act of faith in Jesus Christ and of dedication to His will, and that, if this personal act of dedication is not made by a sufficient number of people, the Church will decline and die away. In each generation the Church has to be reconverted. And since there is no firm division between generations, and one hungry generation is always pressing forward to tread down that which has gone before, the work of reconversion has to go on continuously and without intermission.'

(NEILL 1948:134)

Whatever our churchmanship this universal problem of nominality has to be faced and overcome in the process of renewal and growth. Often the nominal Christian will turn hostile as the claims of Christ are presented, no matter how graciously, and the local church may experience numerical decline as nominal members leave and spiritual vitality grows.

A wise strategy for the evangelisation of nominal Christians is *to call them to re-dedicate their lives to Christ* or *to re-affirm their baptismal vows*.

As the evangelisation of nominal church members does not require the crossing of cultural barriers it is termed E_O *Evangelism* (E for evangelism and O for 'zero' cultural barriers). People in the pew, however irregularly they may come, generally understand the traditional language and liturgy of the church and possess a basic knowledge of the facts of the gospel message.

2. Expansion Growth

Expansion Growth describes the numerical increase of the local church by Biological, Transfer, Restoration and Conversion Growth. The Conversion Growth, however, results from the *evangelisation of unbelievers of a similar culture* to the evangelising church and only requires the crossing of the cultural barrier between the church and the world – the *'stained-glass'* barrier. Called E_1 evangelism, it recognises the need to communicate the gospel in intelligible terms to those outside the Church.

Dr Michael Green reminds us of the relevance of the gospel message for twentieth century man in his book *Salvation* and draws attention to the obstacle of language when he writes:

'Of course, it does not make sense if words like "saved" are used without interpretation. Modern man thinks he knows what is meant by "Salvation" and he does not want it. The unexplained use of religious language is a major factor in the dismissal by most modern men of Christianity as irrelevant.

(GREEN 1965:236)

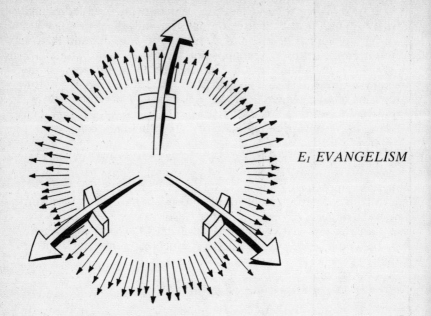

E₁ EVANGELISM

Figure 46. Expansion Growth

Religious language is only one of many factors that make up the 'stained-glass' barrier, for the Church communicates by deeds as well as words. In fact, as the proverb maintains, actions speak louder than words, so archaic dress and ritual and culturally irrelevant activity, such as unintelligible hymn-singing, creates a cultural capsule in which the Church lives in isolation from the world it is called to serve.

The ancient *inclusi* sought to express their devotion to Christ by retreating from the world and bricking themselves into caves. Many modern Christians do not realise that their refusal to face the challenge of communicating the gospel today is equally irresponsible. It is imperative that all cultural, i.e. man-made, obstacles to effective evangelism be identified and overcome if large numbers of those outside the Church are to be won for Christ. The 'stained-glass' barrier needs removing pane by pane!

3. Extension Growth

Extension Growth describes *church planting among people of a similar* culture to those of the evangelising church. In this case new converts are nurtured in a new congregation rather than incorporated into the existing church. As the 'stained-glass' barrier still has to be crossed, E₁ evangelism is required.

Church planting is a neglected but major strategy for evangelisa-

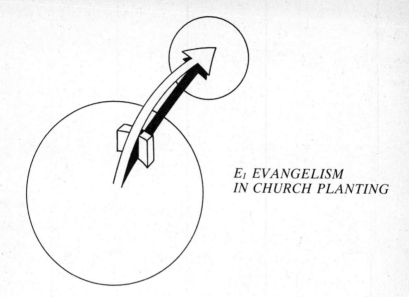

E_1 EVANGELISM
IN CHURCH PLANTING

Figure 47. Extension Growth

tion and all denominational advances have included Extension
Growth. When the London Baptist Association was formed in 1865
it had three primary objectives: 'Fellowship – co-operation and unity;
evangelism – to advance the Kingdom of Christ; and church extension – a continuing programme of church building.' It is not surprising, therefore, that in the first hundred years of its history it grew
from a fellowship of 59 to 279 churches.

4. Bridging Growth

Bridging Growth describes *cross-cultural church planting*. When a
church or group of churches send a team or individuals to plant
a church within a different culture. Two classifications of cultural
boundaries are made:

Class 1 cultures have some similarities with the culture of the
evangelising church and require E_2 evangelism (2 = 'stained-glass'
barrier + Class 1 cultural barrier).

Class 2 cultures are very different from the culture of the evangelising church, and require E_3 evangelism (3 = 'stained-glass' barrier
+ Class 2 cultural barrier).

If British missionaries were sent to another Western European
country to plant churches, the task would require E_2 evangelism, for
our cultures are similar. If the same missionaries were sent to Thailand, the task would require E_3 evangelism, as the differences

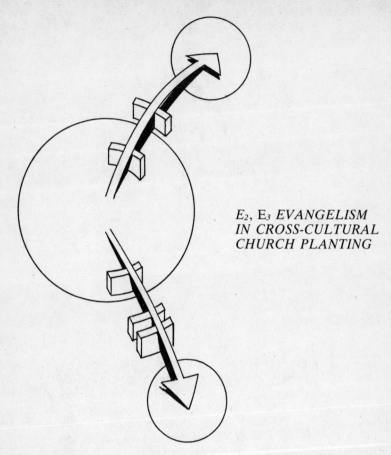

E_2, E_3 EVANGELISM IN CROSS-CULTURAL CHURCH PLANTING

Figure 48. Bridging Growth

between British and Thai cultures, especially those of the tribal peoples, are so great.

With the advent of the 'global village' and our multicultural society, it is no longer necessary to travel thousands of miles to face the challenge of E_2 and E_3 evangelism. Often our next-door-neighbour is culturally distant from us and our witness must be sensitive to these barriers to good communication and therefore effective evangelism.

We obviously want to avoid the misunderstandings that cross-cultural communication can produce. When American President Nixon visited Panama, relations between the two countries were tense. As he disembarked from his aeroplane the watching crowd whistled in derision. The President thought they were whistling in welcome, so smiled and waved. Infuriated, the crowd whistled louder. Delighted, Nixon's smile broadened and he waved back vigorously. Convinced the Yankee was being provocative the enraged crowd rioted. Finally Nixon got the message and beat a hasty retreat in a fast car!

Culture is not transmitted biologically; it is not carried by the genes of a certain race or class of mankind. A person is born culturally 'neutral' and *learns his culture* as he relates to his environment. A simple model of a culture may be drawn to illustrate three interrelated, interacting and constantly changing spheres (see Figure 49, A Model of Culture):

– the *ideological* sphere with a particular culture's belief system, religions, traditional ideas, attitudes, values, etc.

– the *technological* sphere with the culture's tools, clothes, media forms, transport, etc.

– the *sociological* sphere which describes the culture's relationships, government, courtship and marriage, accepted behaviour, etc.

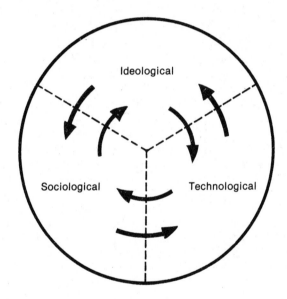

Figure 49. A Model of Culture

Dr Winter's insights into the evangelistic tasks confronting a local church highlights these cultural issues and identifies areas where solutions to problems in cross-cultural evangelism may be found. The widespread use of video among the British working classes has considerable implications for their evangelisation. If television and video are the main media of entertainment and information-gathering, then British churches ought to develop evangelistic programmes that use them.

When evangelising Urdu-speaking Muslim Pakistanis, it is not simply a matter of translating an evangelistic tract into Urdu, as some Christians imagine. A sensitive and genuine attempt must be made to love and understand Pakistani people. It will be necessary to learn about the religion and traditional ideas, their attitude to sacred writings such as the Bible and Koran, their strict patterns of behaviour between the sexes, their generous hospitality, forbidden foods, etc., etc. All of these cultural factors will effect evangelism.

If a middle-class church evangelises a working-class estate, cultural issues will have to be faced yet again. Cultural insensitivity to different value systems, use of media, or patterns of behaviour, will cause frustration to both groups and seriously hinder effective evangelism. If the cultural distance is too great Expansion or even Extension Growth (both E_1) will be unsuitable. The task may not require E_2 but perhaps $E_{1.5}$ Bridging Growth, and the new church will be very different from the one which planted it.

SEEK THE RECEPTIVE

Churches grow and become agents of growth when their evangelism respects the cultural identity of other peoples. As various groups are revealed by the community survey so the evangelistic task needs to be identified and put into effect as resources allow. If resources were unlimited and a local church had all the personnel, time, finances, evangelistic programmes and materials, cross-cultural workers, suitable premises, etc. to evangelise the whole community, then it could draw up a comprehensive strategy for evangelisation. In reality, resources are limited, in some cases very limited indeed, and therefore priorities for the use of evangelistic resources have to be established on the basis of receptivity or resistance to the gospel.

The ultimate goal of discipling 36 million unchurched British people means that each church must reach the unchurched in its own neighbourhood. The local community survey should have identified these people and the groups to which they belong – and they could add up to tens of thousands. Each person is in need of Christ and the local church has the task of taking the gospel to them. Where do they begin?

When Jesus sent out the twelve and seventy-two (Luke 9.1–6; 10.1–20) to preach the gospel of the Kingdom of God they had clear instructions to stay and minister to the receptive but to 'shake the dust off your feet as a warning' to the resistant. Even Jesus did not press himself upon the unwelcoming Samaritan villagers (Luke 10.51–56).

When the apostles continued the mission after Pentecost they constantly sought the ripened harvest by going to the receptive and turning from the resistant (Acts 10.22–29; 13.13–14; 14.1–7, 19–20; 17.2, etc.). They believed that the Holy Spirit prepared the harvest, directed the mission and controlled the harvesting (Acts 14.27; 16.6–10; 1 Cor. 3.5–9).

The 'times and occasions' (Acts 1.7) are in God's hands and peoples are ripe at one time but not at another. God alone knows when and because he controls the harvest, the task of the harvester is to follow the Holy Spirit and sensitively seek the ripened field. Soil-testing techniques are designed to do just that.

Who is Receptive?

The Resistance-Receptivity Scale endeavours to provide a model for classifying the response of particular groups or individuals to the gospel. Evangelistic strategies are developed accordingly (see figure 50, Resistance-Receptivity Scale).

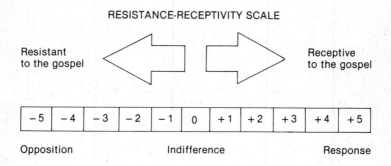

Figure 50. Resistance-Receptivity Scale

If a door-to-door survey or Scripture distribution or street evangelism revealed considerable interest in the gospel among young married couples or West Indian families or unemployed youth or prostitutes then they would be placed in the responsive category. Further categorisation may be possible between groups, so that priorities in planning may be established. As a general rule the resources for evangelism should be concentrated where response is found. When that harvest has been gathered in it will increase the available resources for the continuing task of evangelisation.

Groups may be identified as possessing common characteristics that cause them to feel they are distinct and set apart from others. The cause of their unity and identity may be such characteristics as language, religion, occupation, ethnic origin, economic status, social position or geographical location. For example, a distinct group formed by ethnic, linguistic and religious factors may be a Sikh community; a sociologically defined group may be college students associated with a local university, or urban industrial workers from a steelworks; a geographical group might be agricultural workers living together in a closeknit village community. The community

survey of Appendix 5 'Understanding Your Church', should attempt
to identify these groups as accurately as possible.

When are People Receptive?

Anthropologists have discovered that people are open to spiritual
issues and willing to consider religious matters at certain periods of
life. These are the so-called *'rites of passage' and the passing of the
seasons.*

Anthropologist Arnold van Gennup noted that most societies have
rituals for individuals and groups that mark their transition from one
important status to another. He coined the term 'rites of passage'
and those associated with the biological cycle of birth, puberty,
adulthood, marriage, birth of children, death of loved ones, and
dying are special occasions of spiritual appraisal and religious awareness. Today we should add the traumatic experience of divorce.

In addition, most societies also mark the passing of the seasons
with religious ceremony indicating spiritual sensitivity. Those who
first evangelised these islands and converted our ancestors were quick
to take the heathen rites and replace them with the Christian
calendar. Today the main Christian festivals continue to offer opportunities for evangelism among people who become 'religious' just
because of the time of year!

These periods of religious awareness and spiritual openness
provide *windows of receptivity* that the Church could make much
more use of. Every minister knows the opportunities for spiritual
counsel and evangelism that arise among the parents of infants reque-
sting baptism or dedication, couples preparing for marriage, the
dying and the bereaved.

An appraisal of the use and availability of Christian rites is urgently
required and would considerably help in the re-evangelisation of
these British Isles. Their indiscriminate and cheapened use among
the nominal and unbelieving simply hinders the task. The evangelistic
potential of the main Christian festivals remains to be fully exploited.

Why are People Resistant?

The Church Growth Movement has been accused of overstressing
the importance of concentrating on the receptive to the detriment
of the resistant. A typical quote to illlustrate the point, which Dr
Wagner now considers 'somewhat embarrassing', is taken from his
Frontiers of Missionary Strategy (p. 108):

'. . . the law of sowing tells us that time and resources are not
wisely spent on sowing seed in soil which obviously will never
produce fruit.'

If this principle were adhered to then most Muslim evangelisation would cease forthwith! In fact, the neglect of the resistant is not, and never was, a position advocated by the measurement of receptivity. Resistant groups must never be bypassed or left unevangelised but 'held lightly' praying and trusting that the group will turn responsive. The gospel should be preached to all peoples everywhere but as long as resources remain limited they ought to be concentrated where there is a response.

When there is no response to the preaching of the gospel there are two basic questions that need to be asked, *'Is the group resistant?'* and *'Is the group receptive, but we are evangelising them wrongly?'*

Two anthropological terms are used to distinguish between the two types of resistance:

(a) Emic Resistance (or receptivity) is determined by factors within the groups or individuals themselves. Reasons for their resistance are complex and ultimately rest with the Lord of the harvest. If or when the group turn receptive, factors may be identified which, in the providence of God, have contributed to the response but they lie with the group rather than the missionary.

During the Vietnam War many resistant peoples were driven from their ancestral lands and only then became responsive to the Gospel brought to them by the same missionaries they had previously rejected.

(b) *Etic Resistance* (or receptivity) is determined by factors introduced by the evangelising agent. In this case the group or individuals are or would be responsive to the gospel but the methods used fail to communicate it effectively, so that no disciples are made or churches planted. Cultural distance between the missionary or church and the unevangelised group is often the cause. In many British churches there is also the self-imposed exile of the church from the people.

In 1969, the Rev. Gavin Reid warned about the failure of the Church to communicate in the television age. In his book *The Gagging of God* he wrote:

'What is happening is that most local churches are working on the monastic principle. Their activities revolve round the central building and the clergyman. The faithful need to be kept "unspotted from the world" which is true enough, but this is equated with the maximum of exposure to spiritually disinfected atmospheres. The faithful are kept near their pastor and encouraged to clock in at the maximum of in-group activities.

'The result of this is that Christians usually think of communicating their message on their own terms, and if possible on their own premises. For them the church is their bolt-hole and womb.'

(REID 1969:89)

We cannot say that British people are resistant to the gospel if the Church has failed to declare it or if its institutionalised form is an obstacle to faith. In fact, there is considerable evidence to suggest that where British Christians have been bold and daring enough to move beyond the boundaries of their churches and share the gospel sensitively they find a willingness, if not eagerness, to listen and a positive response from many. They would say, with the apostle Paul, 'I have complete confidence in the gospel; it is God's power to save all who believe. . . For the gospel reveals how God puts people right with himself: it is through faith from beginning to end' (Rom. 1.16,17).

In his *Good News Down Your Street* (Grove Booklet No. 59) the Rev. Michael Wooderson, Vicar of Chasetown, describes an effective programme of evangelistic Bible study courses that his trained church members lead in the homes of interested people.

The programme was also used with considerable success in his former church of St Thomas', Aldridge, and he writes of the willingness of people to be visited:

'Our experience was quite simply that when as a church we were ready for this form of evangelism, then the openings came. I am convinced that that would be the case in most other places too.'

And to confirm Michael Wooderson's conviction, a Methodist minister who has also used the programme writes:

'For the church as a whole it has brought a fresh encouragement, as new people are seen in church and testimonies are given in services. And in the community it has aroused interest and comment (people talk!); not long after we started we had a request from a relation of one of the families to whom we had sent a team: "Could you send me a team, too?" That has been our experience. The fire, once started, has spread far more quickly and burned hotter than my meagre faith in the Holy Spirit ever led me to expect.'

I am convinced that British peoples are far more receptive to the gospel than most Christians dare to believe. The 'hardness of heart' that so many lament in our nation is largely *etic resistance* and the main cause of the problem is the failure of British Christians to evangelise in appropriate ways.

BEGIN WHERE PEOPLE ARE

A basic rule of all communication is that you must begin where people are. This is as true for communicating the gospel as any other message.

In his book *They Converted Our Ancestors* Dr John Foster argues that Christianity probably first came to the British Isles before 200 AD through Celtic converts. These first missionaries may have been converts of Irenaeus, Bishop of Smyrna and a disciple of Polycarp, who was himself a disciple of the apostle John.

There are traditions of earlier introductions of the christian faith to Britain but whether truth lies behind them or not, Christianity has been known to successive generations of British peoples for about 1800 years. The fortunes of the faith have waxed and waned through the centuries and the gospel has triumphed at one time and not at another, but how much of the gospel is known and understood today?

How do they hear?

During the centuries the way peoples have made sense of their environment and understood the universe has varied. A peoples' 'world view' not only differs from culture to culture but from age to age. The way that the English working classes of the eighteenth century viewed their world is very different from the English working classes of today. The context into which Wesley and Whitefield preached the gospel is not the same as the contemporary context.

Dr Eugene Nida, Translations Consultant of the United Bible Societies, illustrates the importance of recognising a person's world view from an experience in Thailand. A missionary gave a New Testament to a Thai Buddhist. Some time later when they met again, the missionary asked, 'How did you like the book?'

'Oh,' the man replied, 'this is a wonderful book and such a remarkable man! He was born and he died, he was born and he died, born and died, born and died. Why, this man Jesus made it to Nirvana in four reincarnations, while Buddha required one thousand.' For this man the four Gospels represented four different lives of Jesus!

In 1981 a European Values Systems Study was undertaken by Louvain, Belgium, and Gallup UK. The purpose of the study was, 'to analyse and describe the moral, political, religious and social value systems in Europe today and to provide a model for future studies in order to monitor change in value systems over time.'

Countries surveyed were Belgium, France, Great Britain, Holland, Denmark, Italy, Northern Ireland, the Republic of Ireland, Spain and West Germany.

Compared to the rest of Europe, British people declared themselves to be most satisfied with life; felt themselves secure, safe and sound; were generally satisfied with their work; were the happiest; considered marriage was not outdated and that freedom was more important than equality.

In answer to the question, 'Which, if any, of the following do you believe in?' British people said 'yes' to:

God	76%
Life after death	45%
A soul	59%
The Devil	30%
Hell	27%
Heaven	57%
Sin	69%
Re-incarnation	27%

The following percentages thought the Ten Commandments applied to themselves:

1.	No other gods	48%
2.	God's name in vain	43%
3.	Keep Sabbath	35%
4.	Honour parents	83%
5.	Not kill	90%
6.	No adultery	78%
7.	Not steal	87%
8.	No false witness	78%
9.	Not covet another's wife	79%
10.	Not covet another's goods	79%

On the basis of this research project and using much more data than recorded here, the Rev. Tom Houston, Executive Director of Bible Society, attempted to describe the Biblical content of the Gospel for the United Kingdom in the eighties. He based his outline on the minimum content of the gospel in 1 Corinthians 15.1–11 and presented the following to the Evangelical Alliance's Evangelists' Conference at Swanwick in December 1982:

1. Show us a Father who is faithful
2. Show us a Saviour who sets us free
3. Show us a Saviour who died for others
4. Show us a Spirit who brings life under control
5. The need of forgiveness is likely to come from the importance of people's own standards at first
6. The commitment we ask for may be to fight evil in self and the world under a leader who can win.

While this was a 'first stab' at the task of 'contextualising' the gospel for the United Kingdom in the 1980s, it is the sort of exercise that should engage all who are concerned to help our peoples hear the Good News today.

What have they heard?

If we are concerned to begin where people are it is not only important to know how people hear, but also what they have already heard and believe. While seventy-six per cent of British people believe in God, the same survey reveals that only thirty-one per cent believe in a personal God and thirty-nine per cent believe there is some sort of spirit or life force.

The appropriate message and methods for effective evangelism could be more clearly defined and carefully selected if the answers to questions about people's knowledge and beliefs were known. What people believe about God or know about Jesus Christ or understand about the Christian life affects our approach to them.

A simple tool to help the communicator answer these and similar questions has been devised and is called the 'Engel Scale' (see figure 51, Engel's Evangelism Guide).

This tool is an attempt by Dr James Engel to explore the 'Spiritual Decision Process'. Dr Engel justifies the use of the model theologically and practically in his book *Contemporary Christian Communications*, but nevertheless it is unpopular with many. A notable critic is Dr Peter Cotterell who writes in his book *Church Alive*:

'Whatever the intentions of Engel when he formulated the scale, it is inevitable that the scale will suggest something that is quite unbiblical, that a man who scores minus ten is further from God than the man who scores minus three. But that is not so. Both are equally dead, both are equally unsaved. There is no certainty that either will, in fact, come to Christ, or any likelihood at all that the minus three man will come to faith in Christ before the minus ten man. Nor does one have to slide down the scale from minus ten to minus nine and so on, gradually passing through each supposed stage until at last the moment of conversion is reached. Even a decision to act, at minus two, is not the same as action, and all of us know of people who are quite decided to act. . .but never get any further.

'The only valid use of the Engel Scale might be as an indicator of how I might speak to a particular person to whom I was trying to be Christ's witness. But even here there is real danger of the introduction of a mechanical approach, passing through the ten or so stages in the expectation that when at last the end is reached the person *must* be saved. The Holy Spirit of God, not a mechanical system, must lead us in our privilege of witnessing for Christ.'

(COTTERELL 1982.121)

I have quoted Dr Cotterell at length because I am in complete agreement with his cautionary remarks. However, the value of 'an indicator of how I might seek to a particular person' is so important that it cannot be lightly dismissed, especially when such a tool might correct so much of what is wrong with contemporary evangelism. The fact that my young children use my large screwdriver to dig holes in the lawn and extricate woodlice from the patio does not mean that I throw it away. The screwdriver is a very useful tool when used properly and so is the 'Engel Scale'.

Jesus taught in the Parable of the Sower (Matt. 13.1–9, 18–23), that hearing the 'message of the Kingdom' precedes understanding and growth (v.23). The apostle Paul says the same in Romans 10.10–17, where he briefly summarises the process by which people are brought to faith in Christ. Messengers are sent out (v.15), the message is proclaimed (v.14, 15), people hear the message (v.14) which they then believe. Not all who hear believe (v.16) and those who do not, remain spiritually dead and unsaved (v.10, 13). Paul concludes by writing (v. 17), 'So then, faith comes from hearing the message, and the message comes through preaching Christ.'

In context, Paul is arguing that the Jews have had an opportunity to accept the gospel and be saved and their failure to do so makes them, and not God, responsible for their plight. He is also implying that communication (of the gospel) precedes conversion and the Christian witness must endeavour to help the unbeliever hear and understand it. This involves sensitivity to what the unbeliever knows and needs to know about the gospel before he can respond and be put right with God through faith in Christ.

In practice, this is precisely what Paul did. As the apostle preached to different groups of people during his missionary journeys he adapted his preaching to the knowledge of his audience. For example, when preaching to the Jews and God-fearers of Antioch in Pisidia (Acts 13.16–41) he assumed their knowledge of God and the Old Testament, but at Athens among the idolatrous Greeks and their philosophers (Acts 17.16–34) he began with their concept of God (v.23).

The 'Engel Scale' tries to identify what people know or need to know of the Christian message before coming to faith in Christ. I do not believe that all the stages have to be passed through sequentially or that a particular period of time has to elapse before conversion. It is possible for illiterate, biblically ignorant and grossly sinful people to be converted the first time they hear the gospel. If this were not so, then education, knowledge of the Bible and respectability would qualify people for conversion. A great variety of doctrinal and ethical agendas could then be placed before potential converts and the sovereign and secret work of the Holy Spirit would be replaced by a book of rules. Salvation is all of grace and as soon as conditions for conversion (not growth in Christ) are laid down the gospel ceases to be the Good News of God's grace and mercy to sinners. The gospel is no longer good or newsworthy!

While it remains possible for people to be converted the first time they hear the gospel, this is most unusual. The Holy Spirit generally 'woos' people before they are won. The 'Engel Scale' explores this period of 'courtship' between the Holy Spirit and the unbeliever and helps the Christian witness to focus more precisely upon his role in the process. Perhaps the term 'Scale' is therefore inappropriate and liable to abuse. Engel himself seems to prefer the term 'model' but possibly a more accurate title is 'Evangelism Guide'.

– 10	AWARENESS OF SUPERNATURAL
– 9	NO EFFECTIVE KNOWLEDGE OF XTY
– 8	INITIAL AWARENESS OF XTY
– 7	INTEREST IN XTY
– 6	AWARE OF BASIC FACTS OF GOSPEL
– 5	GRASP OF IMPLICATIONS
– 4	POSITIVE ATTITUDE
– 3	AWARE OF PERSONAL NEED
– 2	CHALLENGE AND DECISION TO ACT
– 1	REPENTANCE AND FAITH
0	A NEW DISCIPLE IS BORN
+ 1	EVALUATION OF DECISION
+ 2	INITIATION INTO THE CHURCH

Figure 51. Engel's Evangelism Guide

Engel's Evangelism Guide

– 10. Awareness of the Supernatural
We have already noted, in chapter 2, the widespread belief and experience of the psychic and supernatural among British people. While this may be viewed with suspicion and be related to a mechanistic view of the universe and therefore be unrelated to belief in God, it nevertheless indicates where evangelism may begin.

The Bible encourages the Christian witness to believe that all people are addressable. To some extent they all stand in awe of their environment and conscious of their sin.

At Lystra and Athens, the apostle Paul pointed to order in creation in order to focus on the Creator and the responsibility of man as creature (Acts 14.15–17; 17.22–31). God speaks to all men through Creation and 'gives evidence of his existence' (v. 17) or, as the Psalmist expresses it:

'How clearly the sky reveals God's glory!
How plainly he shows what he has done!
Each day announces it to the following day;
    each night repeats it to the next.
No speech or words are used,
    no sound is heard;
yet their voice goes out to all the world and is
heard to the ends of the earth.'

Psalm 19.1–4

In addition, man is morally aware. (Rom 2.15). The Holy Spirit lays the Law upon the human heart and community and the Ten Commandments become the pressure points of alienation and conviction.

Reflecting on his missionary experience in Papua, New Guinea, Roman Catholic priest Lester Knoll identified 'Four Faith Convictions for Evangelism' that his activities are based upon. They are:

1. The Spirit of God has already been at work.
2. The certainty that personal conversion is essential.
3. The conviction that the Father desires to reveal his love personally to each person.
4. The expectation that when the Spirit breaks through to consciousness, there will be evident signs of changed lives.

As the British Church takes up the challenge of evangelising 36 million unchurched people it could well embrace those same 'Convictions', especially the first, that 'the Spirit of God has already been at work!'

– 9. No effective knowledge of Christianity

I believe it was G.K. Chesterton who said the British people had not rejected Christianity but a caricature of it, and this represents the position of millions within our population.

All British peoples surely have some knowledge of Christianity, from the media if not from the Church, though for many it is a gross misrepresentation of the real thing. Religious Education and organised 'worship' in many schools has successfully inoculated vast numbers against the Faith. Their knowledge is so misinformed that they have no inclination to act upon what they know or to enquire further.

The Christian Heritage Year (May 1984 to May 1985) is an attempt to remind and inform the British people about the great influence for good of the Faith upon the nation and the contribution British Christians have made to the world Church. If all churches and Christians could back this project and join in educating our peoples about

Christ and Christianity this combined venture could prepare the way for further evangelistic endeavour.

– 8. Initial Awareness of Christianity

An unbeliever becomes aware of the reality of Christianity through the influence of the people and the Word of God. The Holy Spirit uses these two agencies as the unbeliever contacts Christians and reads or hears the Scriptures.

Hopefully, the initial contact is both positive and influential. This is where first impressions and 'stained-glass barrier' issues are of vital importance. When Christian profession is not matched by genuine Christian living then the 'credibility gap' makes the gospel unbelievable.

At the 1966 World Congress on Evangelism, Professor Walter Kunneth of Erlangen University spoke on 'Hindrances to Evangelism in the Church'. High upon his list as a serious hindrance was the state of Christian people. He said:

'Because Christians appear so "unredeemed" and act as if they had no faith, the death sentence is passed upon the Church and thus upon the Gospel itself. The disfigured image that these false representatives give to the life of the Church makes the proclamation of the Gospel untrustworthy and counteracts the unfolding and outworking of the Gospel that would arouse men and women to faith.'

(KUNNETH 1967: Vol 2, 176)

Obviously, Christians should be very concerned about their image and their use of the Scriptures, for quality counts!

– 7. Interest in Christianity

Unbelievers who are interested in Christianity may be more curious about Christians than the Faith, but whatever the cause it is often the prelude to faith. Nicodemus appears at first to have been intrigued with the person of Jesus Christ. He subsequently defended him before other religious leaders and then unashamedly and openly expressed his respect and devotion (John 3.1–21; 7.45–52; 19.38–42).

There is a surprising amount of interest in Christ and Christianity today in the United Kingdom. In the European Values Study only four per cent of British people claimed to be convinced atheists and fifty-eight per cent called themselves religious persons.

The Rev. Tony Barker of Histon Baptist Church, near Cambridge, invited thirty-five men to his home for an informal discussion, described as 'free and frank', about the possibility of personal faith in Christ. All the men were avowed atheists or agnostics and none of them attended church. Twenty-one came the first night and twenty continued to attend weekly for the next few weeks. Of the twenty, ten were subsequently converted and some have become leaders in the church and a further seven now attend the church regularly. This and similar experiences around the country confirms the considerable interest in Christianity that exists. In such a spiritual climate there is obviously considerable scope for the evangelistic meeting, whether formal or informal, that endeavours to answer the questions that people are actually asking!

– 6. *Aware of the Basic Facts of the Gospel*

While there is considerable interest in Christianity there is very little awareness of the gospel. The basic elements of the Good News, as described in chapter 5 are not known, though the facts of the life of Jesus Christ probably are. For example, millions of British people have seen such film epics as Franco Zeffirelli's *Jesus of Nazareth*. However, the significance of who he was and what he did and the response required, is not understood. The evangelistic task when people are at this point is to rectify their ignorance.

If this Evangelism Guide were used to evaluate and plan ecumenical evangelistic projects it is at this point that theological divergence is most likely to commence. All Christians of whatever theological conviction or denomination or churchmanship would surely agree to the general promotion of Christianity but disagreements about the person of Christ, the significance of the Cross, the fact of the Resurrection, the plight of man and the nature of the gospel, etc. would begin to arise. Differences multiply as the evangelistic task for each section is identified – even the most co-operative conservative evangelicals disagree about the post-conversion phase, especially 'initiation' (+2)!

The reason why so many ecumenical ventures into evangelism flounder is the failure to recognise what evangelistic goals and tasks are feasible for the group.

– 5. *Grasp of Implications*

The question to ask at this stage is, 'Do people know what is involved in being a Christian?' Most people are probably aware of micro-ethical issues and suspect a long list of 'don'ts', such as, don't smoke or swear or drink alcohol.

While the ethical demands of the gospel and the need for holy living must always be put before unbelievers, the Holy Spirit, and not the Church or evangelist, actually sets the ethical agenda for conversion. As Dr Lesslie Newbigin writes:

'If the church which is the bearer of the Gospel has also the right to lay down for new converts the ethical implications of conversion, the mission has become simply church extension.'

(NEWBIGIN 1978:153)

The Holy Spirit convicts of particular ethical issues of his choice. For example, unmarried couples who live together may not be convicted about 'living in sin' but about their attitude to each other. Their marriage may follow some time after conversion, and possibly before initiation into the church.

The Church Growth Movement has been accused of advocating 'cheap grace' and 'easy believism' because it recognises this 'delay in ethical awareness'. But even a cursory reading of the Letters of the New Testament shows that new converts were not perfect (1 Cor. 6.9–20) and discipline had to be instituted to maintain the holiness of the fellowship (1 Cor. 5.1–5). Even Christian leaders, such as the apostle Paul, had to 'keep striving' for perfection (Phil. 3.12–21). Fish are caught before being cleaned!

– 4. Positive Attitude
C. H. Spurgeon said you cannot preach the gospel with a clenched fist. He also said, 'There are a great many more flies caught with honey than with vinegar, and there are a great many more persons brought to God by love than by pitiless declamations!'

If the Good News is to be perceived as *good*, it must meet and satisfy a conscious need of the unbeliever and be understood as a positive message. The task of evangelism is to address that need and show that God in Christ can satisfy it. Far too much evangelism fails to do this and is heard as bad news! Dr James F. Engel writes:

'Once individuals begin to grasp the implications (−5), there is growing openness and receptivity to evangelism. They now have sufficient background to understand at least something of what the Bible is saying. Moreover, they have been helped to see that it is relevant for their basic needs and strivings. Once this stage is reached it is probable that there will soon be a positive attitude towards the act of accepting Christ (−4).

(ENGEL 1979.77)

– 3. Aware of Personal Need
The essence of Christianity is a personal commitment to Jesus Christ as Saviour and Lord and a consequent personal knowledge of God (John 14.15–23; 1 Cor. 1.1–9). Before a person reaches this state of commitment he realises how salvation relates to him personally. He becomes aware that God loves *him*, Jesus Christ died for *his sins*, the Holy Spirit will indwell *his heart* and empower *his life* and, there is a place kept in heaven for *him*.

The awareness of a personal need to receive the gift of eternal life through faith in Jesus Christ eludes many people, especially nominal Christians. As the Rev. John Stott testifies in his book *Basic Christianity*:

'I used myself to think that because Jesus had died on the cross, by some kind of rather mechanical transaction the whole world had been automatically saved. I remember how puzzled, even indignant, I was when it was first suggested to me that I needed to receive Christ and His salvation for myself. Thank God, I came to see that, though an acknowledgement that I needed *a* Saviour was good, and a belief that Christ was *the* Saviour of the world was better, best of all was a personal acceptance of Him as *my* Saviour.'

(STOTT 1958:123)

– 2. Challenge and Decision to Act

We have seen that the Good News includes the call to repent and believe. This challenge must be presented so that people are given an opportunity to respond to the claims of Christ. In chapter 5 we mentioned the need for sensitivity and avoidance of manipulation.

When this challenge is presented the responsibilities of proclamation are discharged and the evangelist must await the activity of the Holy Spirit upon the unbelieving mind, sinful heart and rebellious will.

People in this position have had some exposure to Biblical truth and self-appraisal, yet so much evangelism assumes that everybody is at this stage and all they need to know is how to repent and believe. If most people are at −8 or −7 then an evangelistic tract or message or programme that assumes they are all at −3 or −2 is inappropriate.

If an evangelistic encounter increases a person's knowledge of the Gospel and enables him to move from −8 to −5, it has been a very effective encounter. Extended contact with that person, with further opportunities to evangelise, may well succeed in winning him for Christ.

–1. Repentance and Faith

At this stage of repentance and faith the Holy Spirit regenerates the human soul and a person is born again (John 3.3; 1 Pet. 1.3). Just as the becalmed sailor waits and longs for the wind and is powerless to move, so the evangelist awaits the Holy Spirit as he draws people to Christ (John 3.8; 6.44; 15.16).

+1. Evaluation of Decision

Following conversion the new convert faces a period of evaluation. For the apostle Paul it meant a period of isolation and waiting upon God (Acts 9.1–9). Paul's introduction to the Christian community met with some difficulties (Acts 9.13,26) and this is often the case with new converts. Commitment to Christ is one thing, commitment to a church is something else!

In *The Screwtape Letters*, C. S. Lewis deals with the Devil's tactics to destroy the new disciple. Screwtape says, 'All the habits of the patient, both mental and bodily, are still in our favour.' And more serious still, 'One of our great allies at present, is the Church itself.' As the new convert is confronted by all that is wrong with the church, so his faith is undermined, and it is at this stage that the small welcoming group of Spirit-filled Christians can offer so much to the new Christian. He needs to see the reality of Christian living and have examples to follow toward maturity in Christ.

This stage of care for the new convert is often neglected. Many converts are left to fend for themselves and are consequently lost between the evangelistic activity and the local church. This so-called 'follow-up gap' must be bridged by 'persuasion activities' as described in chapter 5.

+2. Initiation into the Church

This has also been described in chapter 5.

Once initiated into the fellowship of the church and incorporated into a local church, the new convert who was once so far from Christ, has stepped out on the road of discipleship (+3). In Dr McGavran's terms he has been 'discipled' and now commences the 'perfecting' phase that ceases when he stands complete in heaven before Christ.

When the new convert has been initiated into the church the evangelistic goal has been reached. They are beginning to grow in Christ and are on the way to active discipleship.

Invaluable Tools

Engel's Evangelism Guide, the Resistance-Receptivity Scale, Dr Winter's Phases of Growth and similar tools help the church to evaluate the various evangelistic methods and programmes available today. They also provide practical insights for planning and developing imaginative and bold strategies and plans. We need new methods and programmes that are tailor-made for each local church and specific context.

I have deliberately refrained from listing and commending numerous ways or methods for evangelism in favour of providing insights and principles so that a local church may produce or choose those most suitable. I have listed some agencies and resources in Appendix 1.

High on any list of most helpful books on the 'nuts and bolts' of evangelism must be two by Dr George E. Sweazey, Professor of Homiletics, Emeritus, at Princetown Theological Seminary and former Secretary for Evangelism of the Presbyterian Church in the USA. 'Effective Evangelism' was published in 1953 and 'The Church as Evangelist' in 1979.

'AS THE FATHER SENT ME . . .'

The Great Commission to preach the gospel to all men everywhere and 'make disciples' is still binding upon the Church, and will remain in force until the 'end of the age' and Jesus Christ returns. Therefore the Church is 'sent' and involvement in God's mission is not optional.

As churches respond in obedience and are committed to evangelism and growth they should evangelise boldly in faith.

When the dispirited disciples gathered together after the crucifixion and death of Jesus, they were uncertain about rumours of his resurrection and were amazed when he appeared in their midst (John 20.19–23). They had been fearful and in hiding behind locked doors before he came (v. 19).

In the commissioning that followed, the risen Lord pointed to the *pattern* of their mission: 'As the Father sent me, so I send you', the *power* available for its fulfilment: he breathed on them and said, 'Receive the Holy Spirit'; and the *proclamation* they must make: 'If you forgive people's sins, they are forgiven; if you do not forgive them, they are not forgiven.'

A week later the disciples were still behind locked doors (v. 26). It was not until Pentecost and the coming of the Holy Spirit, when they were all filled with the Spirit, that they overcame their fear and boldly preached the gospel.

Today, many British churches and Christians are like those first disciples with their pre-Pentecost mentality, locked away in fear from the world. They were frightened of opposition and ridicule; of facing facts and the true situation; of losing prestige, position and power; of making mistakes and looking foolish; of not being ready; of having to change; of breaking with traditions; of a simple gospel, and of sacrificing all for the mission of God.

The evidence of the New Testament, church history and the world Church suggests that when churches and Christians obey the command of the risen Christ and follow his example, they discover he dispels their fear and still breathes upon them, and sinners still flock for forgiveness.

As you and your church plan to follow his pattern, in his power, proclaiming his forgiveness you can discover it, too, and that's how churches grow!

Appendix 1. Useful Addresses

1. Church Growth Courses
    Bible Society
    Stonehill Green
    Westlea
    SWINDON   SN5 7DG
  The Bible Society offers Basic and Advanced Courses on Church
Growth throughout England and Wales. Details available on request.
2. British Church Growth Association
    59 Warrington Road
    HARROW   HA1 1SZ
  The BCGA provides a forum for Church Growth researchers,
teachers, practitioners and consultants. The Association publishes
the 'Church Growth Digest', sponsors conferences and co-ordinates
Church Growth activity in Great Britain.
3. One Step Forward
    High House
    Walcote
    LUTTERWORTH
    Leics   LE17 4JW
  One Step Forward offers a local church programme of fellowship,
spiritual growth and commitment, and evangelism based upon principles that produce church growth.
4. Evangelism Explosion (GB)
    228 Shirley Road,
    SOUTHAMPTON   SO1 3HR
  Evangelism Explosion offers an extensive programme of training
in personal evangelism and discipleship based upon Church Growth
principles.
5. Campus Crusade for Christ
    103 Friar Street
    READING
    Berks   RG1 1EP
  Campus Crusade offer church and group-based programmes of
personal evangelism training linked to films and literature.

6.   Administry
     28 Fontmell Close
     ST ALBANS
     Herts   AL3 5HU

Administry is a new Anglican-orientated organisation offering a wealth of ideas and programmes for any local church through its regularly published 'resource papers'.

7.   For a comprehensive list of Christian agencies and groups serving the British Church see 'UK Christian Handbook' 1983 edition, available from MARC EUROPE, 146 Queen Victoria Street, London, EC4V 4BX.

Appendix 2. Books Mentioned in the Text

CHAPTER 1. WHY CHURCH GROWTH?

World Christian Encyclopaedia edited by David B. Barrett (Oxford University Press, 1982, 1010 pp). The most complete and thorough analysis of World Christianity with its 21,000 denominations.

UK Christian Handbook edited by Peter Brierley (Evangelical Alliance/Bible Society/MARC, 1983, 430 pp). A compilation of British Church and Mission statistics with a directory of organisations and institutions. A must for anyone wanting to know what resources are available for mission in and from the United Kingdom.

Prospects for the Eighties Vol 1 (Bible Society, 1980, 96 pp) and Vol 2 (MARC 1983, 80 pp) Reports by denomination and county of the census of English churches undertaken by the Nationwide Initiative in Evangelism in 1979.

Witness in Six Continents edited by Ronald K. Orchard (Edinburgh House Press, 1964, 200 pp). Significant addresses and reports presented at the meeting of the Commission on World Mission and Evangelism of the World Council of Churches held in Mexico City in 1963.

To a Rebellious House (CIO Publishing, 1981, 57 pp). The report of the Church of England's Partners in Mission Consultation in 1981. Stimulating, challenging and important if acted upon.

The Bridges of God by Donald A. McGavran (World Dominion Press, 1955, 158 pp). The book that launched the Church Growth Movement in which McGavran challenged long accepted methods of missions and advocated new strategies for growth.

How Churches Grow by Donald A. McGavran (World Dominion Press, 1959, 188 pp). A book that challenged negative and maintenance attitudes in mission and called for bold and faith-filled plans to take advantage of great opportunities for church growth today.

Open Secret by Lesslie Newbigin (SPCK, 1978, 214 pp). A Trinitarian theology of missions, helpful criticism of Church Growth, and excellent chapter on Christ and other religions by a great British missionary scholar.

Understanding Church Growth by Donald A. McGavran (Eerdmans,

1980, revised edition, 459 pp). A standard textbook of Church Growth with the distilled wisdom and numerous illustrations that accumulate after a lifetime of research and lecturing.

Your Church Can Grow by C. Peter Wagner (Regal, 1976, 171 pp). A popular presentation of 'Seven Vital Signs' discovered in healthy, growing American churches.

Grow or Die edited by Alexander Wedderspoon (SPCK, 1981, 141 pp). An Anglican appeal for church growth to commemorate the 900th anniversary of Winchester Cathedral.

CHAPTER 2. WHAT'S SO SPECIAL ABOUT CHURCH GROWTH?

Lausanne Covenant An exposition and commentary by John Stott (World Wide Publications, 1975, 62 pp). A comprehensive statement about the nature and purpose of Christian mission drawn up and signed by participants, over 2,000 from 150 nations, at the International Congress on World Evangelisation at Lausanne, Switzerland, in 1974.

Contemporary Missiology by Johannes Verkuyl (Eerdmans, 1978, 408 pp). A comprehensive historical, biblical and practical introduction to missiology by the Professor Emeritus of Missiology and Evangelism at the Free University of Amsterdam.

The Church and Its Mission by Orlando Costas (Tyndale, 1974). A significant Third World contribution to the theology and practice of mission, with valuable criticisms of Church Growth.

I Believe in the Great Commission by Max Warren (Hodder and Stoughton, 1976, 183 pp). A lucid biblical, historical and contemporary survey of Christian missions. The 'last testament' of one of the leading British missionary writers and thinkers of this century.

'Towards the Dawn' by Clifford Hill (Collins, 1980, 187 pp). A prophetic view of Britain today and tomorrow.

'But Deliver Us From Evil' by John Richards (The Seabury Press, 1974, 240 pp). An introduction to the demonic dimension in pastoral care.

The Light of the Nations by Edwin Orr (Grand Rapids, Eerdmans, 1965). An historical survey of revival during the 19th century by the world's leading authority on spiritual awakenings.

Can British Methodism Grow Again? by Jeffrey Harris (Methodist Church House Mission Division, 1980, 72 pp). An application of Church Growth theory to specific issues in this declining denomination.

Communicating Christ Cross-Culturally by David Hesselgrave (Zondervan, 1978, 465 pp). A valuable contribution to understanding how to communicate the gospel across cultural boundaries by a former missionary to Japan.

The Communication of Innovations by E. M. Rogers and F. F. Shoemaker (Collier MacMillan, 1971). A classic study of the introduction of change to any group with numerous well-researched case studies from around the world.

CHAPTER 3. SIGNS OF GROWTH

A Theology of the New Testament by George E. Ladd (Lutterworth, 1975, 632 pp). A comprehensive treatment by a scholar renowned for his contribution to the biblical theology of the Kingdom of God.
The Renewal of the Church by W. A. Visser 'T Hooft (SCM, 1956, 124 pp). An important biblical and historical study by a former Secretary General of the World Council of Churches.
The Prayers of the New Testament by Donald Coggan (Hodder and Stoughton, 1967, 188 pp). A scholarly and devotional study by a former Archbishop of Canterbury.
The Bible in World Evangelism by A. M. Chirgwin (SCM, 1954, 162 pp). A challenge to use the Bible in mission, based upon historical and contemporary achievements.
Shaken Foundations by Peter Beyerhaus (Zondervan, 1972, 102 pp). A statement of biblical foundations for mission in contrast to recently advocated concepts, by the Professor of Missions at the University of Tubingen, West Germany.
Why Conservative Churches Are Growing by Dean M. Kelly (Harper and Row, 1972, 179 pp). A sociological study of the growing conservative and declining liberal churches of America.
Methodism by Rupert E. Davies (Epworth, 1976 edition, 196 pp). Methodism's history from its foundation up to the proposed unity with the Church of England.
Turning the Tide by Paul Beasley-Murray and Alan Wilkinson (Bible Society, 1981, 110 pp). A study of 350 English Baptist churches to see if the 'Seven Vital Signs' of American church growth were valid in England.
Haven of the Masses by Christian Lalive d'Epinay (Lutterworth 1969 257 pp). A study of the Pentecostal Movement in Chile commissioned by the World Council of Churches.
The Church by Hans Küng (Image Books edition, 1976, 622 pp). A masterful biblical and historical study by a German Roman Catholic theologian of international and ecumenical renown.
Church Alive by Peter Cotterell (IVP, 1981, 122 pp). A popular and practical introduction to Church Growth by a former missionary who is now Director of Missionary Studies at the London Bible College.
'Your Spiritual Gifts Can Help Your Church Grow' by C. Peter Wagner (Regal, 1979, 263 pp). A popular and comprehensive treatment of a controversial subject vital to church growth.
Look Out! The Pentecostals are Coming by C Peter Wagner (Coverdale, 1974, 181 pp). A sympathetic but objective study of the phenomenal growth of this group of Latin American Christians.
The Church at the End of the Twentieth Century by Francis Shaeffer

(The Norfolk Press, 1970, 190 pp). A stimulating and challenging study by a renowned Christian philosopher and apologist.

CHAPTER 4. LAYING A FOUNDATION FOR GROWTH

Churches and Church-goers by R. Currie, A. Gilbert and L. Horsley (OUP, 1977). A detailed study of the ups and downs of the British Church during the past 300 years.

I Believe in Church Growth by Eddie Gibbs (Hodder and Stoughton, 1981, 453 pp). A very comprehensive introduction to Church Growth principles with British illustrations and application.

Urban Harvest by Roy Joslin (Evangelical Press, 1982, 322 pp). A heartfelt reflection on Christian ministry in the inner-city by a Baptist minister who was actively involved.

CHAPTER 5. ORGANISED FOR GROWTH

Images of the Church in the New Testament by Paul S. Minear (Lutterworth, 1961). Possibly the most thorough study of the New Testament models of the Church ever written (see Appendix 6 for list).

The Growth of the True Church by Charles Van Engen (Rodopi, Amsterdam, 1981, 517 pp). A published doctoral thesis analysing the ecclesiology of the Church Growth Movement.

The Changing Anatomy of Britain by Anthony Sampson (Hodder and Stoughton, 1982). Probably the best known and most quoted analysis of British society that exposes all, or nearly all, about power and privilege and the lack of it.

Christianity in Culture by Charles H. Kraft (Paternoster, 1979, 404 pp). A major contribution to cross-cultural communication of the gospel by a committed conservative evangelical anthropologist.

Ephesians – a commentary in 2 volumes by Markus Barth (Doubleday, 1974). A classic commentary in the Anchor Bible series by one of the world's leading biblical theologians.

Bias to the Poor by David Sheppard (Hodder and Stoughton, 1983, 240 pp). A cry for change in the Church and society in favour of the urban poor of Britain.

Missionary Methods: St Paul's or Ours by Roland Allen (Eerdmans, 1962, 173 pp). A church growth book first written over 50 years ago by a former Anglican missionary to China. It continues to challenge the Church to follow the Acts of the Apostles.

New Wineskins by Howard A Snyder (Marshall, Morgan and Scott 1977, 192 pp). A guide to spiritual and structural renewal of the local church.

Successful House Cell Groups by Paul Yonggi Cho (Logos International, 1981). The testimony of how small cell groups helped to build the largest church in the world – the Full Gospel Church with 341,000 members in 1983 at Seoul, South Korea.

God Can Do It Here by Eileen Vincent (Marshalls 1982). A detailed and exciting description of the Full Gospel Church written with the conviction that it could happen in the United Kingdom.

Frontiers in Missionary Strategy by C. Peter Wagner (Moody Press, 1971, 208 pp). Suggested guidelines for developing effective missionary programmes.

The New Evangelism by Alan Walker (Abingdon, 1975, 112 pp). A restatement of the nature of evangelism for those who had forgotten its place in mission.

The Apostolic Preaching and its Developments by C. H. Dodd (Hodder and Stoughton, 1963 edition, 96 pp). A brief, simple yet scholarly analysis of the Good News the apostles proclaimed.

Evangelism in the Early Church by Michael Green (Hodder and Stoughton, 1970, 338 pp). A scholarly but readable study of evangelism during the first two hundred years of the Church's expansion.

Christian Mission in the Modern World by John Stott (Falcon, 1975, 128 pp). Clear and concise definitions of all the key words used in the current debates about Christian mission. A must for those who want to understand the issues.

I Believe in the Holy Spirit by Michael Green (Hodder and Stoughton, 1975, 222 pp). A comprehensive and biblical study of the Holy Spirit's person and work in mission, personal experience and the life and ministry of the Church.

Baptism in the New Testament by G. R. Beasley-Murray (Paternoster, 1962, 395 pp). A major study by a Baptist New Testament scholar of international repute.

CHAPTER 6. PLANNING FOR GROWTH

The Discipling of a Nation by James H. Montgomery and Donald A. McGavran (Global Church Growth Bulletin, 1980, 175 pp). Examples are given of how it has been done in the past, to show how it may be done in the future.

Christ, His Church and His World by Stephen Neill (Eyre and Spottiswoode, 1948, 157 pp). The post-war vision of this great missionary statesman.

The Meaning of Salvation by Michael Green (Hodder and Stoughton, 1965, 240 pp). The biblical concept of salvation is explored and related to contemporary problems.

The Gagging of God by Gavin Reid (Hodder and Stoughton, 1969, 126 pp). A passionate appeal for the Church to communicate in the television age.

They Converted Our Ancestors by John Foster (SCM, 1965, 125 pp). A thrilling account by an eminent missionary historian, of how the gospel first came to the British Isles.

Contemporary Christian Communications by James Engel (Thomas Nelson, 1979, 326 pp). A careful exposition of the theory and practice of communication in evangelism.

One Race, One Gospel, One Task edited by Carl Henry and Stanley Mooneyham (World Wide Publications 1967, 2 Volumes). The official reference volumes of the World Congress on Evangelism at Berlin in 1966.

Basic Christianity by John Stott (IVP, 1958, 144 pp). A classic and very popular introduction to the christian faith.

The Screwtape Letters by C. S. Lewis (Geoffrey Bles, 1942, 160 pp). A humorous exposé of demonic activity.

Effective Evangelism by George Sweazey (Harper Brothers, 1953, 277 pp). A detailed why and how to evangelise from the local church.

The Church as Evangelist by George Sweazey (Harper and Row, 1978, 249 pp). The theory and practice of church-based evangelism by a master of the subject.

Appendix 3. The Homogeneous Unit Principle (H.U.P.)

The H.U.P. is undoubtedly the most controversial principle to emerge from the Church Growth Movement. For some Christian leaders it is synonymous with Church Growth and because they reject it they dismiss everything else the Movement has to offer.

This is one reason why I have relegated this subject to an appendix! Another, and more important reason, is that Church Growth does not stand or fall on the validity of the H.U.P. Dr Peter Cotterell states unequivocally that he does not believe in the principle and considers it unbiblical (see *Church Alive* p. 111). Even Dr C. Peter Wagner, the staunchest defender of the H.U.P. says, 'By no means is the principle of Homogeneous Unit churches the only, or even the chief, distinguishing characteristic of the movement.' (*Our Kind of People* p. 6). But what is the H.U.P.?

THE ORIGIN OF THE TERM

In Dr McGavran's early writings he identified a universal principle that like-minded people, related in families and socialised in clan, class or caste, turn to Christ together and in large numbers. These relationships are the bridges that God uses to pass over the Good News and receive over the new convert.

By 1959 he was writing about homogeneous units and in his *Understanding Church Growth* (1970 and revised 1980) wrote '(People) like to become Christians without crossing racial, linguistic, or class barriers' (p. 198). This has become the primary statement or 'definition' of the principle.

Dr C. Peter Wagner has vigorously defended the H.U.P. and constantly sought to apply it in the 'stew-pot' of America's cultural mosaic, (See *Our Kind of People*, John Knox Press, 1979 and *Church Growth and the Whole Gospel*, Harper and Row, 1981).

CRITICISMS OF THE H.U.P.

There are two main criticisms of the H.U.P. – that it is unbiblical and unethical.

The H.U.P. is unbiblical because it contradicts the essential unity of the new humanity created in Christ, the classic statements of which are found in Ephesians 2.11–22 and Galatians 3.26–28.

'For Christ himself has brought us peace by making Jews and Gentiles one people. With his own body he broke down the wall that separated them and kept them enemies. He abolished the Jewish Law with its commandments and rules, in order to create out of the two races one new people in union with himself, in this way making peace. By his death on the cross Christ destroyed their enmity; by means of the cross he united both races into one body and brought them back to God.'

(Ephesians 2.14–16)

In this unity of God's family in union with Christ all divisions are healed and all barriers broken down.

'So there is no difference between Jews and Gentiles, between slaves and free men, between men and women; you are all one in union with Christ Jesus.'

(Galatians 3.28)

Critics who maintain that the H.U.P. is unethical challenge McGavran's concern for what potential converts 'like'. Critics say 'Of course they like to; but they must not be allowed to!' Converts must be prepared to cross cultural boundaries if necessary. They must come to see that part of the cost of discipleship is to love those they normally hate and accept those they once rejected. The Church must be a model of reconciliation and a local church must reflect this too. The H.U.P. allows race and class prejudice to exist in the Church, which is unthinkable. Some critics even maintain that churches formed using this principle cannot be genuine churches and 'apartheid' is commonly used to describe the practice of this principle.

DEFENCE OF THE H.U.P.

1. Cultural diversity exists, not merely because of man's sin (Gen. 11.1–9), but also because of God's rich and wonderful creativity. The colourful mosaic of mankind should be celebrated and preserved, not destroyed. Even the worship of heaven is heterogeneous: 'from every race, tribe, nation and language' (Rev. 7.9), as well as united and harmonious.
2. If we insist on monocultural churches, then the minority culture commits cultural genocide and the majority culture is imperialist, which is thoroughly un-Christian.
3. The H.U.P. is sensitive to the needs of unreached peoples and is 'receptor orientated', following God's example in communication (John 1.14) within cultures (Gal. 4.4).

4. All cultures are tainted with sin and some parts of them are
   demonic (1 John 5.19). They are all subject to divine judgement
   and the Holy Spirit's conviction and must submit to God's rule.
   To demand conformity to the missionary's culture is to presume
   perfection for his culture.
5. While the unity of the Church is a fact and must be maintained
   and visible, the unity of the body of Christ does not have to be
   expressed by conformity. The 'wall' that Jesus Christ abolished
   by his death was 'enmity' or 'hostility' (Eph. 2.14) between
   peoples and any form of hatred and bitterness between races and
   classes is incompatible within the Church. However, while there
   were no barriers to fellowship and they all shared a common
   standing in Christ, Jews remained Jews and Gentiles stayed
   Gentiles, slaves and free men could not change their status in the
   Empire and men and women did not change or lose their sex
   (Gal. 3.28). Unity in diversity is undoubtedly the rule.
6. This diversity is best expressed in having a great variety of churches. Linguistic diversity is readily accepted and the validity of
   Chinese, Greek, Hungarian and English speaking churches is not
   questioned. The H.U.P. claims that other cultural factors are
   valid causes of homogeneity, and the task of the Church is to
   plant churches among all of these homogeneous groups.
7. Love respects human dignity and cultures and 'does not insist on
   its own way' (1 Cor. 14.5 RSV). Therefore, it cannot be unethical
   to allow peoples to turn to Christ and follow him in their own
   way. That they confess and obey Jesus Christ and are growing to
   maturity in Christ, are the crucial issues.

CONCLUSION

1. The H.U.P. does attempt to recognise the cultural obstacles to
   faith *perceived by the unconverted*. A Church's preoccupation
   with its own culture and insensitivity to others can blind it to the
   needs of outsiders and frustrate its mission. Dr W. A. Visser 'T
   Hooft suggests that this blinkered approach has led to the decline
   and death of many churches.

   'Thus it would seem that the alliance of the Church with one
   particular culture and its lack of evangelistic and pastoral concern
   for the masses of the population can lead to its annihilation.'
   (The Renewal of the Church p. 71)

   The middle-class captivity of the British Church is undoubtedly a
   problem of homogeneity. Insights using the H.U.P. could lead to
   liberty.
2. I cannot accept the H.U.P. as a 'vital sign' of a growing church
   if that implies that a church must identify its own homogeneous
   group and recruit and evangelise its own kind. There is no doubt

that this interpretation is made and applied. Firstly, and most seriously, it is a denial of the Great Commission to go to all peoples everywhere. Secondly, it is similar to the sinful particularism and racial superiority that defiled the people of Israel. And thirdly, its success is dependent upon the receptivity of the homogeneous group. If the H.U. that the church goes out to evangelise or caters for is unresponsive, the H.U.P. strategy will lead to decline.

3. The causes of homogeneity and the boundaries that create the H.U.P. require careful research. Superficial analysis that defines homogeneity on the basis of race or skin colour or education, etc., leads to false assumptions and unwise strategies. Dr C. Peter Wagner's *Ethclass* model for the USA is a helpful guide but a British equivalent has not yet been produced (see *Our Kind of People*, chapter 3). Until this work has been done the H.U.P. will remain a subject of interest, and continuing controversy, but is unlikely to contribute very much to the evangelisation of the United Kingdom.

Appendix 4. Signs of Growth in our Church

This congregational questionnaire is designed to raise awareness of the Ten Signs of Growth in a church. It may be used in a variety of ways.

COMPLETING THE QUESTIONNAIRE

Each question has a box beside it that should be filled in with a number 1 to 4 selected from the following scale:

| 1 | 2 | 3 | 4 |

Negative   Positive

If the answer to a question is very positive then the maximum score of 4 can be registered, the lower numbers are given accordingly. There are 30 questions, so the highest score is 120.

USING THE QUESTIONNAIRE

The purpose of completing the questionnaire is to provide an opportunity for individual or group evaluation of a church. It is a *subjective* exercise and will record a person's point of view on each particular issue. The collective point of view when a congregation has completed the questionnaire will provide information for leadership discussion and action.

The questionnaire could also form the basis of small group discussion where two or three signs are discussed each week or session. Allow time for the completion of the relevant sections before discussion and then compare and discuss the responses. Reports of the findings and discussions of the groups could be collected for use by the leadership.

GROWTH IN OUR CHURCH

Sign 1. Constant Prayer

1. Our church has well-attended prayer meetings, either in homes or at the church, every week. ☐
2. Individual and personal prayer is encouraged and topics for prayer are regularly given to church members. ☐
3. Prayer for our community and world needs features prominently in the life of our church. ☐

Sign 2. Respect for Biblical Authority

4. When questions arise in our church about the Christian life or our Church activities we turn to the Bible for guidance. ☐
5. The preaching and teaching in our church is based on the Bible and related to life today. ☐
6. The Bible constantly challenges our church about the way we behave and what we believe. ☐

Sign 3. Effective Leadership

7. Our minister/pastor/priest is a person with vision for growth and always reminds us of the need to reach out to others. ☐
8. The leaders in our church are caring and loving and are helpful in times of trouble. ☐
9. Our leaders know where they are going and get things done. ☐

Sign 4. Mobilised Membership

10. Every member of our church is encouraged to discover and use their gifts and talents. ☐
11. Our church recognises the great variety of spiritual gifts, some extraordinary and others not, and we are willing to recognise and accept each other's gifts. ☐
12. We accept the truth that all members have something to contribute to build up the body of Christ and are trying to put it into practice. ☐

Sign 5. Eventful Worship

13. Our worship services are always helpful and uplifting times. ☐
14. Everybody sings enthusiastically and appears joyful during our worship. ☐

15. Someone who had never been to church before would understand what to do and what was being sung or said in our worship. ☐

Sign 6. Continuous Evangelism

16. Most of our church members love Jesus Christ so much they cannot help talking about him to their relatives, friends and neighbours. ☐
17. Our church has an all year round evangelistic programme of visitation, missions, guest services, etc. ☐
18. New converts are regularly welcomed into our church and receive basic Christian instruction in special classes or groups. ☐

Sign 7. Community Life

19. Our church is known for its warm, friendly and caring fellowship. ☐
20. People easily feel 'at home' in our church. ☐
21. Church members mix freely and regularly get together on other occasions than Sunday services. ☐

Sign 8. Compassionate Service

22. We are always looking for practical ways to show God's love in our community. ☐
23. A number of people now come to our church because of the practical help and care we showed them in the past. ☐
24. We have a number of caring and helpful activities on our premises that are open to all and in which church members are active. ☐

Sign 9. Openness to Change

25. There are many testimonies to changed lives in our church. ☐
26. We have seen many changes in our church in the past few years and they have been accepted without bad feelings and divisions. ☐
27. Our church is willing to change the way we do things if it will help outsiders come to know Jesus Christ. ☐

Sign 10. Released Resources

8. People in our church generously give their time as well as their money for God's work. ☐

29. At least 10% of our church's income is given to missions at home and overseas. ☐
30. The financial giving in our church has more than kept pace with inflation. ☐

Appendix 5. 'Understanding Your Church'

A CHURCH GROWTH SURVEY

This survey is designed to provide sufficient information for you to better understand your church (or a group of churches) and plan for mission.

The information gathered will graphically illustrate the past and present condition of your church and the nature of your community. This should lead to fresh insights and new understanding that will encourage future planning and more effective ministry.

As the information requested is the minimum required, those completing the survey should be as thorough as possible. Many statistics may be difficult to obtain and will have to be estimated on occasions. If estimated figures are given, indicate with an 'E' on the form and graphs and check your estimate with others in the church. If any figures are unavailable or irrelevant indicate with 'N/A'.

There are two parts to the survey – STATISTICAL and NARRATIVE INFORMATION – the following guidance is given:

PART 1. STATISTICAL INFORMATION

1. Church Membership

Where an official membership is used this is easily obtained. If not, then membership on the basis of communicant or commitment should be used. Please define the basis of your membership and be consistent throughout the decade.

Biological Growth   This is the result of the children of committed Christian parents coming to faith and active church membership.

Transfer Growth   represents the recruitment of committed Christians from other churches.

Restoration Growth   refers to those who have returned to active membership after disassociating themselves from a church for more than two years.

Conversion Growth takes place when those outside the Church are brought to repentance and faith and join a church as responsible members.

Reversion refers to those who are no longer active church members, they do not attend any church and have apparently ceased to follow Christ.

2. Church Weekly Attendance

If possible take the average attendance during the months of October and November because they are the least affected by the weather, festivals and holidays. Adults refers to 16 years old and over. Youth refers to the total of 14 to 18 year old young people, who attend church organisations, e.g. Brigade, Guides, Convenanters, etc.

3. Church Finances

All financial statistics require correction for inflation for comparison, see page 195. Simply multiply the amount by the correction factor for the appropriate years. Fabric expenses refer to the total cost of the church property, including heating, repairs, loan repayment, etc.

4. Age and Sex of Church and Community

Statistics for the community are available from the National Census, Social Services, Local Government Office, etc. Please check the date of the statistics provided and indicate on your survey for future reference. Total percentage refers to the percentage of the church membership and adherents in the first column, and percentage of all the community population in the second. Ages in the church will probably have to be guessed!

Now complete the following:

1. Church Membership
Membership is defined as ....
....

Total membership	Biological growth	Transfer growth	Restoration growth	Conversion growth	Total gain	Loss by death	Transfer out	Reversion	Total loss

19
19
19
19
19
19
19
19
19
19
*19

* current year

Figure 52. Analyse
Your Church
Membership

The loss and gain figures entered in the preceding table may be presented on a bar graph in the following way:–

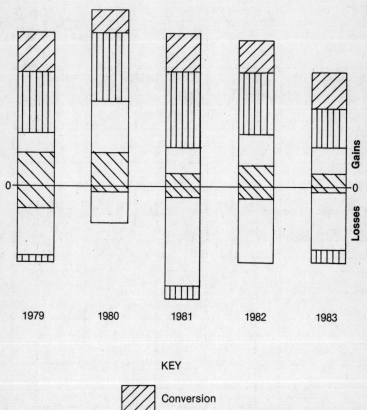

Figure 53. Church Membership Bar Graph

Draw your own bar graph for each year and see what you discover about the annual growth and decline of your church.

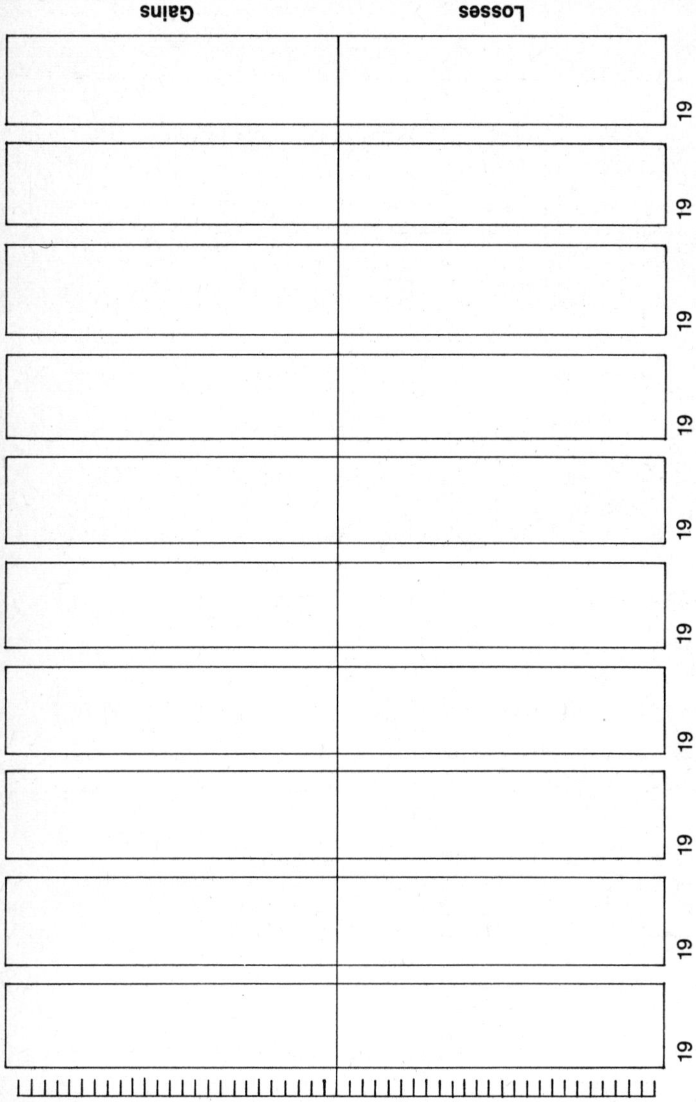

Gains   Losses

19

19

19

19

19

19

19

19

19

19

Figure 54. Draw Your Own Church Membership Bar Graph

2. Church Weekly Attendance

Fill in years for the past 10 years and the current year.

current year

a. Average adult (i.e. 16 years old and over) Sunday morning and evening attendance in October/November of each year above.

a.m.											
p.m.											
TOTAL											

b. Children (15 years old and under) attending church and/or sunday school on a typical Sunday

c. Attendance at your most popular Christmas season service

d. House Groups
Frequency of meeting: Monthly / Fortnightly / Weekly / Occasional (Delete as appropriate)
Purpose(s): Instruction/Fellowship/Evangelism (Delete as appropriate)

Groups										
Attendance										

e. Seating Capacity (overcrowding problems begin when 80% full)

f. Midweek Services (describe type of meeting)

g. Youth

h. Sunday School Children

3. Church Finances

	Total income	Inflation corrected	Total expenditure	Inflation corrected	Fabric expenses	Inflation corrected	Overseas missions	Inflation corrected	Home missions	Inflation corrected
19										
19										
19										
19										
19										
19										
19										
19										
19										
19										
19										

Figure 55. Work Out Your Church Finances

4. Age and Sex of Church and Community

	Church				Community			
	Male	Female	Total % M	F	Male	Female	Total % M	F
0-4								
5-9								
10-14								
15-19								
20-24								
25-29								
30-34								
35-39								
40-44								
45-49								
50-54								
55-59								
60-64								
65-69								
70-74								
75+								

Figure 56. Analyse Age and Sex Percentages

Now fill in the following graphs and pie charts:—

Carefully read this section before completing your graph.

1. Fill in the blanks underneath the graph for the year and the number of members, attenders, youth etc.

2. The dark lines on the graph represent the past ten years.

3. Select your horizontal scale carefully to cover the range of numbers involved.

4. Plot the numbers for each year and then connect the points to draw your graph.

The 'ups and downs' of your church should tell a story. Get together with others in your church and share your discoveries.

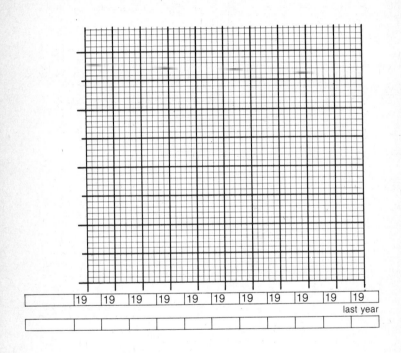

19 | 19 | 19 | 19 | 19 | 19 | 19 | 19 | 19 | 19 | 19

last year

Figure 57. Plot Your Church Membership

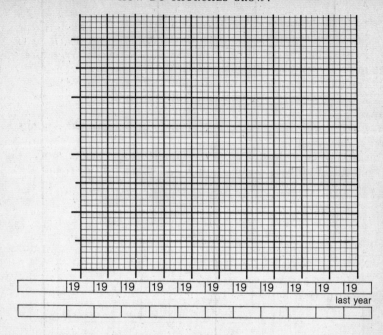

Figure 58. Plot Attendance: Average and Christmas

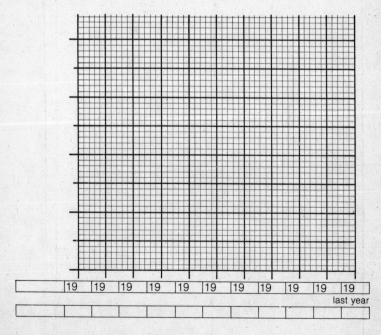

Figure 59. Plot Youth and Children

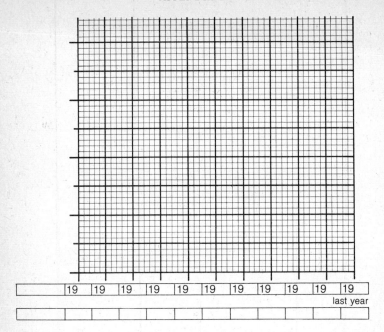

Figure 60. Plot Finances from the information in figure 55

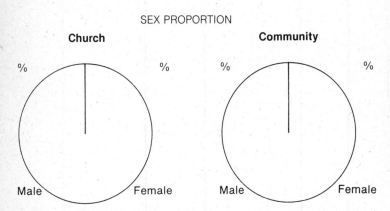

SEX PROPORTION

Total percentages of male and female in the church or community may be represented on this pie chart. Each percentage point is 3.6°, so multiply the actual percentage by 3.6 to discover the segment of the pie for each category. Use a protractor to mark the number of degrees and draw the pie chart.

Figure 61. Sex Proportions of Church and Community

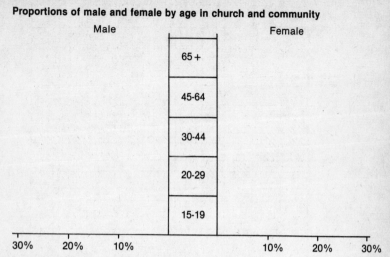

Complete the bar graphs for male and female by age and identify the balance of age and sex in your church. Plot the community in a different colour and compare it with your church.

Figure 62. Proportion of Male and Female by Age

How to Calculate Growth Rates

Standard Church Growth calculations and comparisons use two rates: annual growth rates (AGR) and decadal growth rates (DGR). We will describe them one at a time.

1. Annual Growth Rates (AGR)

Annual growth rates (AGR) compare the growth of the church from one successive year to another. They answer the important question: exactly how much did our church grow in a particular year? AGR is expressed in percent (%). Annual growth rates can be either positive or negative. When they are calculated, they are then plotted on bar graphs like the one below in figure 63.

There is more than one way to calculate AGR, but here is the one we recommend:

Subtract the earlier year's membership from the later year's membership. (Note: your figures must be one year apart, not more.) Divide the answer by the earlier year. Then multiply this answer by 100 (this changes the decimal to *percent*).

Example: A church has: 350 members in 1978
                          475 members in 1979

What is the annual growth rate?

Step 1. $475 - 350 = 125$
Step 2. $125 \div 350 = .357$
Step 3. $.357 \times 100 = 35.7\%$ AGR

Here is how a church's AGR bar graph might look for ten years:

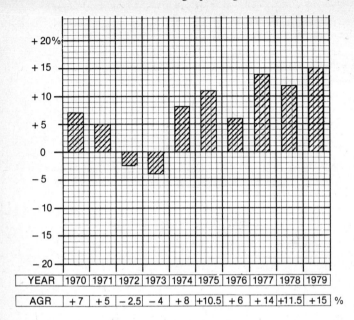

YEAR	1970	1971	1972	1973	1974	1975	1976	1977	1978	1979
AGR	+7	+5	−2.5	−4	+8	+10.5	+6	+14	+11.5	+15	%

Figure 63. Annual Growth Rate Bar Graph

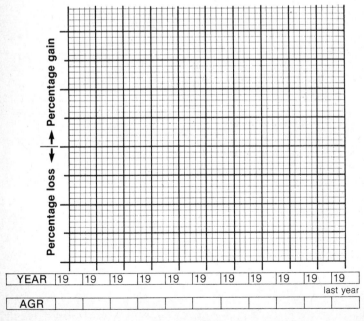

YEAR	19	19	19	19	19	19	19	19	19	19	19
AGR											

last year

Figure 64. Plot Your Annual Growth Rate

2. Decadal Growth Rates (DGR)

Decadal growth rates (DGR) are used for determining the rate of growth across a period of more than one year. DGR is a standard measurement that can be used not only for ten years (a decade, thus "decadal") but for two or five or 20 or any number of years. Converting growth for any period to what the growth *would have been* for ten years allows for ready comparison, and therefore valuable in diagnostic efforts.

A. *Simple calculation*

When you have data that is ten years apart (such as 1969–1979), follow the same procedure as you did for AGR;

Example: A church has 180 members at the end of 1969
                              640 members at the end of 1979 (ten years)

Step 1. 640 − 180 = 460
Step 2. 460 ÷ 180 = 2.56
Step 3. 2.56 × 100 = 256% (DGR)

B. *Calculation for other than a ten year period.*

In order to do this calculation, which is more precise, you will need an electronic calculator which has the y^x and $1/x$ functions.

Here is how to do it. (Caution: push only the buttons indicated:)

Example: 500 in 1976
              700 in 1979 (3 years)

	your display
Step 1. Clear calculator	0
Step 2. 700 (latest membership)	700
Step 3. ÷	700
Step 4. 500 (earliest membership)	500
Step 5. =	1.4
Step 6. y^x	1.4
Step 7. 3 (number of years 1976–1979)	3
Step 8. $1/x$	0.333
Step 9. = (wait until answer shows!)	1.118
Step 10. y^x	1.118
Step 11. 10 (for ten years)	10
Step 12. = (wait until answer shows!)	3.069
Step 13. x	3.069
Step 14. 100	100
Step 15. −	306.9
Step 16. 100	100
Step 17. = (answer is DGR)	206.9 or 207% DGR

NOTE: Further information about the calculation of Growth Rates is available from the Global Church Growth Bulletin, P.O. Box 66, Santa Clara, California 95052 USA.

PART 2. NARRATIVE INFORMATION

Please comment briefly on the following. Responses may be written down or recorded on cassette for reference later. The sections may also be used as the basis for discussion among your church leaders.

1. Local Community

a. What are the geographical limits of your community? Select a socially recognised area or identify your parish and if possible mark up a map with the boundaries clearly defined.

b. How many people live in your community and what are they like? Describe the people in racial, social, economic and educational terms. If you cannot obtain the information locally write to the Offices of Population, Censuses and Surveys at Titchfield, Fareham, Hants.

c. What are the major needs of your community? Local social workers will often provide information.

d. Are your church members involved in community affairs?

e. Are your church buildings used for community purposes?

f. What religious groups are active in your community? List the various churches, sects and other religious groups and estimate the numbers involved in each group.

g. Identify where members live on your map. Mark locations of house groups, other places of worship, distinctive and relevant features and places of interest. Are there any areas or groupings that are significant?

2. Church Membership

a. What percentage of your members live within your community? Are you a local church or do you have many members commuting? Do the leaders commute?

b. Does the membership of the church differ significantly from the community, for example, in occupation, housing, education, race, etc? Does this mean that some groups are unrepresented and therefore unreached? Are these groups that are unreached by you being evangelised by others?

c. How do you account for your gains and losses in membership during the last ten years? Explain why members have transferred in or out, and the reasons for Biological, Transfer, Restoration and Conversion Growth.

3. Church Programmes

a. What have you done in the past, or what are you doing now, and what do you hope to do in the future in the following areas? Comment fully and frankly and mention any difficulties encountered or joys experienced.

1) Worship
2) Sacraments
3) Preaching ministry
4) Pastoral care
5) Evangelism
6) Social concern
7) Sunday school and youth ministries
8) Involvement with other local churches
9) Involvement with denomination
10) Church organisations
11) New members' procedures
12) New leadership
13) Leadership training
14) House groups

c. Describe the Christian education materials (if any) in use in your church and justify this selection.

4. Church Property

a. What properties are used by your church? Does your church own them and are they in good repair? Do you foresee major expenses related to property?

b. Do you have plans for your property?

5. Church Objectives

a. What are the three main objectives of your church for the next 5 years? Place them in order of priority.

1...
2...
3...

b. What must you do or stop doing to achieve your three main objectives?

Appendix 6. Images of the Church in the New Testament

by Paul S Minear

(Lutterworth 1961 London)

Analogies discussed in the book

(1) the salt of the earth
(2) a letter from Christ
(3) fish and fish net
(4) the boat
(5) the ark
(6) unleavened bread
(7) one loaf
(8) the table of the Lord
(9) the altar
(10) the cup of the Lord
(11) wine
(12) branches of the vine
(13) vineyard
(14) the fig tree
(15) the olive tree
(16) God's planting
(17) God's building
(18) building on the rock
(19) pillar and buttress
(20) virgins
(21) the Messiah's mother
(22) the elect lady
(23) the bride of Christ
(24) the wedding feast
(25) wearers of white robes
(26) the choice of clothing
(27) citizens
(28) exiles
(29) the Dispersion
(30) ambassadors
(31) the poor
(32) hosts and guests
(33) the people of God
(34) Israel
(34) a chosen race
(36) a holy nation
(37) twelve tribes
(38) the patriarchs
(39) circumcision
(40) Abraham's sons
(41) the exodus
(42) house of David
(43) remnant
(44) the elect
(45) flock
(46) lambs who rule
(47) the Holy City
(48) the holy temple
(49) priesthood
(50) sacrifice
(51) aroma
(52) festivals
(53) the new creation
(54) first fruits
(55) the new humanity
(56) the last Adam
(57) the Son of Man
(58) the Kingdom of God

(59) fighters against Satan
(60) Sabbath Rest
(61) the coming age
(62) God's glory
(63) light
(64) the name
(65) life
(66) the tree of life
(67) communion in the Holy Spirit
(68) the bond of love
(69) the sanctified
(70) the faithful
(71) the justified
(72) followers
(73) disciples
(74) road
(75) coming and going
(76) witnessing and community
(77) confessors
(78) slaves
(79) friends
(80) servants
(81) "with . . . ."
(82) edification
(83) household of God
(84) sons of God
(85) brotherhood
(86) the body of life
(87) members of Christ
(88) the body and the blood
(89) the diversities of ministers
(90) spiritual body
(91) head of cosmic spirits
(92) head of the church
(93) the body of this head
(94) the unity of Jews and Gentiles
(95) the growth of the body
(96) the fullness of God